AMERICAN MENNONITES and the GREAT WAR *1914-1918*

Studies in
Anabaptist and Mennonite History
No. 34

AMERICAN MENNONITES and the GREAT WAR *1914-1918*

Gerlof D. Homan

Studies in Anabaptist and Mennonite History

Edited by Cornelius J. Dyck, Leonard Gross, Leland Harder, Albert N. Keim, Walter Klaassen, John S. Oyer, H. Wayne Pipkin, Editor-in-Chief Theron F. Schlabach, and John H. Yoder.

Published by Herald Press, Scottdale, Pennsylvania, and Waterloo, Ontario, in cooperation with Mennonite Historical Society, Goshen, Indiana. The Society is primarily responsible for the content of the studies, and Herald Press for their publication.

°*Out of print but available in microfilm or photocopies.*

AMERICAN MENNONITES and the GREAT WAR *1914-1918*

Gerlof D. Homan

Foreword by
James C. Juhnke

HERALD PRESS
Waterloo, Ontario
Scottdale, Pennsylvania

Library of Congress Cataloging-in-Publication Data
Homan, Gerlof D.
    American Mennonites and the Great War, 1914-1918 / Gerlof D.
Homan ; foreword by James C. Juhnke.
       p. cm. — (Studies in Anabaptist and Mennonite history ; no. 34)
    Includes bibliographical references and index.
    ISBN 0-8361-3114-2 (alk. paper)
    1. World War, 1914-1918—Mennonites. 2. Mennonites—United
States—History. I. Title. II. Series.
D639.M37H66 1994
940.4—dc20   94-1375
                                               CIP

The paper used in this publication is recycled and meets the minimum requirements of American National Standard for Information Sciences—Permanence
of Paper for Printed Library Materials, ANSI Z39.48-1984.

AMERICAN MENNONITES AND THE GREAT WAR, 1914–1918
Copyright © 1994 by Herald Press, Waterloo, Ont. N2L 6H7
    Published simultaneously in the United States by Herald Press,
    Scottdale, Pa. 15683. All rights reserved
Library of Congress Catalog Card Number: 94-1375
International Standard Book Number: 0-8361-3114-2
Printed in the United States of America
Cover design by Gwen M. Stamm

02 01 00 99 98 97 96 95 94 10 9 8 7 6 5 4 3 2 1

To my parents
Klaas and Sytske Homan

Contents

Foreword

Mennonites in a World of Progress and War

Gerlof Homan's *American Mennonites and the Great War* is a thoroughly researched narrative of a time of troubles for a particular German-speaking pacifist religious subculture in America. Such a guide to the Mennonite war experience of 1917-1918 is long overdue. World War I was a turning point in Mennonite life as well as in the wider world. That war brought profound changes in the ways Mennonites thought about their country and related to it.

We who live at the end of a century scarred by total war must make a great leap of imagination to understand the buoyant national spirit with which the United States marched off to war in April 1917. Ours is a time of greater disillusion. As the 1991 Gulf War demonstrated, America's enthusiasm for war may still seem to flame brightly for a moment, but it has an extremely short half-life. President George Bush's administration did not dare to propose military conscription or increase war taxes. The notion of an international war so popular that it could be financed mostly by the voluntary and locally collected contributions of citizens, as the Woodrow Wilson administration financed World War I, is almost beyond our comprehension. On this side of World War II, of the Vietnam War, and of the threat of nuclear holocaust, Americans are far more sober and realistic about war's likely outcomes.

War and Progress

It is a major challenge to understand the forces of 1917 that seduced the American people into thinking that a great war crusade would enhance democracy at home and overseas.[1] There was a complex connection between the ideal of progress—an ideal with exceptional power in the prewar years—and the phenomenon of war. The two decades before America's decision for war were an era of reform, the "progressive era." Those were years of confident, reformist, nationalistic zeal.

Progressive leaders, responding to challenges of rapid urbanization and industrialization, believed that the country stood at a crossroads of change. They were confident they knew the sources of evil, the forces of good, and the effective instruments for reform. They optimistically addressed a host of modern problems—corrupt political machines, monopolistic trusts, urban blight, environmental exploitation, child labor, prostitution, alcoholism, and other evils. Progressive reformers intended to transform American politics and make American society more just and more efficient.

One major source of progressive ideals was evangelical Protestantism. Walter Rauschenbusch, a Baptist pastor who had experienced the social disorganization of a depressed area in New York City, called the church to follow a new "Social Gospel." In Topeka, Kansas, a Congregationalist minister named Charles Sheldon organized his congregation to meet the needs of poor Negroes (as African-Americans were then known). Sheldon wrote a best-selling book, *In His Steps*, with the thesis that city life could be transformed if only public officials would chart their course by the teaching and example of Jesus.

By seizing the popular banner of reform, Protestant leaders attempted to maintain their eroding status as moral arbiters of the nation. America might yet become a truly Christian nation, evangelical Protestant progressives believed. They called Christians to work for the kingdom of God—a goal seen, of course, to coincide in large part with the success of the United States.

A more secular but no less inspiring body of progressive-era belief and knowledge found expression in the natural and social sciences. The relatively new fields of sociology, psychology, economics, and statistics rapidly became organized professional disciplines. Large universities expanded rapidly, displacing the earlier dominant role of Christian colleges. University leaders argued that the goal of education was public and community service. Trained experts, moved by ethical concern, could carefully investigate the facts, apply their knowledge to the data, and take the lead in solving problems. Morality, expertise, and efficiency would go hand in hand. In the prewar decades, a network of professional organizations grew up to support the aspirations and autonomy of each profession. At one level the new professionals asserted the ideal of objectivity. At another level, they yearned for opportunities to put their specialized gifts to use in programs of service to the nation.

Every era in U.S. history has seen change and growth in the character of American nationalism. In contrast to laissez-faire thinkers of the late-nineteenth century, the nationalists of the progressive era were willing to turn to government agencies to solve social and economic problems. The ideology of Social Darwinism had argued that government should let the struggle for life go on without interference, among freely competing social and economic forces. But progressive-era reformers saw that the environment of a new urban-industrial order often contradicted freedom. Government could guide the struggle for life by shaping the context for change.

Reformers who directed their energies to such problems as alcoholism, child labor, immigrant slums, or consumer protection often began with strategies of intervention by voluntary agencies. But they eventually moved on to a demand that government agencies take responsibility. Reform became a national crusade under the leadership of presidents Theodore Roosevelt and Woodrow Wilson, both fervent and aggressive nationalists. Roosevelt and Wilson used the coercive power of government to regulate parts of the national economy and social order. On behalf of U.S. national interests, they were also quite willing to intervene in the affairs of other countries, as Roosevelt demonstrated in his drive for the Panama Canal and Wilson showed in his effort to control the politics of Mexico.

Between August 1914 and April 1917, before the United States entered the war, many U.S. progressive leaders were critical of the war. A few pacifist progressives such as Jane Addams, founder of the Hull House settlement work in Chicago, maintained their antiwar stance throughout the war and beyond. Soon after President Woodrow Wilson called the nation to arms, however, most of the reformers were caught up in the exciting war effort. John Dewey, philosopher of pragmatism, overcame his pacifist instincts by reasoning that the war would offer opportunities to apply creative human intelligence to social problems and a chance for more organized cooperation in the postwar world. The war would extend human progress.

America's wartime mobilization called on the kind of expertise in social control that was the hallmark of progressive concern. Municipal reformers organized the military training camps along lines of community organization they had dreamed of for their cities. Industrial mobilization, government takeover of the railroads, and other economic controls afforded fresh arenas for reform. The fields of wartime labor-management relations, urban housing, social insurance, and campaigns against alcohol and prostitution were newly opened for progressive reconstruction.

If reforming idealists came around to support the war, it was not just that they became persuaded it was possible to achieve good ends through evil means. Rather, their wartime attitudes fitted well with their idea that government should act for social justice and democratic reform. Militant nationalism and social reform had not been so integrally linked since Americans had fought their Civil War to preserve the Union and end slavery. The First World War brought, in the words of historian Allen F. Davis, the "Flowering of Progressivism."

The raising of a national mass army revealed the connections between the spirit of progressivism and the new nationalism. America raised more than 3 1/2 million troops in World War I, 72 percent of them conscripts. Conscription was a great success, even though it involved a massive abridgement of young men's personal liberties.

The government's willingness to initiate such a massive intervention, and people's willingness to accept it, demonstrated that both government and people identified U.S. nationalism with democratic idealism. The Selective Service System was able to count upon the volunteer labor of some 14,000 local draft board members, plus 179,000 other paid and unpaid staff members. The system was a decentralized one, operated by willing workers who believed in what they were doing. As a triumph of efficient organization directed toward a high national purpose, it reflected values that were at the heart of the progressive movement.

The Mennonite Subculture

Few U.S. Mennonites and Amish in the first decades of the twentieth century were directly affected by the progressive movement's response to the problems of urbanization and industrialization.[2] Mennonites were a rural people. They had prospered in America, developing farm communities in their Pennsylvania-German heartland and extending outward to the midwestern frontier, north to Ontario, and south into the Shenandoah Valley. In the 1870s and 1880s, their numbers had been strengthened by immigrants from Eastern Europe to the Great Plains frontier, who settled along a line from Kansas to Manitoba. The Mennonites had also benefited from U.S. freedom and toleration, which allowed them to take their place as a legitimate denomination rather than as the barely tolerated sect they had been in Europe.

Though they were a relatively isolated, rural people, Mennonites adapted to the U.S. environment. In the late nineteenth and early twentieth centuries, the more forward-looking of the Mennonites organized national conferences to carry out more aggressive and systematic projects of education, publication, and mission. They established Christian colleges, educating new leaders who served as intermediaries between traditional ways and the outside world. They sent mission workers to foreign and domestic fields, where they learned the ways and the theology of Protestant evangelical missions.

Even when Mennonites intended their organizations to serve the cause of a conservative tradition, the changes bespoke Americanization. The aggressive style of American denominations and the sense of religion as activity ran counter to traditional Mennonite ideals of humility and simplicity. Mennonites disagreed among themselves and divided into subgroups over the extent of accommodation to U.S. society. But they were all grateful for freedom of religion. They believed in nonresistance. And they were shocked when their country went to war.

Progressives Encounter Nonresistants

The national government officials encountered by Mennonites in their wartime quest for military exemption and humane treatment in military camps were, for the most part, idealistic progressive reformers rather than autocratic militarists. Men such as Woodrow Wilson (president), Newton D. Baker (secretary of war), and Frederick P. Keppel (assistant in charge of conscientious objector affairs), were convinced of their own democratic enlightenment. They viewed Mennonites and other sectarian pacifists with a kind of benevolent paternalistic condescension. Mennonites and Amish, Baker believed, were victims of culture lag. The government needed only to get their young men out of their narrow-minded, traditionalist communities and explain to them the high ideals of this great war for democracy. Then they would gladly join the crusade.

Some Mennonites did answer America's call to arms. A few took up weapons and left the church. On the whole, however, Mennonite draftees steadfastly refused combatant military service. This refusal greatly complicated the responsibilities of military camp commanders, who were not oriented to human rights. Modern armies, including those fighting for democracy, do not prepare for war with democratic command structures. As Gerlof Homan's episodes from the military camps make clear, the mix of pacifists and soldiers in the cantonments was a volatile one.

America's progressive leaders miscalculated regarding the pacifists' depth of conviction; they also miscalculated the amount of intolerance and violence Americans would wreak upon nonconformists, both in military camps and in local communities across the country. The treatment of war resisters in World War I became a discreditable chapter in the history of civil rights in America.

The problem was not that Woodrow Wilson and his administration sat down in advance and planned a systematic program to suppress dissent. It was rather that such officials had misjudged the extent of the popular fanaticism which would be unleashed by a righteous war crusade in a democratic society. Wilson and Baker became hostages to a hysterical populace. They eventually justified their repressive measures. They failed to speak out against blatant violations of human rights, accurately observing that their political opponents demanded even more severe repression. Wilson and Baker felt they were doing all they could do for the Mennonites, given the situation the progressive politicians had done so much to create.

America's progressive leaders in the Great War also miscalculated at a more profound level. Their limiting of civil liberties in wartime could be rationalized as a temporary measure. Even though they refused to acknowledge the extent of their responsibility for America's wartime intolerance, they could make a reasonable case for limiting democracy temporarily in order to make democracy secure in the long run. But the deeper question was the ultimate relationship of democracy and war. Wilson, Baker, and their idealistic generation had not taken account of the contradiction between modern total warfare and democratic reform. The Great War, as it turned out, did not make the world safe for democracy or foster American inclinations to accept global responsibility. Instead, the war set the conditions for future warfare that was even more destructive.

The reasons for this failure are subject to historical debate. A narrow view blames the unwise and vindictive Versailles Treaty for upsetting the European balance of power and inviting the rise of German nationalist militarism. A broader view blames the Second World War upon the first. The Great War of 1914-1918 itself, more than the Versailles Treaty, prepared the way for military dictators such as Hitler and Mussolini.

John Dewey and a host of like-minded American progressive leaders badly misjudged the inclination and the capacity of the United States to influence the postwar international order. Overseas, European diplomats rejected most of President Wilson's proposals for a postwar settlement. At home, the American people refused to accept Wilson's plans for a League of Nations. The war had undermined America's benevolent democratic idealism. The war which had promised to be, and in some sense was, the "Flowering of Progressivism," in fact marked the exhaustion and death of the progressive movement. Modern total war does not beget constructive reform. Instead, it begets a host of evils, not least of which is even more destructive war.

Mennonite draftees who faced court-martial officials during the war cited Bible quotations which were at the foundation of their identity as nonresistant people: "Love your enemies" (Matt. 5:44); "Thou shalt not kill" (Exod. 20:13); "All they that take the sword shall perish with the sword" (Matt. 26:52, KJV). Quoted by Mennonites in the World War I context, these Scripture verses had a double disadvantage. They were often said in a German accent at a time when America was at war against Germany. And they pitted the nonresistant defendants against an American civil religion which blessed warfare as an instrument for achieving God's democratic will. Mennonites in 1917-1918 were not equipped to make an articulate critique of connections between worldly progress and modern war.

The abrasive encounter between nonresistant Mennonites and patriotic Americans in local communities during the war was confusing to both sides. One issue, whether or not to purchase war bonds, was especially fraught with ambiguity. If the government had chosen to finance the war with direct taxes upon citizens, Mennonites would have paid without protest. The Bible said to pay taxes, at least as read by that generation. But the war-bond drives were not official taxation, even though they often collected their money through local coercion, as this book amply documents.

Some Mennonite leaders said the bonds were akin to a tax, and so they counseled their people to participate in the drives. Others refused. A mediating position was for Mennonites to offer funds to local banks in exchange for the promise that the funds would be used only for nonmilitary purpose. However, both parties were well aware that the transaction would release other funds to help finance the war. Patriotic Americans, eager to have a role in military mobilization, had no patience for such fine distinctions. It was a confused and painful confrontation.

In the decades after World War I, Mennonites did little to celebrate their wartime witness and experience. Indeed, they often seemed to suppress it. For many individuals the war had been a time of public embarrassment and personal confusion. Notwithstanding their Anabaptist-derived tradition of separation from the world, wartime Mennonites wanted to be accepted by America as good citizens. Many of the stories of persecution reported in this volume remained hidden until the participants were senior citizens or, in some cases, had died. Times of pain and confusion are often eminently forgettable. Given the strong historical consciousness of Mennonite people, it is remarkable and significant that a comprehensive history of their World War I experiences has not been published until nearly seventy-five years after the event.

Entering the world of those who lived through the Great War is like visiting a foreign country. Since 1917-1918 Mennonites have undergone a major cultural transformation. The idea of progress, so confidently promoted by both evangelical Christianity and secular culture, is no longer so persuasive. The once-unquestioned assumption that the nation could promote liberal democracy through international warfare now faces withering critique. Progressive Mennonites have emerged from rural isolation to participate in the main currents of American life.

In 1917-1918 Mennonites were not as well equipped as contemporary pacifists are (or should be) to make an articulate critique of the connections between worldly progress and modern war. Yet the unhappy story of military destruction and the spiraling arms races of the twentieth century have done more to vindicate than to discredit the nonresistant witness of World War I. The stories on these pages can inspire us to be faithful in our own time.

—*James C. Juhnke*
North Newton, Kansas

Series Editor's Preface

Modern nationalism is insidious. In their own way, progressives in the United States in the decades leading to World War I were nationalists. To be sure, they were not romantic nationalists of the National Socialist or Fascist variety. They were not the kind, that is, who built national loyalty mainly around visual symbols and irrational appeals to a common biological race with roots in an ancient soil and primal loyalty to the tribal group. Instead, the nationalism of U.S. progressives in the early twentieth century took its cues largely from the American version of the eighteenth-century Enlightenment. So it called upon the individual to give one's loyalty and one's life to a nation defined not so much by irrational, romantic symbols as by rational constitutionalism, respect for democratic rights, and benevolent reforms.

But for all its rationality and enlightenment, the progressives' nationalism could also be insidious. It claimed respect for the individual, yet asked individuals to melt their own ethnicities and heritages into one national whole. It claimed respect for democratic rights, but easily overruled the basic right of dissent in order to recast the populace into one vast, modern, rationalized war machine. All of that happened in World War I, and conscientious objectors were chief among the victims. Many of those conscientious objectors were Christians known as Mennonites.

For Christians, modern nationalism is more than insidious; very often it is idolatry. Nation-states demand ultimate loyalty. They demand the right to define whom individuals, including Christians, will treat as enemies. At least in times of military draft, they demand that Christians allow the state rather than the work of God's kingdom to define their vocation. They demand worship, in the form of rituals such as flag salutes and singing of national hymns. They subordinate the salvation of persons to the salvation of the state. And ultimately, by claiming God's special favor, they try to define the very God whom Christians will worship.

21

Whatever their limitations and their small numbers, from the time of their Anabaptist origins, Mennonites have pioneered in resisting such claims on the part of emerging modern states. To be sure, in their theology and political thought, Mennonites made a place for secular rulers. Mennonites saw these rulers as God's agents for keeping order among the unredeemed. The rulers were ordained by God to create a climate in which Christians could go about their kingdom work.

In America, during most of the time up to World War I, Mennonites had not felt that their loyalty to God was at odds with a certain respect for government and loyalty to the state. But in wartimes, notably in the American Revolution and the Civil War, they had felt the clash. They certainly felt it in World War I.

Such, ultimately, is the story that Gerlof Homan tells. The editors of the Studies in Anabaptist and Mennonite History series are glad to offer a book that speaks to large modern questions. These include modern nationalism, religion and state, the problems of modern total war, and how individuals with strong loyalties to a religious group (and to God as understood by that group) relate to modern social and political orders.

Seen directly, Homan's book is a story of Mennonites' troubles, harassment, and sometimes real suffering for their pacifism. Seen in a larger way, it is a story of how a modern nation-state with strong claims of respecting human rights fell prey to irrational elements in its supposedly rational and enlightened nationalism.

It may well be that Mennonites came into the story naively, having failed to prepare themselves for what they might face in a modern, all-embracing state. But the story is more than a Mennonite story; it is an American story. It is more than a Mennonite tragedy; it is an American tragedy.

—Theron F. Schlabach
SAMH Editor-in-Chief

Author's Preface
and Acknowledgments

In almost every U.S. war, when patriotism demanded conformity and commitment to flag and nation, Mennonites and others have revived their conviction that they must remain faithful to Christ the Peacemaker. For many Mennonites, wars have been stark and often painful reminders of minority status in a sea of patriotic fervor. In some wars, such as the Gulf War of 1991, they and other pacifists have suffered little harassment. Yet even in such wars they have felt a sense of civic isolation. On the other hand, some wartime Mennonites have expressed anger or frustration over the lack of Mennonite support for the nation's effort.

And some wars have left serious scars. World War I tested Mennonites as severely as any. Perhaps at no other time has American patriotism been more intense and intolerant. Persons and groups who did not meet various tests of patriotism were often denounced and even physically harmed. Mennonites had always considered themselves lawful and productive citizens, yet the period 1917-1918 was a time when their fellow citizens found their patriotism wanting.

Historians and other commentators have not ignored the story of the Mennonite experience in World War I. In 1921 Jonas (J. S.) Hartzler, a member of the important "old" Mennonite Military Problems Committee (later renamed Peace Problems Committee), wrote *Mennonites in the World War: Or Nonresistance Under Test*. Hartzler based his book on various sources, including his own wartime experiences. Since Hartzler's book, much periodical literature and many personal accounts have appeared. Yet there is no recent, comprehensive account based on up-to-date discoveries in archives and other places. This study tries to meet this need.

One question addressed in this book's early chapters is whether

Mennonites were well prepared to face the challenges of the World War I period. There have been many charges that they had neglected their traditional peace stance. Had they? Other chapters assess the Mennonite response to World War I, or "the Great War" as Americans commonly called it at the time. They tell of the struggle to remain faithful to Christ's call to peacemaking and of ways in which American involvement affected the Mennonite community.

Many individuals have assisted and encouraged me in my research. I owe much to Allan Teichroew, archivist in the Manuscript Division of the Library of Congress. His own important studies of the war period led him to many valuable documents, which in many cases have been copied and the copies deposited in the Mennonite Library and Archives at Bethel College (North Newton, Kansas). Teichroew has been patient and untiring in advising me.

James C. Juhnke, of the Bethel College history department, initially encouraged me to undertake this study and gave me much assistance. He suggested important changes in my first draft. I very much appreciate his help; moreover, I have drawn heavily from his important articles on the World War I experience.

Among the many archivists who assisted me I especially thank Leonard Gross and Dennis Stoesz of the Archives of the Mennonite Church (Goshen, Indiana), and Barbara Thiessen of the Mennonite Library and Archives. Deep thanks go also to my son Robert G. Homan for reading the manuscript carefully and offering changes and corrections, to my spouse, Roelie, for proofreading it, and to Theron Schlabach of Goshen College for his final, thorough editing. Their help transformed the manuscript into a publishable one.

Finally, I thank my former mentor Cornelius Krahn (1902-1990), who first kindled my interest in Anabaptist history at Bethel College. Not only did he teach and write; for many years he labored hard and successfully to make the Mennonite Library and Archives one of our premier Mennonite research centers. I am a beneficiary of his important contributions to Anabaptist and Mennonite history.

—*Gerlof D. Homan*
Normal, Illinois
Summer 1993

Abbreviations

Archival Abbreviations
AMC—Archives of the Mennonite Church, Goshen Indiana.
BCHC—Bluffton College Historical Collection, Bluffton College, Bluffton Ohio.
CMBS—Center for Mennonite Brethren Studies, Fresno, California or Hillsboro, Kansas.
GHR—Guy Hershberger Research: Professor Guy F. Hershberger's collection of World War I materials in AMC.
MLA—Mennonite Library and Archives, Bethel College, North Newton, Kansas.
MRF—Mennonite Research Foundation: Project #24 consists of questionnaires received from many World War I Mennonite draftees; in AMC.
MSLA—Menno Simons Library and Archives, Eastern Mennonite College, Harrisonburg, Virginia.
NA—National Archives, Washington, D.C.
PPC—Peace Problems Committee: Papers of the Peace Problems Committee of the (MC) Mennonite Church (formerly named the Military Problems Committee); in AMC.
RG—Record Group.
SOHC—Schowalter Oral History Collection: A collection of 270 interviews with World War I Mennonite draftees; in MLA. Unless otherwise indicated all interviews in SOHC and AMC were conducted by individuals associated with MLA or AMC.
(Other archival depositories, consulted less frequently, are not abbreviated.)

Journal and Encyclopedia Abbreviations

GH—Gospel Herald (official paper of the "old" of MC Mennonite
Church).

ME—The Mennonite Encyclopedia.

MHB—Mennonite Historical Bulletin (published by AMC).

ML—Mennonite Life.

MQR—The Mennonite Quarterly Review.

TM—The Mennonite (official paper of the General Conference [GC]
Mennonite Church).

AMERICAN MENNONITES and the GREAT WAR 1914-1918

1

The Mennonite Peace Witness Prior to 1917

The Anabaptist movement began in the early part of the sixteenth century during the time of the Protestant Reformation in Europe. In the 1520s in Zurich, Switzerland, Conrad Grebel, Georg Blaurock, and others disagreed with the influential church reformer Ulrich Zwingli. Points of contention included infant baptism, separation of church and state, the swearing of oaths, and nonresistance.

The dissenters launched a more radical movement of the Reformation. Soon they and their followers were dubbed Anabaptists, or Rebaptisers. Anabaptists suffered bitter persecution, yet their movement spread to various parts of Europe, including Germany, Austria, and the Netherlands. In the Netherlands and Germany, the movement suffered serious divisions and turmoil, but then from 1536 until 1561 a Dutch former Roman Catholic priest, Menno Simons, provided good leadership. Thereafter most (although not all) of these radical church reformers took Menno's name and became known as Mennonites. Because the primary focus of this book is on that branch of Anabaptists who became Mennonites, all Anabaptists will be referred to simply as Mennonites.

However, several other Anabaptist groups deserve brief comment. In Austria most of the Anabaptists followed Jakob Hutter who advocated the creation of Christian communal living; his followers received the label Hutterites. In the 1690s in Alsace, France, as well as in Switzerland and in southern Germany, some conservative Mennonites led by a minister named Jakob Ammann seceded from the mainstream. Ammann's group became known as the Amish.

Despite differences, all Anabaptist groups covered in this book believed in separation of church and state, adult or believers baptism, a certain degree of nonconformity, and nonresistance. They based their ideas of separation of church and state and nonconformity on a belief in two kingdoms. These were the kingdom of this world, and the kingdom of the true followers of Christ. In the Anabaptist view, these two kingdoms were antithetical and antagonistic. The kingdom of this world was even beyond redemption. The Anabaptist idea of nonresistance rested on New Testament teachings. The model was the life of Jesus and his teaching that his followers should love their enemies, turn the other cheek, go the extra mile, and repay evil with good.[1]

War and military conscription affected Mennonite principles of nonconformity, separation of church and state, and nonresistance. But especially tested was nonresistance. Unlike various other denominations, which at one time or another embraced then discarded nonresistance, Mennonites made this belief central to their creed and a principle for which they were ready to suffer and sacrifice. In 1914-1918, modern, total war would impose demands on the individual who took Jesus' commands so literally.

In Europe authorities had long been unwilling to exempt Mennonites from bearing arms or performing some alternative kind of military service. In the sixteenth, seventeenth, and eighteenth centuries, Mennonites in the Netherlands were among the first to secure exemption from actual arms-bearing—but often they agreed to make financial or noncombatant contributions to war efforts. France and most German states soon granted similar provisions, while in Switzerland they were finally granted at the beginning of the nineteenth century. But even as European Mennonites won a measure of exemption, by the middle of that century most were becoming acculturated in their nations' values. By 1914 they did not object to performing military service or to the revoking of noncombatant alternatives.

Only in Russia did European Mennonites cling to their traditional belief in nonresistance. When in the 1870s the Imperial Czarist government considered revoking Mennonites' complete exemption from military service, about one-third of the Mennonite population left and migrated to the United States and Canada. However, economic factors, in addition to such cultural factors as a requirement to use the Russian language in schools, also influenced the Mennonite decision to leave. Fortunately, the Mennonites who remained and the Russian government worked out a system of alternative service. Instead of military service, Mennonite young men were allowed to work in forestry, in a program largely financed and administered by the Mennonites themselves. In World War I many Mennonite young men did medical duty as well.[2]

In the eighteenth and nineteenth centuries, Mennonite nonresistance was tested also in the New World. Beginning in 1683 and continuing in the early part of the seventeenth century, many Mennonites fleeing severe persecution in Switzerland and parts of southern Germany migrated to Pennsylvania. There they lived and prospered among their fellow-pacifists, the Quakers, who welcomed various groups seeking religious freedom.

A few decades later many Amish settled nearby. Eventually Mennonites and Amish settled as well in such states as Virginia, North Carolina, Ohio, Indiana, and Illinois. In the nineteenth century, other Mennonites settled in North America. Some who came from Alsace, France, settled mainly in Illinois. Others came from Germany and Switzerland and established themselves in various midwestern states. Then in the 1870s, large numbers of Mennonites and some Hutterites arrived from the Russian empire. Unlike the Mennonites and Amish already in North America, most of the new arrivals were of Dutch and north German descent. They settled on the western prairies, especially in Manitoba, Minnesota, South Dakota, Nebraska, and Kansas.[3]

Thus in 1914 Mennonites in the U.S. consisted of a great variety of ethnic groups, each with their own distinct cultural identity. In addition, they were divided over religious issues—not so much over theology as over church discipline, especially questions of nonconformity. Consequently, when faced with World War I militarism, Mennonites gave varied responses. The responses did not necessarily reflect the length of a group's stay in the American environment. One might expect greater compliance with the demands of American patriotism if a group of Mennonites had stayed some 150 years in North America, with a long time to acculturate—but such was not the case. Furthermore, one could expect greater opposition to military conscription on the part of those who had left Germany and Russia because of their opposition to military conscription. Again, such was not always the case.

The total number of Mennonites in the U.S. in 1916 was some 79,000 members (not including the Brethren in Christ, a related group with Anabaptist roots). The oldest and largest group for many years was known informally as the "old" Mennonites but is now more officially referred to as the Mennonite Church (MC). At the time of World War I, this group numbered about 35,000 members. Located mostly in Pennsylvania, they also had congregations in Virginia, Ohio, Indiana, Michigan, Illinois, Iowa, Missouri, Nebraska, Kansas, Oregon, and other states.

Having lived in North America as many as 150 years, most "old"

Mennonite members and congregations had acculturated in certain ways and no longer used the German language. Yet in other ways they remained nonconformist. To the outside world they seemed simple and rural—even austere—in their dress, worship, and style of life, although most were willing to adopt modern technology. The "old" Mennonites were better organized than some other Mennonite groups and thus more able to face the challenge of military conscription.[4]

The next largest group, the General Conference (or GC) Mennonites, counted about 15,500 members. The GC denomination had begun in 1860 among a small group of German immigrants in Iowa. It had grown rapidly. First it attracted Mennonite congregations elsewhere who wanted progressive programs such as missions and higher education, plus more liberal discipline. Then, especially in the 1870s, many of the Mennonites arriving from the Russian empire also joined.

Although they had some congregations in Pennsylvania, Indiana, Ohio, and elsewhere, most GC Mennonites resided in Kansas, Nebraska, and Oklahoma. Compared to the "old" Mennonites, they tended to be less nonconformist and more progressive in matters such as attire, education, and political participation. However, because of the large 1870s immigration, at the time of World War I a great many GC Mennonites still spoke the German language or some variant. Furthermore, it was a principle of GC polity to allow considerable congregational autonomy and diversity. Therefore, the GCs faced the war with weaker central authority.[5]

The Amish, at that time already known as the Old Order Amish, numbered about 7,700 and resided mostly in somewhat separated communities in Pennsylvania, Ohio, Indiana, and Iowa, plus some scattered ones in Illinois, Kansas, Oklahoma, and elsewhere. Actually, in a complex set of divisions occurring especially in the 1860s and 1870s, most Amish in North America had not become Old Order Amish but some variant of what might be termed Amish Mennonites. At one time there were about 11,000 Amish Mennonites. Among them were the Central Conference Mennonites in Illinois, who numbered about 2,100 in 1914.

In the first half of the twentieth century most Amish Mennonites joined the "old" or MC Mennonite church in a process that, except in Canada, was completed by 1927. However, some congregations either joined smaller denominations such as the Defenseless (now renamed the Evangelical) Mennonite Church (EMC) or joined the GC branch. The Central Conference Mennonites joined the GC in 1946. In fact, many Amish Mennonites were more progressive and less nonconformist than the "old" Mennonite Church.[6]

Next in size were the Mennonite Brethren Church of North America. In the 1860s these Mennonites had seceded from the main Mennonite church in the Russian empire. Strongly influenced by the Baptists, they accepted a more pietistic and evangelical theology. However, they were not more nonconformist than GC or other "liberal" Mennonites. In 1916 they numbered about 5,000 and resided mostly in Kansas, Nebraska, and Oklahoma. Although somewhat similar in name and emphasis to the Mennonite Brethren in Christ, they were ethnically Dutch-north German rather than Swiss-south German, and their evangelicalism had grown out of European Pietism rather than from American revivalism.

The Mennonite Brethren in Christ (MBC), by contrast, dated from the 1880s in the United States, when two groups of Mennonites with a newly revivalistic form of evangelicalism merged. In 1916 the MBC numbered about 4,700 members, most of whom lived in Ohio and Indiana.[7]

Some other smaller groups with memberships of fewer than 2,000 were the Evangelical Mennonite Brethren; Krimmer Mennonite Brethren; Church of God in Christ, Mennonite (Holdemans); Hutterites; and the Defenseless, Wisler, Reformed, and Old Order Mennonites. Hutterites differed from other Mennonite groups because of their communal organization. They traced their origins back to the time of the Reformation and migrated in the 1870s from the Russian empire to South Dakota, Montana, and Manitoba, where they established prosperous colonies.

Another group closely associated with Mennonites were and are the Brethren in Christ (BIC), often nicknamed "River Brethren" because of origins in the eighteenth century in a region along the Susquehanna River in Pennsylvania. Although somewhat different from most Mennonites in their mix of Anabaptism and Pietism, they and Mennonites share much in common. Their history of nonresistance and nonconformity was much like that of Mennonites, and in the twentieth century they would cooperate and identify with Mennonites in various ways. In 1916 the BIC had about 5,300 members, residing mostly in Pennsylvania and Ontario.[8]

Together these various Mennonite and related groups made up an interesting tapestry whose subtle shadings were often difficult for outsiders and even insiders to understand. Despite the variety, Mennonite groups shared many values. They were still overwhelmingly rural and, to one degree or another, nonconformist. Rural isolation, nonconformity, and limited education meant that they frequently had a poor understanding of the outside world. True, the more "progressive" Mennonites sought education and had launched Bethel, Goshen, Bluffton, Tabor, and Hesston colleges, plus Eastern Mennonite School. But in 1917 few Mennonites had education beyond elementary school or were well informed about the affairs of the other kingdom.

Thus, while it was often difficult for non-Mennonites to understand Mennonite mentality, many Mennonites found it equally difficult to understand the mentality of the "kingdom of this world." Yet as long as the state and society did not make too many demands upon them, the Mennonite and related groups could retain their nonconformity and live quite well.

Although many if not most Mennonites preferred to live within their own networks and communities, they could not prevent the modern world from impinging. The latter part of the nineteenth century and the first decade of the twentieth were periods of rapid industrialization and urbanization, which brought a revolution in communication and transportation. These and other changes altered the political and social landscape. In the 1890s much of rural America witnessed an agrarian rebellion in the form of Populism, soon followed by the Progressive movement. Some Kansas Mennonites supported Populists who demanded an activist government which would offer federal protection of and assistance to depressed farmers. Soon thereafter Progressives also championed government activism.

Not only did national leaders propose and achieve various social, economic, and political reforms; they also championed moral crusades abroad to "civilize" and teach democracy to Latin Americans, Filipinos, and later the Germans. Progressive leaders such as presidents Theodore Roosevelt and Woodrow Wilson and their supporters felt that using military force to teach Latinos, Asians, and Germans the principles of democracy was not much different from the domestic crusades to establish social and economic justice. So under Wilson, World War I became a moral crusade to save and civilize the world.

Not many Mennonites were actively involved in Progressive politics, although many of those who voted supported the Progressive Republican Theodore Roosevelt. But some Mennonites were affected by Progressivism's moral overtones. Thus, during the Great War, some even considered the use of arms a legitimate means of establishing a better world order.

Furthermore, new religious, theological, and moral currents such as revivalism, fundamentalism, modernism, and the temperance movement influenced many Mennonites. Some Mennonites received pastoral training at the proto-fundamentalist Moody Bible Institute in Chicago, and, like many other budding fundamentalists, they frequently were more concerned with saving souls than with nonresistance. Finally, Mennonites had recently embarked upon missions at home and abroad, and when the Great War broke out, they were very active in places such as Chicago, Kansas City, China, and India.[9]

By that time Mennonites had made some progress in overcoming their internal feuds and divisions and in beginning to cooperate. Thus, in August of 1913, at Berne, Indiana, there was a so-called All-Mennonite Convention. Since some groups had no representatives, the conference was not really "all-Mennonite." But some 143 delegates from various branches did meet. In 1916 a second such conference occurred at Carlock, Illinois, with 519 delegates present.[10]

However, inter-Mennonite cooperation was only a weak infant in 1917. Unlike in World War II, in 1917-1918 there was no Mennonite Central Committee to negotiate with federal authorities about the fate of Mennonite draftees.

How well had the Mennonite principle of nonresistance been upheld in the New World? Among all the expressions of Mennonite nonconformity, in many respects nonresistance proved to be one of the most difficult to maintain. Already in colonial times, an emerging spirit of nationalism had severely tested nonresistance, and Mennonites had occasionally made compromises. In 1755, for example, Mennonites had provided General Edward Braddock with teamster services in his well-known campaign against French outposts in western Pennsylvania. During the American Revolution, patriots attempted to conscript Mennonites and members of other nonresistant groups. Apparently almost no Mennonites yielded, although some rendered noncombatant services.[11]

In the years following, until the outbreak of the Civil War, there were no drafts. Throughout the early decades of the nineteenth century, Mennonites faced some pressure to drill with state and local militias, but state laws allowed them to escape this service by paying fines or other monetary contributions. During the Civil War some Mennonite men, or at least sons of Mennonites and Amish, enlisted, and a few were conscripted against their wills. But as the U.S. and the Confederate governments established national drafts, they allowed Mennonites and others either to hire substitutes or to escape the draft by paying money known as commutation fees.[12] After the Civil War Mennonites faced no draft until the summer of 1917.

Although during colonial times and in the nineteenth century, Mennonites upheld the principle of nonresistance, they could have done more to make their peace teaching vital. Too often they passed their nonresistance on to the next generation merely as a matter of tradition. Especially in the first half of the nineteenth century Mennonites wrote little on the subject of peace. Among the authors who did write was a Lancaster County, Pennsylvania, pastor named Christian Burkholder, who in 1804 published a small but oft-reprinted and influential book entitled *Nützliche und erbauliche Anrede an die Jugend der wahren Busse* [Useful and Edifying Address to the Young Regarding True Repentance].[13]

More than thirty years later Peter Burkholder, a prominent Virginia bishop, reiterated the Anabaptist peace position in a larger book entitled *The Confession of Faith of the Christians Known by the Name of Mennonites.*[14] During and after the Civil War other Mennonites wrote much more about peace. In 1863 the Ohio bishop John M. Brenneman wrote *Christianity and War: A Sermon Setting Forth the Suffering of Christians.*[15]

Also in 1863, the future publisher and "old" Mennonite leader John F. Funk wrote *Warfare Its Evils, Our Duty: Addressed to the Mennonite Churches of the United States and All Others Who Sincerly [sic] Seek and Love the Truth.*[16] In the following year a Reformed Mennonite physician and historian, Daniel Musser, published *Non-Resistance Asserted: Or the Kingdom of Christ and the Kingdom of This World Separated.*"[17] Such publications were among the first American Mennonite writings whose main purpose was to promote the idea of peace.

From 1865 until 1917 the United States did enjoy a long period of relative peace—except for conflicts with Indian tribes, a short war with Spain, and a colonial war in the Philippine Islands. During this period various west European nations and the United States had rather strong peace movements and many peace activists. But Mennonites scarcely became involved in such "secular" peace activities. Most of them preferred nonconformity.

Mennonites did not neglect their peace concerns, however. They expressed their traditional nonresistance in various conference resolutions, periodical literature, and a few other writings. Not all Mennonite conference resolutions have been preserved and studied to determine post-Civil War Mennonite concern for peace. However, the "old" Mennonites' Indiana-Michigan Conference was more or less typical. The conference did not deliberate peace concerns at every meeting, yet it frequently did express or reiterate its commitment to nonresistance.[18] Mennonite periodicals also carried numerous articles on peace, albeit often borrowed from non-Mennonite sources.[19]

Some Mennonite leaders at least occasionally thought and wrote about peace—among them, for instance, John S. Coffman, the "old" Mennonites' leading evangelist in the late nineteenth century, and Daniel Kauffman, a man who in the twentieth century would be an influential "old" Mennonite editor and leader. In 1898 the latter published a systematic statement of Mennonite belief, entitled *Manual of Bible Doctrine. . .* , in which he included the biblical basis for peace and had a section entitled "The Gospel of Peace."[20]

Meanwhile in 1884 a GC missionary and thought-leader, Samuel S. Haury, restated Mennonite nonresistance in a pamphlet called *Die Wehrlosigkeit in der Sontagschule* [Nonresistance in the Sunday School]. His was an eloquent statement, although he did not spell out exactly what young men should do if and when conscripted in time of war.[21] Two years later the key peace writing of Daniel Musser reappeared, this time entitled *Non-Resistance Asserted: As Taught by Christ and His Apostles.*[22]

In 1888 a manuscript that Old Order Amish bishop David Beiler had written in the 1850s was published with the title *Das Wahre Christentum* [True Christianity]. In a chapter entitled "Von den Rache oder Gegenwehr" [On Revenge or Resistance], Beiler discussed nonresistance in some detail.[23] Three years later John Holdeman, main founder of the Church of God in Christ, Mennonite, discussed the same in a work called *A Treatise on Magistracy and War.*[24]

One of the most articulate expressions of Mennonite peace concern in the post-Civil War era came in 1895 from a prominent GC in Kansas, Henry P. Krehbiel. Among various roles Krehbiel later became editor of *The Mennonite Weekly Review*. In World War I he gave very important assistance to Mennonite draftees. Thereafter, in the 1920s and 1930s, he was a leading Mennonite promoter of peace concerns. In his 1895 essay, "War Inconsistent with the Spirit and Teaching of Christ, and Hence Unwise and Unnecessary," Krehbiel carefully examined Old Testament passages that seemed to support war and compared them with the life and work of Jesus the Prince of Peace.[25]

Mennonites could and should have written more on peace concerns and reinterpreted this Anabaptist principle in the light of new experiences. But one cannot argue that in the pre-World War I era Mennonites neglected their concern for peace.

The Spanish-American War of 1898 provided Mennonites with further opportunity to reaffirm their peace principles. The war was too brief to make a significant domestic impact and did not arouse much criticism or interest among Mennonites. Nonetheless, on May 17, 1898, the GC Western District Conference met in a special session in Newton, Kansas, to determine their attitude toward the war. The meeting reaffirmed Mennonite nonresistance, but it also offered medical services under the Red Cross.[26]

Meanwhile Menno S. Steiner, an influential young leader among "old" Mennonites, especially blamed Spain for the outbreak of war. Although he urged his fellow Mennonites to love and to feed the needy, he also viewed the conflict as an opportunity to bring the gospel to Spain.[27] In 1900 Henry Krehbiel and many other Americans denounced American imperialism, yet later he and many Kansas Mennonites supported and voted for President Theodore Roosevelt—even though Roosevelt was an avowed anti-pacifist, militarist, and imperialist.[28]

In 1913, shortly before the outbreak of World War I, some 148 Mennonites gathered in Berne, Indiana, for that first All-Mennonite Convention. Here delegates not only tried to become acquainted with other Mennonite denominations but also discussed a variety of concerns such as nonresistance. The conferees listed nonresistance as a fundamental Mennonite principle and spoke in favor of it "without exception." Yet the delegates could not agree either on a definition or on its application.[29] Soon events would call for such application and different Mennonites would respond differently.

War broke out in Europe in July and August 1914. For many years the big powers had engaged in various rivalries and often reached the brink of war. The underlying causes of the war were complex, going back at least to the 1870s. Generally, all the big powers who became involved in the war in 1914 were responsible for letting hostilities break out, yet Austria-Hungary and Germany were especially guilty because of reckless policies they pursued toward Serbia.

Americans at first paid little attention to the war but soon began to take sides. Although many Americans resented the rigid policies Great Britain established to limit freedom of the seas, most supported the Allies, that is, Britain and France. But among Americans of German extraction, of whom there were many, quite a few sympathized with Germany and her friends—the Central Powers

Initially anti-German feeling was strong because of Germany's invasion or "rape" of Belgium, with atrocities by German troops well-publicized in the U.S. In the summer of 1915, after the sinking by a German submarine of a British passenger liner *The Lusitania*, resentment toward Germany became more intense. Americans considered submarines "immoral" weapons and were incensed over the loss of many innocent lives, including several American citizens.

Much to the chagrin of Secretary of State William Jennings Bryan, a peace advocate who favored restraint, President Woodrow Wilson's administration, which was pro-British, strongly warned the German government. Eventually Bryan resigned in protest of what he considered to be one-sided policies. By June 1915, Germany and the United States seemed to be on the brink of war. However, the German government made some concessions, and for the time being a military confrontation was averted.

Americans soon profited from the war, which brought prosperity to the economy. Furthermore, the American stake in the Allied cause grew with the extension of large private loans to France and Britain. Early in 1917 anti-German feeling increased considerably after Germany reneged on a pledge not to resume unrestricted submarine warfare, and on discovery of a German plan to involve Mexico in a war with the United States. In early April 1917, President Wilson concluded that he had exhausted all avenues to maintain peace. So he asked Congress to declare war. On April 6, Congress complied.[30]

Like most Americans, Mennonites had decried and lamented the outbreak of war in 1914. The *Gospel Herald*, principal publication of the "old" Mennonite Church, blamed the war on human greed, jealousy of races, and pride "mixed here and there with a tinge of religious fanaticism." The nations were now reaping what they had been sowing.[31] After the sinking of the *Lusitania*, the paper severely criticized Germany and called the incident an "act of willful, malicious, savage murder upon a vast scale." But the *Gospel Herald* added that it considered all nations capable of committing such atrocities and continued to urge American neutrality and support for Bryan's resignation.[32]

The Mennonite, a periodical speaking for many General Conference Mennonites, blamed all the big powers for the outbreak of war.[33] After the *Lusitania* incident it expressed shame upon discovering the atrocity was the work of individuals who, like almost all Mennonites, were of German blood and culture. *The Mennonite*'s editor felt like a child "horrified to discover that the hand of its parent has become stained with blood and murder."[34] Ironically, however, in 1916 *The Mennonite* did not oppose U.S. intervention, or "police measures" as they were called, against Mexico. The editor considered Mexico a "priest-ridden country" ruled by "fanatical and selfish, and half-balanced leaders."[35]

Although both of these influential publications reemphasized the Mennonite peace position, *The Mennonite* was wrong in assuming that most of its readers were neutral. Probably many Mennonites of Swiss and south German extraction, whose families had lived in the U.S. for generations, were neutral or not pro-German. But in the early years, before the U.S. entered the war, many Dutch-north German Mennonites, being only a generation or two away from living in the Russian empire, took pride in their German culture and favored the Central Powers.

An outspoken supporter of the Central Powers was *Vorwärts*, a German newspaper edited by Abraham L. Schellenberg and published in Hillsboro, Kansas, for and by Mennonites. Schellenberg was the manager of the Mennonite Brethren Publishing House and editor of a Mennonite Brethren (MB) paper *Zionsbote*. He considered especially France and "barbarous" Russia to have been the chief instigators of the war and defended Germany against the charges of atrocity. He criticized the U.S. government for not having warned American passengers on the *Lusitania* that its crossing would be dangerous. And he urged his readers to contribute funds for the German Red Cross. His appeal won some response not only among MB readers but also among GCs, in the GC Western District Conference.[36]

A paper similar in readership and sympathy was *Der Herold*, edited by Henry P. Krehbiel and his brother Christian. *Der Herold* argued the war's outbreak was due to despotic Russia's expansionism, France's desire for revenge, and Britain's jealousy of Germany's economic strength. Like Schellenberg, Krehbiel also assisted with the collection of funds for the German Red Cross.[37]

Despite some partisanship, on many occasions during the three-year period prior to U.S. involvement in the war, Mennonites reiterated their traditional peace position and their denunciation of war as a means of settling international conflict. Mennonite publications carried many articles on peace and many pleas not to become involved in the current conflict. They argued correctly that "sham Christianity" had failed to give peace to the world and that placing one's faith in Christ and in the so-called preparedness policy were irreconcilable objectives. They also admonished Mennonites not to succumb to cheap slogans, and urged them to declare they were "too humble" or "too Christ-like to fight."

Furthermore, Mennonite publications reminded readers that, for citizens of the heavenly kingdom, patriotism meant the love of God and "the highest spiritual welfare of all people." Instead of calling for military preparedness, as many Americans were insisting upon, Mennonite leaders argued that preparing for war could only lead to war. Finally, Mennonite papers insisted that nonresistance, far from being an expression of cowardice, required a double portion of courage. It took double courage to face death and not try to inflict violence upon one's enemy.[38]

In August 1915 the "old" Mennonites' general conference, meeting in Archbold, Ohio, reiterated its opposition to carnal warfare and urged "a meek, quiet, and submissive attitude" towards the government if war would come. It admonished young men not to enlist in military service and threatened to disown those who did. Turning to what Christians could do positively, it recommended extending relief to war sufferers.[39] One year later the All-Mennonite Convention in Carlock, Illinois, passed and sent a petition to President Wilson expressing its opposition to military training. "War," it pleaded, "can never serve as an effective solution to international complications"—because war was "unscriptural, unjust, ineffective, and a great social and economic waste."[40]

Both these Mennonite gatherings were reacting to the National Defense Act, a law passed by Congress in June 1916, and to subsequent proposals to introduce compulsory military training. The National Defense Act supplemented the Militia Act of 1903. It established compulsory militia duty in case of national emergency but, like the act of 1903, it released from combatant duty all persons who claimed exemption on the basis of religious belief. However, it did not exempt them from noncombatant duty. The law allowed the president to define such duty.[41] The two acts foreshadowed an even more important law, the controversial Selective Service Act of May 1917, which established the World War I draft and again failed to exempt conscientious objectors from noncombatant duty under military direction.

During the debates on the National Defense Bill, many peace activists testified against the proposal. Included were persons such as William I. Hill and Joseph Swain of Swarthmore College, a Quaker institution; and prominent progressive social reformers Oscar Villard and Lillian Wald.[42] But Mennonites did not testify or protest, possibly because they failed to understand how little the law offered to persons with scruples against any kind of military service. However in March of 1917, just as Congress was considering the possibility of introducing compulsory military conscription, a committee of the All-Mennonite Convention went to Washington. Committee members Jacob Snyder and Jasper (J. A.) Huffman presented to both President Wilson and var-

ious congressmen and senators what they considered a "splendid petition." The petition requested complete exemption from military service. In Washington the men were assured that their cause was just and
right, and some officials promised to support the proposal. White
House officials told the Mennonites that their petition would have the
President's "most earnest consideration." In the same month the Mennonite Brethren Church presented a similar petition.[43]

When war came in April of 1917, how well prepared were Mennonites to uphold their nonresistance? Had the amount of literature
and sermonizing on the subject—especially since the beginning of the
war in August 1914—been sufficient? Had it reached the membership?
Mennonite draftees for World War I have left conflicting testimony on
their preparedness. Many later said that they had been well-grounded
in Mennonite nonresistance at home, in their churches or college, and
by articles in their church papers.

Perhaps "old" Mennonite Christian (C. L.) Graber best summed
up the positive testimony. He said he could not say who had influenced
his decision. The fact was, he declared later, "I was taught nonresistance at home, in Sunday School, in church all my life and it never entered my mind to do anything else except to refuse military service."[44]
Another "old" Mennonite, Isaac M. Baer, even felt that the memories of
Civil War still lingered and influenced him. "Although 51 years had
lapsed," he wrote later, "the test and suffering experienced by Mennonites during the Civil War [in Pennsylvania] were not wholly forgotten."[45]

However many other men later complained that their churches
had not prepared them. For instance, Wilmer Shelly of the Upper Milford Mennonite Church in eastern Pennsylvania stated after the war
that "when World War I came, up until that time in my home church I
had never heard anything about conscientious objectors [or] of the
Mennonite position on war. I had never received any instruction or
mention of a conscientious objector."[46]

Henry Krehbiel's sister, Susan, voiced a similar complaint. In September of 1918, she wrote her brother that she was not surprised if
Mennonite boys were experiencing much trouble. They had grown up,
she charged, "without ever hearing much said about this, now so all important subject." All they had learned, she wrote, was a few verses; she
could not recall a sermon on the subject.[47]

In a similar vein *The Mennonite*, an important General Conference Mennonite publication, lamented that the church had neglected
the "foundation," and now the house was "shaking and dangerously

near seriously hurt." Perhaps with some justification the editor decried "old and threadbare" traditions, but he exaggerated when he complained further. One could not point with pride to a "single noted piece of [Mennonite] peace literature," he continued.[48] Obviously the editor failed to recall Funk, Musser, Beiler, Krehbiel, and others. Finally, some Mennonites complained that many of their people had paid more attention to salvation, evangelism, missions, and pietism than to teachings about war.[49]

More could and should have been to done to maintain and reinterpret Mennonite nonresistance and to provide good peace literature for young people. There was some peace literature once war came, but often it was hastily prepared. Too often Mennonites had simply relied on nonresistance as a time-honored tradition.

Despite such criticisms, most Mennonite men who arrived in military camps knew about nonresistance as a way of life even if they did not always find it easy to articulate their reasons for believing in it. Clearly they could not explain their opposition to war and violence as well as some other conscientious objectors did. Their parents and congregations could have done more to prepare them for their ordeal. But against considerable odds, most World War I Mennonite draftees remained faithful to Mennonite nonresistance.

2

The Initial Response to U.S. Involvement in the War, 1917

The United States entered World War I with unbounded zeal, energy, and enthusiasm. Led by President Wilson's slogans, many Americans considered the war a great progressive crusade: to make the world safe for democracy; to end all wars; and to exterminate German authoritarianism, "barbarism," "Kaiserism," and militarism. Seldom has American patriotism been more intense or generated more intolerance. But the crusade required large military forces—which in turn meant drafting all available manpower.

The Wilson administration had been considering compulsory military service for some time. The Militia Act of January 1903 and the Defense Act of 1916 foreshadowed such a contingency, even though Wilson had been saying he was opposed to conscription. Many southern and western congressmen and senators also claimed to be opposed.[1]

But early in 1917 Wilson reversed himself, and in April the War Department introduced a proposal to Congress for drafting all males between ages eighteen and twenty-five. In line with the 1903 and 1916 laws, the bill provided for conscientious objection—in fact, its language allowed complete exemption, without even demanding noncombatant or alternative service. To qualify, one would have to be a member of a well-recognized religious sect or organization whose creed forbade service in any of the armed forces or participation in war.[2]

During congressional hearings, various individuals expressed their opposition to compulsory military service. Jane Addams, leading feminist, social reformer, and peace activist, even predicted draft riots. She was supported by the Socialist Norman M. Thomas, who himself soon faced conscription and a jail term. Hollingsworth Wood of the Society of Friends said conscientious objection should not be based on tradition but on conviction and sincerity—tested, as in Great Britain, by special tribunals.[3]

Unfortunately no Mennonites testified. Some did attempt to influence the proposed legislation by sending delegates to Washington, D.C. But on the whole Mennonites were slow to realize that the war was rapidly breaking down their semi-isolation and semi-separation. With less naïveté they might have sensed that war—especially modern, total war—imposes special demands, sacrifices, and conformity. Moreover, they lacked experience in communicating and articulating their special concerns to the authorities; so they failed to convince non-Mennonites of their loyalty and patriotism. April to September 1917 foreshadowed much of what was to come during the war.

The first Mennonite reaction to the prospect of a draft came on April 11-12, 1917. On those two days, delegates of the GCs' Western District, plus representatives of the Krimmer Mennonite Brethren, Mennonite Brethren, Holdeman Mennonites, and one group of Defenseless Mennonites, met in special session at North Newton, Kansas.

The sessions began with an encouraging report by Peter H. Richert and Peter H. Unruh, who had just returned from Washington, D.C., and a letter by Henry W. Lohrenz, president of Tabor College. Soon the delegates decided to appoint a special committee of seven, charged with trying to preserve freedom from military service. Specifically, the committee, soon dubbed the "Committee of Seven" or the "Exemption Committee," was to petition the authorities and to establish contact with other district conferences, Mennonite groups, and historic peace churches. The seven were Peter H. Richert, Gerhard Penner, Joseph C. Goering, Peter H. Unruh, Henry P. Krehbiel, William J. Ewert, and H. D. Penner.

Then "after a prolonged lively discussion," the delegates reaffirmed the statement that the Western District Conference had made on May 17, 1898. They reiterated Mennonite refusal to participate in war but also stated that if Mennonite men wished to do medical service or serve with the Red Cross, the church could not dissuade them.[4]

In fact the meeting failed sadly in its first major statement of Mennonite nonresistance. It provided no guidelines or instructions for drafted men. It seemed to accept, or at least clearly to condone, noncombatant service—an option that later caused controversy among Mennonites and members of other historic peace churches, as well as between Mennonites and authorities. The meeting "deeply disappointed" one Mennonite pastor and leader, Jacob Klaassen of Cordell, Oklahoma. During the long years of peace, he lamented, Mennonites had apparently forgotten their own history. He thought the delegates had been more concerned about being faithful to country than about loyalty to their own confession of faith.[5]

Shortly after the April 10-11 meeting, Richert and Unruh left for Washington, D.C. There Maxwell Kratz, a Mennonite lawyer from Philadelphia who presumably had contacts among legislators, and Peter Jansen, a Mennonite who was a prominent Republican politician in Nebraska, joined them. Their principal task was to represent Mennonite interests during the debates on the proposed draft. But unfortunately, Mennonites did not cooperate with each other. With their arrival there were at least three Mennonite delegations in the capital, operating somewhat independently.[6]

In addition to the four representatives of the GC's Western Conference, Henry W. Lohrenz, president of Tabor College, and Martin M. Just were in Washington representing the Mennonite Brethren. Also still present were Huffman and Snyder of the All-Mennonite Convention. The Convention represented the more acculturated Mennonites and the Huffman-Snyder team made the unfortunate mistake of assuring various congressmen that Mennonites were willing to accept any military duty except the bearing of arms.

Perhaps with the assistance of Peter Jansen, Richert and his fellow delegates were able to see Representative Charles H. Sloan from Nebraska. Sloan had many Mennonites in his congressional district and was helpful. He even promised the petitioners that he would introduce an amendment exempting conscientious objectors from military service. Later he arranged for them to meet all the members of the House Military Affairs Committee. The Committee seemed favorably disposed to the Mennonites' concern.[7]

The delegates also saw Christian W. Ramseyer, a Mennonite congressman from Pulaski, Iowa. But he was of little help. He was so politically acculturated that he was not even a conscientious objector, and he had supported the declaration of war. Although opposed to conscripting men under the age of twenty-five, Ramseyer objected to exempting men up to age sixty. In other words, he opposed *selective* service, saying he favored a draft of all men in the age range "so as to give all classes of healthy, able-bodied men an opportunity to serve in the army."[8]

Nor could Mennonites count much on Benjamin F. Welty, an Ohio representative and a "Bluffton boy," as Snyder and Huffman referred to him. Although reared Mennonite, Welty was no longer one and had served as a lieutenant-colonel in the Ohio National Guard.

Certainly he was no conscientious objector.[9] A more helpful congressman was William W. Griest, whose district included Lancaster County, Pennsylvania. Although not a Mennonite, during the entire war he worked hard and conscientiously on behalf of his Mennonite and other pacifist constituents.[10]

In addition to the pleas of the Mennonite delegations, Congress received a number of petitions. One was from John W. Kliewer, president of the Western District General Conference and of Bethel College. Kliewer reminded Congress of the Mennonites' loyalty and mistakenly claimed that in the early 1870s President Ulysses S. Grant had promised to exempt Mennonites from military service. The Mennonite "lobbying" had little impact except on one point: the petitioners got the word "military" deleted from a reference to noncombatant service. Potentially that seemed to be an important change, although in the way the government would interpret the Selective Service Act, it was not.[11]

On April 28 the House deliberated and voted on the proposal of its Military Affairs Committee. That committee's version was similar to the original War Department proposal in only exempting those who belonged to "well-recognized religious sects or organizations" whose existing creed or principles forbade them from participating in war. But it was also different, especially because it would not have granted conscientious objectors complete exemption.

During the debates Representative Edward Keating of Colorado offered a plan of genuinely alternative service. Like the plan Russia had long since worked out with its Mennonites, it would have allowed conscientious objectors to do agricultural, forestry, relief, reconstruction, or other civilian work. Keating's plan, in the form of an amendment, had been drafted by Norman M. Thomas, William Fricke, and John E. Steen, three Presbyterian ministers who represented the Fellowship of Reconciliation.

Keating urged his colleagues to take this amendment seriously because it came from Presbyterians, a "hard-hitting and hard-fighting sect," even if the three were pleading the case of conscientious objectors. However, the House of Representatives rejected his proposal by the lopsided vote of 152 to 31. On the same day it accepted the Committee's bill by a vote of 397 to 24.[12]

On April 28 the Senate debated its bill, which was virtually identical to the original War Department's proposal and so would have provided complete exemption of conscientious objectors from all military duty. Surprisingly, that section did not evoke much criticism or discussion. Indeed, there were a few attempts to liberalize it. For example, senator Charles S. Thomas from Colorado believed that, because of its religious restriction, the proposed exemption provision was "confined within . . . narrow limits" and undemocratic. Therefore, he offered an amendment to require no person to render service in the armed forces who was "conscientiously opposed to engaging in such service."[13]

Unfortunately, Thomas allowed his amendment to be set aside in favor of one by Robert M. LaFollette, the well-known progressive Republican senator from Wisconsin. LaFollette had strongly opposed U.S. entry into the war. Now he proposed that there should be special tribunals formed solely to grant exemptions from military service on the basis of various criteria. His idea followed a plan that the British had established in 1916. However, the progressive senator did not list religious, humanitarian, or philosophical scruples as his criteria. Instead, he would have allowed objection based on the particular war. No doubt with his own heavily German-American constituency in mind, he would have granted persons of German extraction and other nationals of enemy states to be exempt from fighting against their own kind. Not surprisingly, that idea evoked considerable opposition—and defeat. U.S. law has never honored such selective objection.[14]

George E. Chamberlain, a senator from Oregon and chairman of the Military Affairs Committee, was "entirely in sympathy" with excusing conscientious objectors. He had, he said, "great patience with a man of that kind." So he too offered an amendment to exempt objectors other than those who belonged to well-recognized religious sects or organizations. It is not clear if he also intended to exempt them from noncombatant service. In any case, the Senate rejected his plan. On the other hand, the Senate did not go to the other extreme.

The strongest attack on the whole idea of exemption came from senator Porter J. McCumber of North Dakota, who introduced an amendment to delete it. Saying that exemption only favored slackers and traitors, he argued that every American owed the country the duty of serving, even to the extent of giving one's life. He dubbed conscientious objectors "copperheads," whose only place was "in the trenches, at the front, making them serve their country." Such rhetoric foreshadowed public contempt for conscientious objectors as World War I continued. McCumber's attempt failed, by a vote of fifty-four to seventeen. However, during subsequent conference committee meetings a few days later, the negotiators dropped the original, generous Senate provision on conscientious objection and kept the House version instead. On May 18 President Wilson signed this measure into law.[15]

The Selective Service Act required all men from ages twenty-one to thirty-one to register. In August 1918 the Act was amended to include men aged eighteen to forty-six. Actual conscription would be selective. Officials could grant exemptions for physical and professional reasons. As for pacifists, a draftee could be exempted if he belonged to a well-organized religious sect or organization whose creed forbade its members to participate in war—but he would be exempted only from combatant, not from so-called noncombatant duty. The law did not define noncombatant service. Instead, it gave the president the authority to form a definition at a later time.[16]

The law shocked Mennonites. "We had not believed that this would be possible in the United States," declared Christian E. Krehbiel, brother of Henry P. and a prominent Kansas GC Mennonite in his own right. Probably he spoke for many others. Pastor Klaassen of Cordell, Oklahoma, felt that government officials had intentionally "confused" Mennonites "by innocent-sounding promises."[17] However, throughout much of the summer of 1917, most Mennonites kept hoping that somehow the government would interpret its law so generously and liberally that their young men might still escape all military obligation. Their first attempt to influence national legislation had not taught them much. They had yet to understand national political realities or the mood of the nation.

June 5 had been scheduled as the day of registration under the Selective Service Act. On that day about 10 million men took the step. In the next eighteen months, 2.8 million men would be dispatched to military camps. Of Mennonite draftees, the first contingent did not leave until September. Meanwhile in June some two hundred thousand to nine hundred thousand men refused or failed to register, and many more refused or failed in 1918.[18]

But authorities rightly considered registration a success. Most eligible Mennonites registered, even though many might still have left for Canada. In general, church leaders thought it best to comply and register. The strongest criticism of the draft came from E. H. Sprunger, editor of the *The Berne* (Indiana) *Witness*—a local paper largely by and for Mennonites. Sprunger argued that there should have been a referendum on the draft. Shortly after June 5, he lamented that conscription would pluck the flower of the nation and make them eligible for slaughter or break down their moral fiber. War would leave a wake of "moral wrecks."[19] In fact, his words were not so very different from many remarks Wilson had made earlier, when he was still trying to keep the U.S. neutral. But before long Sprunger would fall silent and begin to march with the patriotic mainstream.

Individual churches and conferences assisted young men in preparing for draft registration. Especially the Western District Exemption Committee took that task seriously. As early as May 16, the committee decided to publish a special pamphlet in German and English. The booklet would instruct prospective draftees about how to answer certain questions and would list scriptural passages supporting religious conscientious objection.[20]

At about the same time, church leaders reminded young men to submit certificates of membership in order to substantiate their applications for exemption. For men who had to register but had not yet been baptized and therefore were not church members, there was a serious problem. In such instances, President Lohrenz suggested, the registrant should say, "I claim exemption because of my Mennonite creed." However, many draft and military officials were suspicious of such registrants. The same suspicion applied to those baptized after April 6 or May 18, 1917.[21]

There were at least two opportunities for registrants to indicate their religious scruples against military service. Question 12 of each registration card of 1917 asked the registrant to indicate if he claimed exemption on the basis of religious belief. Most Mennonite men did so. Probably having received some coaching by their local church leaders, many gave the same answer. However, it seems that in some instances, at the suggestion of local sheriffs—albeit in clear violation of the law—draft boards ignored this question.[22]

More important was form 174, for those requesting noncombatant status. It is not known how many of these applications were rejected by local draft boards. However, even if a registrant was refused noncombatant status, he could still try to persuade military camp commanders to recognize him as a conscientious objector. Local draft boards also had the option of accepting or rejecting the applications of those who sought exemptions for economic reasons. In certain counties in Pennsylvania, boards treated such applications with exceptional sympathy. If such registrants had scruples against fighting, the boards apparently considered them to be more useful at home on the farm than in the military.[23]

Elsewhere most draft boards were not as generous. For example in Cordell, Oklahoma, Jacob Klaassen considered the local board to be made up of "hateful draft officials" especially prejudiced against Mennonites. That board rejected his son's application for a farm exemption even though Klaassen thought his son was entitled to one.[24] Local prejudice also seems to have moved boards in South Dakota to deny many

Hutterite registrants' exemptions for occupational or marital reasons. As a result, during the entire war a relatively high proportion of married Hutterite men had to go to military camps.[25]

During the summer of 1917, Mennonites experienced disappointment and frustration not only when they sought economic deferments but also on the question of complete exemption. They still hoped to persuade federal authorities to interpret the Selective Service Act liberally as exempting conscientious objectors from all military-related service.

By September they learned much about the new realities and demands of the war. One major problem was that as yet there existed no representative committee—no Mennonite Central Committee—to explain their historic peace position and present their case. Instead, various delegations descended upon Washington, each trying to plead its case with the president, Secretary of War Newton D. Baker, Provost Marshal-General Enoch H. Crowder, and various congressmen. President Wilson did not have much "sympathy with the conscientious objector" but preferred to avoid unnecessary harshness and injustice.[26]

By early 1918 the president looked favorably on farm furloughs for the men, and Secretary of War Baker agreed. Baker had been a lawyer and mayor of Cleveland, Ohio. As a progressive he supported Wilson and in 1916 was appointed secretary of war. Although at one time he had been a pacifist of sorts, he did not have a high opinion of conscientious objectors. But he hoped that through patient effort and by treating the objectors fairly, he and military camp officers could bring them to be "in harmony with the thought" of his generation.

While President Wilson was inclined to define noncombatant status as soon as possible, Baker proposed to postpone the definition. Any early announcement, he felt, would encourage further conscientious objection. He preferred to proceed with the draft and find suitable work for the men in the camps. Crowder supported this policy. He felt no great sympathy toward conscientious objectors, even though at one time he seemed to have favored exempting them from all military service.[27]

By late June representatives of the GCs' Western District, of the Mennonite Brethren, and of the Krimmer Mennonite Brethren agreed on a proposal to accept agricultural or Red Cross work. Moreover, if the government would not accept these suggestions, they were even willing to consider noncombatant work.[28] On June 17 a three-man delegation consisting of John W. Kliewer, H. P. Krehbiel, and P. H. Richert arrived in Washington and in the next few days saw various congressmen as well as Crowder and Baker.

The delegation achieved nothing. Crowder promised only vaguely to find a way to respect their conscience. Baker gave the impression of a friendly person who promised to do everything possible for them. He told the delegates that it would be "a sad, sad affair" if Mennonite young men would leave the country, as Krehbiel threatened they might if drafted. At Baker's suggestion the delegates informed Crowder that Mennonite draftees might be able to do such work as irrigation, draining, farming, restoration work abroad, or other service "outside the military establishment which aims to support and save life" and which would not result in "personal injury or loss of life."[29] But the talks reached no agreement.

Except for its Western District Conference, the General Conference church was rather slow in responding to the conscription issue. Not until late August, at a meeting at Noble, Iowa, did the Middle District discuss the matter. There, "in the shade of a hickory tree in the pasture," the conferees deliberated the question. "The suspense was getting very heavy" as the delegates listened carefully to an "old" Mennonite bishop, Simon Gingerich of Wayland, Iowa, give a report on the military draft.

Later in the meeting a committee of three—J. H. Langenwalter, J. F. Lehman, and Bluffton College President Samuel K. Mosiman— recommended that the government should place draftees who refused any type of service in a detention camp or a civilian prison, but not in a military prison.[30] About two weeks later, this resolution was presented to the GCs' overall General Conference which was meeting in Reedley, California. This was the same meeting at which the GC denomination severed its ties with the Federal Council of Churches because of the latter's support for the war effort.

But the conference failed to provide future draftees with specific guidelines about how far they could or could not obey their military officers in the camps. Instead, it left the men in camp to decide when they were or were not acting against the word of God and their confession of faith.[31] Draftees, however, wanted guidance and direction, not vague generalities.

In late June, Aaron Loucks, a leader in the "old" Mennonite Church who had helped found the Mennonite Publishing House in Scottdale, Pennsylvania; and a Holdeman delegation consisting of Jacob Dirks, D. B. Holdeman, and Frederick C. Fricke, also went to Washington.[32] In July and August Hutterites and the Franconia "old" Mennonites sent petitions to President Wilson requesting exemption from participation in war in any form. In early August the Franconians dispatched a delegation to Washington. Here Baker received them and suggested that they let the men go to the camps, where they could do what their consciences permitted them to do.[33]

However, not until late August did "old" Mennonites in the East offer real advice to their young men. On August 20 Franconia Mennonites met at Souderton, Pennsylvania, where they rejected any service, combatant or noncombatant, under the military arm of the government. Furthermore, they created a committee of three to work with the Lancaster "old" Mennonite Conference, the Church of the Brethren, and the Brethren in Christ to negotiate with officials in Washington. Two days later the Lancaster Conference passed a similar resolution.[34]

Then on August 29, 184 "old" Mennonite delegates representing sixteen district conferences (plus some Mennonite Brethren in Christ and some Defenseless Mennonite observers), gathered in the Yellow Creek meetinghouse near Goshen, Indiana. Here they reaffirmed the traditional Mennonite nonresistant position by declaring their church had "continually stood for the surrendered life, a consistent separation from the world, and an attitude of peace toward all men." The delegates rejected all forms of military service and advised young men to present themselves when drafted. But the men were to inform the authorities that under "no circumstances" could they consent to service, either combatant or noncombatant, under the military arm of the government.[35]

Thus the "old" Mennonite church took a firmer position than had the General Conference and the Mennonite Brethren—a difference that would complicate possible cooperation among the various Mennonite groups. Such cooperation would also depend much on the War Problems Committee which was established at this meeting. This "old" Mennonite committee consisted of Aaron Loucks, Daniel (D. D.) Miller, and Sanford (S. G.) Shetler, while Jonas (J. S.) Hartzler would serve as its secretary. Its mandate was quite similar to that of the Western District Exemption Committee, and in the course of the war it did a vast amount of work on behalf of the draftees. Most influential was Aaron Loucks's—so influential that some government officials began to consider him a threat to the nation.[36]

One of the first tasks of the War Problems Committee was to negotiate with Washington authorities about conscription. In Washington Loucks's Committee met members of the Franconia Conference delegation and also members of an Old Order Amish one. Upon the advice of Senator Atlee Pomerene of Ohio, the various delegates agreed to send a small committee consisting of D. D. Miller, Loucks's, and Shetler to see Secretary Baker. On September 1 the three men met with Baker, who opened the meeting by asking what the "boys" wanted. Apparently the men had a "very satisfactory conversation." Baker said that Mennonite draftees would be "tried on conscience," but he also assured them that Mennonites in camps would not be forced "to cross over" and to wear the military uniform because they already wore a "distinctive garb" (a point of course not true of nearly all Mennonites, especially males).

In the end Baker and the delegates seemed to have agreed on ten points. In sum, conscientious objectors were to be held in special detention units where they did not have to wear uniforms, drill, or serve in any capacity that violated their creed and conscience. And they would not have to accept noncombatant service but could be assigned to other tasks not under the military arm of the government.

The delegates must have been elated. Apparently their efforts to secure fair treatment had finally been successful. However, a few weeks later Baker informed Loucks's committee that there had been a serious misunderstanding. Draftees who refused any kind of service would not be assigned nonmilitary work but were to remain in detention camps. There they would have to wait for "such disposition as the government may decide upon."[37]

On October 23, in another meeting with Secretary of War Baker, the committee tried to change Baker's mind. They did not succeed. Nor was he swayed by a letter from Loucks, dated October 31. In it Loucks accurately summed up the Mennonite position. He denied, as other Mennonites had done in previous weeks and months, that they were disloyal, unpatriotic, or cowardly. To maintain their position in the present circumstances, Loucks pointed out, required greater courage than accepting noncombatant service. Loucks assured Baker the men would "cheerfully" accept any service for the government that was consistent with their faith, but they could not accept anything under the military establishment. However, they were willing to accept the penalties that might result from disobedience.[38]

Despite Loucks's and other Mennonites' many efforts to secure complete exemption from military service, Mennonites received no satisfaction by the time of the first draft calls. Had they been misled by government officials and lulled into false beliefs? Or was it true that the draftees would probably not have to do anything against their consciences, would not have to become part of the military?

Michael Klaassen, a GC pastor at Cordell, Oklahoma, and a brother of Jacob, believed that his people had been "deceived, deluded," and drawn into the net while the enemy drew tight the snare. However, he blamed the Mennonites themselves; they should have kept their distance from the very beginning. His church's general conference, he argued, should have indicated how far it wanted to go without acting against God's laws and the Mennonite faith. He charged that the conference had been more concerned with how it could show loyalty to the government. As a result, "it all came to a head and the clouds of trouble increased."[39]

Had Mennonites been drawn into a conscription trap or net? Should they have done more to press for a precise federal policy before allowing the men to go to the camps?[40] It is doubtful that the government cleverly misled Mennonite leaders with false assurances to segregate the men and treat them generously. Instead, Baker hoped to be able to keep the number of conscientious objectors relatively small by urging the president to wait before he clarified noncombatant status. Perhaps Baker could have interpreted and applied the Selective Service Act as liberally as he would later, in 1918. But he had good reasons not to do so at that time. Moreover, when Baker told Loucks that the men would be tried "on conscience," he was being honest. And he and other high officials never approved the inhumane treatment that conscientious objectors began to receive in various camps—although to be sure, they did far too little to prevent or correct such abuse.

Even if Mennonite leaders had known precisely what was awaiting the men in camp, what could they have done? They surely were not ready to urge the men to disobey outright, refuse the draft, and not go to military camps. Most Mennonites were much too law-abiding to consider civil disobedience. A few Mennonites did escape to Canada, but they were a small minority and most probably went without registering for the draft. One could argue Mennonites might have achieved more in Washington if the different delegations had cooperated. At times federal officials must have been quite confused by all the Mennonite groups descending upon them. But it is doubtful if one representative Mennonite committee skilled in negotiating with federal officials would have accomplished more. Even the "worldly" Quakers failed.

In September 1917 the first group of men left for military camps where they were indeed "tried on conscience." Already in February 1917, *The Mennonite* had predicted that if war were to come Mennonites would surely get "their fiery trial of persecution." Some Mennonites might take up arms, the editor warned. But he also hoped that Mennonites would place their trust in God to preserve and to assist them "to remain true to our principles whatever may befall."[41]

In fact, the trial came not only to the young men who were called upon to render military service but also to their parents and others who stayed home.

3

Mennonites and Patriots

World War I swept the United States up in a wave of superpatriotism and mass hysteria as never before. Prior to April 1917, the United States had not been harmed much by the Great War in Europe and had profited considerably by supplying the Allies with loans and material. But now, in the words of historian John Higham, the struggle with Germany "called for the most strenuous nationalism and the most pervasive nativism that the United States had ever known."[1]

In a mass of propaganda, the government demonized the enemy as the embodiment of all evil, and in so doing did much to mold and shape public opinion not only toward the enemy but also toward any wartime dissidents, including conscientious objectors. A special agency, euphemistically titled the "Committee on Public Information," chaired by a journalist named George Creel and often called the "Creel Committee," successfully waged psychological warfare. This agency convinced the great mass of Americans that Germany represented militaristic, aggressive authoritarianism and a serious threat to American freedom and security.

The government's propaganda machine went on to persuade the public that the U.S. was in the war to make the world "safe for democracy" and "to end all wars." Today a more critical if not cynical public might view government propaganda more skeptically. But in World War I Americans were more naive, innocent, or gullible, and so more trusting of their government. They readily swallowed their political leaders' line about the enemy and the demands to make huge sacrifices to rid the world of Prussian militarism and Kaiserism.

Various superpatriotic organizations worked hand in hand with the Creel Committee and with other government efforts to enforce a maximum of patriotic conformity. The climate brought heavy pressures for uniformity in both thought and deed, whether from government or from voluntary organizations. Among such organizations were the

American Defense Society, the National Security League, the American Protective League, the Liberty League, and many others, including newspapers. The American Protective League was actually sponsored by the Department of Justice and became an arm of the federal government.

These organizations, in addition to the official Bureau of Investigation and the Military Intelligence Department, spied on neighbors, reported suspects to the authorities, assisted in the sale of Liberty Bonds, organized patriotic rallies, and "requested" citizens to sign loyalty pledges. Many, many members of the clergy became noisy in their support of the war effort, telling their people that Christ would gladly have donned a uniform and participated in combat against the despicable Hun. Putting Christ in uniform was not something new, but perhaps never before had American clergy been so ardent in support of a U.S. military crusade.[2]

Finally another pressure came from mob action. Mobs had often played an important role in American history—to impose uniformity and to neutralize if not eliminate what were conceived to be threats to the American way of life. In the nineteenth century, mobs had terrorized Irish and Chinese immigrants, Mormons, and African-Americans. Now in World War I, they often terrorized those suspected of harboring unpatriotic thoughts or considered guilty of un-American behavior.[3]

All of these sources communicated a message that loyalty would cost very little but that the cost would be high if one decided otherwise. In sum, by persuasion, fear, and intimidation, various forces imposed superpatriotism and rigid conformity upon most American communities. As Attorney General A. Mitchell Palmer stated approvingly in 1918, "It is safe to say that never in its history has this country been so thoroughly policed."[4]

Soon many individuals were arrested, dismissed from their positions, physically threatened, and in some cases prosecuted, imprisoned, or even lynched. Prosecution was made easy by the terms of two laws passed by Congress and President Wilson, the Espionage Act of 1917 and the Sedition Act of 1918. These acts forbade a host of activities, such as obstructing the armed forces' recruitment or making false statements on the sale of war bonds. They imposed penalties for willfully uttering, printing, writing, or publishing any "disloyal, scurrilous, or abusive language" about the American form of government, the flag, the federal constitution, or the military uniform.[5]

Such laws fell heavily on German-speaking Americans, including

Mennonites, especially those on the western prairies who were only a generation or two away from their immigration from the Russian empire. Such German-American communities fell victim to self-appointed superpatriots and vigilantes.[6] Moreover, because of their nonconformity and nonresistance, Mennonites often suffered even more than other German-Americans. However, not all Mennonite communities came under such harassment. In some localities they were tolerated, at least during the first year of the war.

In the World War I era, popular demands, commitments, and conformity took many forms. Loyal citizens were expected to help finance the war by generous purchases of Liberty Bonds and Thrift Stamps. They were to contribute to the Red Cross or local "war chests" and to display the flag and attend patriotic rallies. Frieda Suderman Pankratz recalls the "almost hysterical frenzy" of a crowd in Moundridge, Kansas, after it had repeatedly sung the wartime theme song "Over There" in the local opera house.[7] Furthermore, some communities outlawed or brought great pressure against using certain languages in church, school, and stores—especially German.

The most important act of patriotism was service in the armed forces. Perhaps because of Wilsonian rhetoric about making the world safe for democracy and ending all wars, many young Americans entered the war with unbounded enthusiasm and zeal. To them the war became a crusade or mighty adventure to eradicate German militarism, the barbarian Hun, and Kaiserism. They also felt that their youth and vigor would achieve these ends quickly. The cruel realities of modern war would soon teach them that military victories came only at great cost. But no issue inflamed patriotic public opinion more than refusing to fight for God, nation, and flag—and to make the supreme sacrifice. Those who refused were considered cowards, slackers, parasites, scoundrels, traitors, and individuals not worthy of holding American citizenship.

In such a climate, could Mennonites profess their faith? On April 5, 1917, the day before the U.S. declared war, *The Mennonite* vowed that Mennonites would reaffirm their opposition to bearing arms, be ready to submit to punishment, and not compromise as most peace advocates were doing.[8] But would they? Many if not most Mennonites hoped the Allies would win the war. Yet their response to all the demands was rather negative. They did not want openly to criticize U.S. involvement in the war for fear of possible prosecution under the provisions of the Espionage and Sedition Acts. They did not wish to antagonize or inflame public opinion more then they were already doing just by their nonresistance. As J. S. Hartzler, then president of Goshen College, wrote in 1918, "In these days of patriotism, it is best that we do not say much about our position but quietly live it."[9]

However, until about mid-1918, Mennonites were not afraid or reluctant to reaffirm Mennonite values; some did so rather vocally. It was only as the pressures built that they became reticent. Various Mennonite editorials and articles reminded readers that they were pilgrims and strangers on this earth and that the Christian kingdom had nothing in common with political realms. Furthermore, they reaffirmed New Testament nonresistance as exemplified in the life of Christ. Mennonites should remember that Christians could not "go to kill in the spirit of Christ" or use carnal weapons, because war was foreign to Christ's spirit and "irreconcilable with his end and purposes."

War, Mennonite readers were told, had no room for love of the enemy. Instead it "enthrones hatred and anger and dethrones love." Mennonite editors and writers insisted that their people did not choose nonresistance to escape hardships and dangers of military service; they did so because they understood nonresistance to be the "plain and positive teaching of Christ." Furthermore, they would watch for opportunities to help relieve suffering.[10]

However, in the summer and fall of 1918 such reaffirmations of the nonresistant faith became less frequent and criticism of the war effort even more so. In late September 1918, *The Mennonite* announced that an "active propagation of peace doctrines in the face of military rule would injure the cause just now." It suggested that the best strategy was to wait and work for peace after the war, in order to prevent another war.[11]

But most Mennonites also realized it was impossible to isolate themselves completely from the war effort. World War I was a modern, total war that demanded some kind of commitment from every citizen. Mennonites knew that the government was spending a large share of their taxes on the war and that their farm products helped feed the military machine. But were they also expected to make all sorts of declarations or manifestations of loyalty such as displaying the flag at home and in their churches? Must they also purchase Liberty Bonds and Thrift Stamps and attend patriotic rallies?

Many Mennonites were eager to display some patriotism in one form or another. Often when addressing government authorities, they expressed their patriotism by referring to their "beloved land or country." As mentioned above, most Mennonites also hoped the Allies would win the war, even if they did not think they could participate in it. Frequently and eagerly they pointed out that many of their ancestors had left Europe to escape militaristic Germany. Many of them did make various sorts of patriotic compromises. For instance, many agreed to purchase the so-called Liberty Bonds and several young men were willing to don uniforms and serve as noncombatants or even as combatants.

Some Mennonite papers approved such compromises—among them the *The Berne Witness*. Initially this paper demonstrated no enthusiasm for the war effort and military conscription. But after some criticism, it denied ever having been unpatriotic. It even went on to support the war effort by publishing many pro-war cartoons and advertising Liberty Loans.[12] *Der Herold* was a similar paper published by and for Mennonites in Newton, Kansas. Prior to April 1917, it took pride in the Mennonites' Germanic culture, but during the war it tried to demonstrate its patriotism in the same way as *The Berne Witness*. It carried no more critical editorials, published pro-war cartoons, and after October 11, 1917, dropped a slogan from its masthead which said, *"Die beste Zeit Frieden zu schlieszen ist Heute"* (the best time to make peace is now).[13]

A few Mennonite congregations took strongly patriotic stands. The Germantown Mennonite Church at Philadelphia had already furnished men for the Union Army during the Civil War and would send soldiers for World War I.[14] The West Zion congregation at Moundridge, Kansas, consisted of descendants from Germany who settled in the New World because of their dislike of Prussian militarism. However, over time its members developed strong American loyalties and supported noncombatant service during the war. At one time the congregation even allowed a speaker to deliver a pro-war harangue.[15]

The General Conference Mennonite institutions of higher learning, Bluffton College in Ohio and Bethel College in Kansas, displayed certain amounts of patriotism. Both colleges actively supported Liberty loan drives and Thrift Stamp sales and contributed to the Red Cross and the war-oriented YMCA. Neither the Bluffton College paper, *The Witmarsum*, nor the *Bethel College Monthly* ever decried the war; in fact, the former frequently praised those who went off to serve their country.[16]

At Bethel College a group of younger faculty who had been affected by the progressive movement supported the war effort. Among them was Samuel Burkhard, head of the department of philosophy and education and acting dean. In the spring of 1918, Burkhard told an audience at nearby Hesston that the current struggle was a clash between two very different ideals of life—German *Kultur* and democracy—which could never live together in the same world. Burkhard decried the war and expressed his hatred for "the whole process"—but said he saw no other alternative. The world had to be made safe for men rather than for Kaisers, he contended.[17]

In some cases members of the congregation might have been more patriotic than their pastors and were probably even embarrassed over their spiritual leaders' antiwar stance. Such was the case in a Central District Conference (later, GC) congregation at Carlock, Illinois. There pastor Joseph H. King denounced the war strongly from the very beginning, refused to display the flag, and advised young men in his congregation not to serve as combatants.

In June 1917 a member of the congregation informed John H. Kerrick, the local Bureau of Investigation agent in Bloomington, Illinois, of her pastor's unpatriotic behavior. She claimed to speak also on behalf of several other members who objected to King's harsh and "vicious" criticism of the government, the president, and the Red Cross. Kerrick arranged a meeting with King who promised to mend his ways. But the complaints continued. In late September Kerrick went to Carlock and met with "all prominent people," three of whom were members of the congregation, and with King. Not one individual spoke up on King's behalf. The pastor then apologized for all the criticism against him and promised "to make everything right in the future." Thereafter the Carlock Mennonite congregation moved toward the mainstream of American patriotism.[18]

But of all the Mennonite congregations, none was more patriotic and supportive of the war effort than two GC congregations of Wayland, Iowa—the Wayland congregation and the Eicher Emmanuel congregation only a few miles away. Many members of the two congregations were of Swiss and Alsatian extraction; unlike the nearby Sugar Creek congregation of the "old" Mennonites, they had become quite acculturated.[19] Few church publications could have sounded more patriotic and supportive of the war than the two congregations' monthly newsletter, *The Pastor's Assistant*.

In December 1917 *The Pastor's Assistant* urged its readers not to discuss whether they liked the war but to ask themselves what special burden they could bear during the current struggle. The pastoral paper reminded members that it was not enough to let the boys fight their battles—those who stayed home had many opportunities to express their patriotism by contributing to the Red Cross and the YMCA and by purchasing Liberty Bonds.

On July 4, 1918, a Sunday school class of the Eicher congregation unfurled a service flag to which were attached seven stars, representing seven boys in military service. In 1918 the local community held its Memorial Day celebration in the Wayland Mennonite church building. Mennonite minister Samuel M. Musselman gave the sermon, which the local newspaper praised as "one of the best addresses ever heard in this community."

In November 1918, Private Walter Lodder gave a "splendid talk" at the Eicher church and shortly thereafter *The Pastor's Assistant* expressed its grief over the death of its secretary's brother who had been killed in France. Holding up the young man's "supreme sacrifice for the nation's ideals to which he had dedicated his life," the paper suggested that it was better to die as a soldier than to live as a slacker. After all, the writer thought, it was "sweeter to die in the performance of duty, than to live with the consciousness of having shirked that duty."[20]

But to many Mennonites, wartime pressure for conformity brought considerable agony and soul-searching. Among the pressures was the public outcry against using the German language. In 1917 millions of German-named Americans used some form of German in their homes and churches. Among them were many Lutherans, Roman Catholics, and others as well as Mennonites. Most Mennonites who were strongly tied to the language, for worship as well as in the home, lived in Kansas, Pennsylvania, and Ohio. Except for the Old Order groups, most other American Mennonites had almost completely shifted to English for worship and much of their public life, although they still might speak a dialect in their families and neighborhoods.

Most Kansas Mennonites spoke high and/or a low German dialect while the Amish in Pennsylvania, Ohio, and elsewhere spoke Pennsylvania German, or, as it was often called, "Pennsylvania Dutch." World War I hysteria and demands for conformity could not tolerate the use of German and its dialects. The intolerance took many different forms. For English speakers, there was great pressure to "purge" the American language of German words such as sauerkraut, dachshund, etc.

Much more troublesome, a few states such as South Dakota specifically forbade the use of German in sermons or public worship. But in most cases, the public pressure was informal, not by law. Local citizens warned or threatened German-speaking residents to stop speaking the language of the despised Hun in their churches, on the street, or even over the telephone.[21]

One day near Moundridge, Kansas, members of the First Mennonite Church of Christian found a typewritten note posted on their meetinghouse door, saying, "No more German service will be allowed at this church."[22] In Dallas, Oregon, the local chapter of the National Council of Defense told the Zion Mennonite congregation to change from German to English. The congregation yielded, but the pastor, J. P. Neufeld, resigned because he could not preach in another language.[23]

In Aberdeen, Idaho, delegates from the local Defense Council visited the First Mennonite Church and requested them to discontinue using German in any setting. Mennonites responded by saying that it would take time to make such a change, since many members did not understand or speak English.[24]

Other congregations facing similar pressures often compromised by introducing one English-language service. In at least one instance pressure to change did not come from local superpatriots but from members of a congregation itself. This happened when several members of a Central District Mennonite congregation at Meadows, Illinois, asked a federal official to convince their pastor, Joseph Kinsinger, to see "the error of his ways."[25]

Local pressure groups were even more successful in persuading Mennonite congregations to discontinue German schools. In April 1918, James A. Ray, superintendent of schools in Marion County, Kansas, and a person who had been very supportive of Mennonites in the past, requested them not to continue their private German schools. He admitted that he had no legal grounds to forbid private religious instruction in German, but on practical grounds he warned that plans were afoot "to burn the books and otherwise break up the school."

By November 1918, all German schools in the jurisdiction of the GCs' Western District Conference were closed.[26] Meanwhile in the same region Bethel College became suspect as a center of German culture. Local Newton patriots did allow the First Mennonite congregation to keep using the German language, but public hostility toward the college remained. This was the case even though some Bethel faculty supported the war effort and the purchase of Thrift Stamps and students had taken up a collection for the YMCA. At one time students became so fearful that they chose to remain overnight in the administration building because they considered that structure safer. No violence occurred, but in September 1918 a committee of the local Loyalty League demanded that Bethel stop its German classes.

The faculty complied; they adopted a resolution which declared, "Whereas the use of the German language calls the loyalty of Bethel College into question at this time, be it resolved that the German language be eliminated from this curriculum."[27]

Because various Mennonite papers were in German, they aroused suspicion and were investigated by the authorities. In the end, none were forbidden to publish, but critics filed various complaints. In September 1917 C. G. Wiens, most likely of Mennonite extraction, drew the attention of the Department of Justice to Abraham L. Schellenberg, editor of the *Zionsbote*, a Mennonite Brethren weekly published in Hillsboro, Kansas. Schellenberg, said Wiens, was "radically pro-German" and always made light of the government. But no action was taken against the paper.[28] Schellenberg, who was also editor of the pro-German *Vorwärts*, learned to be more circumspect.[29]

As for *Der Herold* in neighboring Newton, despite its eventual patriotism, it had some difficulty getting clearance from George Creel's Committee on Public Information, whose thought-control mandate included a requirement that all foreign-language publications be licensed. In its application the paper professed the "highest type of loyalty to the principles of the Constitution" consistent with Christian duty toward "the great government" under which it was an "inestimable privilege to live." But the paper's manager, none other than Henry P. Krehbiel, made a special trip to Washington, D.C., to plead his case. Meanwhile his brother Christian, *Der Herold*'s editor, wrote to Professor Guy Stanton Ford, a member of the Creel Committee. Another brother, Edward P. Krehbiel, professor of history at Stanford University, may also have pleaded *Der Herold*'s case.

Edward Krehbiel knew Ford and was a highly respected member of his profession who served briefly as a member of The Inquiry, a body of scholars and experts selected to advise President Wilson in his future negotiations with the Allies in Paris. Perhaps the purchase of some $15,000 of Liberty Bonds by the Geary Milling and Elevator Company, of which Christian Krehbiel was vice-president, helped *Der Herold* to obtain its license. However, in January of 1919, Edward Krehbiel lost his position as a member of The Inquiry, probably because he had been too active for peace before the U.S. actually entered the war.[30]

In the end, the fact that some Mennonites received licenses to publish in German and others quit using German in church and school did not remove all suspicion of German-speakers. Many of their neighbors still viewed German-Americans as supporting the culture of the despised Hun.

At least three serious incidents against Mennonites resulted from such popular suspicion—although other factors contributed, such as the Mennonites' nonresistant faith or unwillingness to buy Liberty Bonds and contribute to the Red Cross. In April 1918 John Franz, pastor of the Bethlehem Mennonite congregation (GC) located near Bloomfield, Montana, was almost lynched. One factor may simply have been that he encouraged young men in his congregation to become conscientious objectors. But for some time neighbors had been complaining about what they considered to be Franz's pro-German sympathies and about the use of the German language in his church.

At the request of the local sheriff, Franz had agreed to discontinue using German. Nevertheless, one Saturday afternoon a group of twelve vigilantes including two attorneys, a banker, several businessmen, a cattleman, and even the sheriff grabbed Franz and forced him into a car. His wife tried to climb onto the running board of the automobile but was pushed away and thrown to the ground. The men, many of whom seem to have had too much to drink, took Franz to a tree where they tried to place a noose around his neck.

But somehow Franz grabbed the rope and would not release it. While he and the vigilantes struggled, Franz also tried to reason with them and asked the men if they really wanted a record of this hanging to go down in the history of the county. Finally, the sheriff struck a deal. If the men would spare Franz, the sheriff would put him in jail in nearby Glendive. There the sheriff allowed Franz's wife and two children to visit him, and, after speaking to members of the congregation, decided to "try" the pastor.

The "trial" consisted of intense grilling about Franz's alleged use of the German language, his German background, war bonds, etc. A few days later the sheriff released Franz, after insisting that he post a $3,000 bond, promise not to use the German language, and report four times per year to the local district court. The congregation helped raise the bond and gave the sheriff all its German Bibles. Later the bond was revoked, and five families who had falsely accused Franz of harboring pro-German sympathies left the area. After the war Franz refused to sue anyone. One ringleader asked Franz to forgive him, and Franz did.[31]

Anti-German sentiment was also a principal cause of the burning of two Mennonite church buildings near Inola, Oklahoma. In December 1912 the Mennonite Brethren organized a congregation there. Initially the members met in different homes and in the local Baptist meetinghouse, but in 1917 they purchased a building on the northeast side of the town. The congregation numbered about sixty people. Meanwhile in November 1914, General Conference Mennonites organized a congregation they named Eden. They bought an old schoolhouse which they moved to a location between Inola and Chouteau.

That congregation had twenty-seven members. In addition, already in 1906 a few Older Order Amish communities had settled in neighboring Mayes County.[32]

Although Oklahoma had relatively few inhabitants of German extraction, few states could match it in patriotic hysteria and anti-German sentiment. In September 1917, Mayes County patriots formed a Council of Defense. Like similar organizations the council assisted local authorities with recruitment and Liberty loan drives, and ferretted out or exposed "unpatriotic" or suspicious elements. The *Mayes County Republican* added a journalistic voice to the patriotic chorus. In February 1918 its editor criticized those who were not willing to fight. Christ himself would not have stood by unmoved or refused "to lift his hand to right these dastardly wrongs," he argued. One month later the paper complained that the patience of the county had about "frazzled out."

The county's people could not understand why the Mennonites were unwilling to contribute to the Red Cross, the YMCA, and so forth. It was about time for people "to wake up and purge the community of pro-Germanism." For, wrote the editor, "those who are not for us must surely be against us." In late April representatives of the Mayes County Council of Defense met with members of the District Council to discuss possible visits with "Minnonite" *[sic]* leaders. The *Mayes County Republican* opined that apparently "these long whiskered geezers" did not realize "that they are in danger of being handled without gloves by their neighbors." That same month the Mennonite Brethren congregation in Inola allowed a "patriotic mass meeting" in its house of worship, which German-Americans attended.[33]

Despite that meeting, local patriots remained suspicious of the Mennonites and offered to pay an Inola resident $5.00 if he would burn down the Eden church building. The arsonist did so one Saturday in June. Shortly thereafter the Mennonite Brethren building also went up in flames. George Voth, an Eden member, offered his barn in neighboring Mayes County as a place for the Eden congregation to meet. Shortly thereafter the "patriots" burned the barn as well.

Both the local sheriff and members of the congregation knew who was guilty, and the sheriff wanted the Voth family to press charges. But the Voths refused, and the congregation also preferred to suffer in silence. Perhaps this attitude later helped to restore relations with their non-German neighbors. After the barn burned, the congregation worshiped in a schoolhouse. There they were not disturbed—perhaps because the building contained a flag. In 1920 they rebuilt their meetinghouse. As for the MBs, after the destruction of their building they met in homes. Then in 1919-1920 they built a new facility several miles east of Inola.[34]

A source of controversy and irritation between Mennonites and their neighbors was Mennonite reluctance to display the American flag and perform other ceremonial acts. As in other wars, in World War I most Americans considered display of the flag at home and in church a necessary expression of support for the war effort. The same Americans sang patriotic songs whenever the occasion arose. Historically, Mennonites and their Anabaptist predecessors had been pioneers in separation of church and state. They were not anti-government or anarchist—far from it. Yet to them, especially those who still made a sharp separation between the two kingdoms and saw the state as at best a God-ordained instrument for the kingdom of the unredeemed, flags and patriotic ceremonies seemed to raise doubts about where their primary loyalty lay—with God or with the state?

So unlike many if not most American Christians, Mennonites seldom put flags in their houses of worship. Of course, many of their neighbors saw refusal to display the flag either at home or in church as yet more evidence of pro-German and disloyal sentiments. Efforts of local patriots to force Mennonites to display and salute the flag often grew ugly.

One of the first cases occurred in November 1917, on the campus of the "old" Mennonites' college at Hesston, Kansas. A mob of about twenty to twenty-five men put up a flag and placed a note at the bottom of it warning dire results if it were removed. The next day President Daniel H. Bender ordered its removal anyhow. Before long a person threatened to get the local sheriff to arrest him, and to run the college community out of town.

After consulting with the faculty, Bender informed city officials they would indeed leave if the city viewed them a menace. However, the officials urged them to stay, and condemned the flag incident. Some time later a mob again mulled over the possibility of "getting" Bender. But reportedly a local tough prevented it, saying, "You will not take Mr. Bender, unless you do it over my dead body." Bender concluded that the "Lord used a member of the enemy's gang to protect his servant."[35]

Bishop Simon Gingerich of the Sugar Creek "old" Mennonite congregation, whose meetinghouse was a few miles southeast of Wayland, Iowa, became the victim of similar patriotic zeal. Local citizens organized the Henry County Council of National Defense with a Dr. J. C. Stone, a local physician and a rabid superpatriot, as its head.

New as a medical doctor in the community, Stone may have tried to use superpatriotism to build up his clientele. If so he apparently failed, for he lost most of his Mennonite patients and left Wayland shortly after the war.

In any case he was the same person who later, in March of 1918, induced Gingerich to accept an agreement advising conscientious objectors in Camp Dodge to wear military uniforms. In Stone's eyes Gingerich was "thoroughly disloyal in everything" and had to be removed as a Mennonite bishop. Others agreed, and early in February 1918 Stone's "gangs of hoodlums"—as Gingerich later described them—forced the bishop and other ministers to put up flags at their homes and keep them there or be visited with violence.

The gang put a flag up for Gingerich by spiking its staff to one of the bishop's porch posts. The action drew praise from the *Burlington Hawkeye Gazette*. Referring to Gingerich as "the most suspected and much-warned German minister," the paper's editor called upon him to show allegiance to the government, cease "making pro-Germans and disloyalists out the drafted boys," fly the flag in front of the window of his home, and become a member of the Red Cross. The editor further advised members of Gingerich's congregation to inform their bishop, "Simon says, 'thumbs up,' or we will say to you 'Simon, wiggle, waggle.'"

Despite the spikes, by the next day the wind had blown the flag down, and it lay in the front yard. Gingerich picked it up and hung it up to dry, not outside but in his basement. A few days later two men asked him where it was. He told them what had happened. After making threats and accusations, they departed. Many other local citizens were disturbed over the incident, convinced that Gingerich himself had taken the flag down.

The incident caused some kind of "riot" in Wayland and it is surprising Gingerich was not harmed by what he called the "local rabble." In fact Gingerich promised a federal official and Stone that he and his people would fly flags at the doors of their meetinghouse and on their homes. That action may have defused the immediate tension, but the whole flag incident apparently made Gingerich's ministry to men in Camp Dodge much more difficult if not dangerous. It may well help explain why he, a bishop in the "old" Mennonite church, which was still quite nonconformist in attire, nevertheless advised conscientious objectors in that camp to wear military uniforms.[36]

In April 1918, near Collinsville, Oklahoma, there was a near lynching over a flag incident. In 1913 the Mennonite Brethren had established a congregation at Collinsville, a town about fifteen miles north of Tulsa. One member, John Reimer, operated a 160-acre farm and a large threshing business between Collinsville and Skiatook. Reimer had come from the Russian empire to the United States as late as 1891 and had never learned to speak English well. The local Council of Defense refused to let his congregation hold a German Bible school, and apparently he became very unhappy. A rather blunt and outspoken man, he apparently got so angry at the local patriots that he told them, "It won't be long and the Kaiser will be here and then you will have to learn the German."

"When the war is over," he apparently continued, ". . . it will all be German, there will be no English." Naturally local patriots did not appreciate these outbursts, and two delegates of the Council of Defense went to speak with Reimer.[37]

It seems that during that conversation Reimer aggravated the situation by telling the patriots God was on the side of the Kaiser. He did agree to display a flag in his window or on his rural mailbox, but then a few weeks later he removed it. When questioned about this, he supposedly said openly that he did not like the flag and had torn it down. According to at least one account, he also said, "I hate the United States flag, I don't want it around."

Whatever the exact words, on April 19, 1918, two members of the Council of Defense went to his home and fetched him to Collinsville's city hall for questioning. He was placed in the local jail. Then at about 10:45 p.m. a mob of about fifty overpowered the assistant chief of police, Charles Miller, and two patrolmen and took the prisoner to the city hall's second floor. There they wrapped a double electrical cord around his neck and forced him to apologize and to kiss a flag. Then they proceeded to hang him by removing a chair upon which he stood. His "writhing body" swung two times past a basketball post. But the assistant police chief pleaded with the mob to allow Reimer to answer more questions the next morning. The mob relented and lowered Reimer who by then had lost consciousness.

After Reimer revived, officials returned him to jail. Thereafter a few local businessmen and Peter C. Hiebert, a prominent Mennonite Brethren leader from Hillsboro, Kansas, tried to intervene. Hiebert organized a public meeting in a school building at which he affirmed his loyalty to the United States, explained the Mennonite position on war, and pointed out that Mennonites were not Germans but had come from Russia. Apparently, this meeting was successful and Reimer was soon released on bond. He spent the rest of the war with a brother-in-law in Oklahoma City.[38]

Sometimes the pro-flag patriots were confounded. According to one tale that circulates in various versions (but which is no doubt in the main true), a mob near Whitewater, Kansas, decided in April 1918 to go to the home of a local minister and force him to put up a flag. He did, then suggested they all sing "America." Since his tormentors knew the words of only the first verse, soon he was the only person singing![39] In Grabill, Indiana, patriots planted a flag in bishop John Schmucker's yard and promised to return on a certain day to see if he would get up and salute it. They threatened that if he would not do so, they would tar and feather him. On the appointed day several hundred people gathered and shouted and swore at the bishop. But he remained inside reading his Bible, and fortunately nothing happened.[40]

Equally threatening were patriotic attempts to place flags in church buildings. One evening during a meeting of the youth organization Christian Endeavor, an ex-Mennonite (some of whom outdid their neighbors in superpatriotism) planted a flag on the pulpit in the Ebenfels Mennonite Church (MB) in Hillsboro, Kansas. No one said a word, but after the service the flag was removed.[41]

In 1918 a similar incident occurred in an "old" Mennonite church at Protection, Kansas. During a Sunday morning service, while the congregation watched in silence, four men in army uniforms placed a large American flag behind the pulpit. The flag remained there for several months until one of the members quietly took it down. Later the four apologized for what they had done and expressed great respect for their Mennonite neighbors. Currently some of their descendants are good friends of Mennonites and a few have joined the congregation.[42]

In June 1918, in Allen County, Ohio, some 300 citizens from Lima and other communities placed flags on three Mennonite church buildings in the area. The first to be so "honored" was the Pike Mennonite meetinghouse, where a flag was placed over the entrance. One of the participants gave a speech, declaring that he was only doing what "red-blooded Americans" would have done on their own accord. He warned that if the flag offended anyone, the United States was no place for him to stay. Next the crowd sang "The Star-Spangled Banner" and left a note that read,

> To the members of this church. The manhood of America is fighting to make it possible for you to continue unmolested your services in this church. The removal of the Stars and Stripes from this house of worship will be taken as an indication that you desire to go on record as opposing those now fighting for you and will be taken as evidence that reports of un-American sentiment among members of this congregation are true.

Then the crowd went to the Salem Mennonite Church and held a similar "ceremony." There the speaker chided the congregation for not contributing to the Red Cross and for refusal or reluctance to purchase Liberty Bonds. The last congregation visited was the Oak Grove Mennonite Church. From there the crowd left, singing.[43]

Some congregations displayed the flag voluntarily. At Bethel College, faculty and students purchased one; the Bethel College Mennonite congregation placed it in the sanctuary, along with a Christian flag. After the war the flags were removed.[44] In the meetinghouse of the East White Oak church, a Central Conference congregation near Bloomington, Illinois, Pastor Emmanuel Troyer draped a flag over his pulpit but also reminded his congregation that the U.S. Constitution guaranteed freedom of conscience. However, the flag became a point of sharp division when some members wanted to enroll on it the names of those who were serving as regular soldiers but not the conscientious objectors. Finally the congregation agreed not to place any names on it.[45]

It is difficult to determine how many Mennonite congregations yielded and put flags in or outside their houses of worship. Perhaps some did, especially those who were quite acculturated and not very nonconformist. Most likely quite a few of them quietly removed their flags after the war.

Saluting the flag was another issue. While many adults could escape that ritual, their children, attending public schools, had a harder time. Many Mennonite families instructed their children not to salute, and some Mennonite teachers refused. No doubt a great many Mennonites allowed the salutes, but there were some instances of conflict. One example was at West Liberty, Ohio. In March 1918 the community's school board ordered all children to give the salute before entering the building; therefore, many Mennonite families kept their children from school.

That "unpatriotic" behavior stirred up strong public opinion. In a letter to the editor of the *Urbana, [Ohio] Citizen* an indignant citizen lashed out against this "sect of people, so narrow and bigoted." By forbidding the children "to take part in patriotic exercises," protested the writer, and by "carry[ing] their religion into the public school," the Mennonites were teaching their children "the spirit of disloyalty."

In late March there was a meeting between such Mennonite leaders as Clayton (C. F.) Derstine and bishop Samuel (S. E.) Allgyer on the one hand and the county superintendent, Judge T. B. Owen, the sheriff, a representative of the local paper, and other local citizens on the other. Before it ended the Mennonite leaders agreed that the children could go ahead and salute.[46]

But at least one ordinary Mennonite, named Ora Troyer, still refused to let his nine-year-old daughter take part in that and other patriotic rituals. So in late May 1918, Troyer was arrested. Later that month he was put on trial in a local court, where he explained that saluting the flag would promote a militant spirit in his child. The court rejected the defense, found Troyer guilty, and sentenced him to twenty-five days in jail. A few weeks later a county court in Bellefontaine refused to review the sentence, but did suspend it so that Troyer could file a petition in a higher court. The final outcome is not known.[47]

At least one Mennonite teacher had similar difficulty. Roy Kauffman, a sixth-grade teacher at Kings Creek a few miles south of West Liberty, also refused the pledge of allegiance to the flag. In response his superintendent warned that some of the older boys in his school might "handle him." Thereupon Kauffman decided to leave the school building via the fire escape and not return.[48] In a somewhat similar vein, Archibald T. Yoder, a member of the school board in West Liberty, ran into difficulties when he tried to prevent a teacher from inculcating her pupils with patriotic values by such rituals. In May 1918 public pressure induced Yoder to resign.[49]

Mennonites ran into difficulty, not only because of their actions or their refusals to act, but just because of their nonresistant beliefs. Traditionally most Americans have had little understanding of or regard for conscientious objectors; some seem to have seen them as even more contemptible than ordinary criminals. World War I was no exception. Uncomprehending neighbors called conscientious objectors parasites, yellow bellies, cowards, slackers, shirkers, and similar names. Such people, many said or implied, were either too callous to heed the call of suffering and dying humanity, or too selfish to play their part in a great, necessary national enterprise. So they did not deserve the rights and privileges of citizens.

Elkhart, Indiana, had long had exceptionally able and articulate Mennonites because until recently it had been the site of John F. Funk's Mennonite Publishing Company. Nevertheless, the draft board in that city recommended that conscientious objectors be put in uniform and sent as soon as possible to the trenches in France at the earliest possible moment.[50] In so saying, it spoke for many other Americans. According to *The New York Times*, "the conscientious objector wants something for nothing, he is a voluntary insolvent debtor. His claim to moral superiority is the wildest of absurdity. At the worst he is a public enemy."[51]

Instead of exempting conscientious objectors from combat, many local draft boards favored drafting them. One board opined that if these men were really as religious as they claimed, their influence at the front would be beneficial.[52] Local hostility often made conscientious objectors reluctant to go home on furlough. If they went, they might receive the kind of "welcome" given to Samuel Yoder, a conscientious objector at Camp Meade. In July 1918, he went home to Belleville, Pennsylvania, on leave. There he was greeted with a sign in his front yard: "Sam Yoder a slacker, ashamed of the U.S. uniform, is home, lives here. We are ashamed of him. Leave, for the people don't want you."

As if that were not enough, a local citizen referred to conscientious objectors as "contemptible milk sops, peace-at-any price polliwags, slackers, and Red Cross non-supporters." In the minds of such citizens, it would be better if the shirkers left the community and joined their friends and masters in Germany.[53]

In some communities people watched local pastors carefully and forbade them to give Mennonite youths draft counseling. Some of the charges against Pastor King of the Carlock congregation in Illinois were that he had spoken against the war and called the Selective Service Act unconstitutional.[54] Similarly, former pastor and later elder Christian R. Egle of the Salem Defenseless Mennonite congregation near Gridley, Illinois, was investigated and interrogated by agents of the American Protective League and the Livingston County War Board. Although his congregation had contributed the generous sum of $10,000 to the Fourth Liberty Bond drive, plus purchasing some $3,000 in war stamps, Egle's stand against military service aroused his neighbors' ire.

Apparently Egle and others had indeed instructed prospective draftees that they would not have to drill or wear the uniform if they could convince authorities that they were sincere. In the summer of 1918, quite a few Mennonite men from Central Illinois in Camp Wheeler, Georgia, took such advice seriously. An angry L. W. Steele, local agent of the Toledo, Peoria, and Western Railway, informed Secretary of War Baker that some Mennonites in his area were acting like "babys" [sic]. Ministers such as Egle should "be called down." "In the name of God and all that is holy and just," Baker should not to be influenced by these people, who Steele thought were interested not in religion but only in "dollars and cents."

Steele was not alone. Anti-Mennonite feeling became so intense that a number of superpatriots decided to daub the Salem church building. During the night of July 10-11, they smeared both the exteri-

or and the interior with "copious daubs." Still not satisfied, on one side of the building they wrote "No more slackers," and on the other side "No more German preaching." On the floor of the anteroom, in large letters, they painted, "Wear U.S. Uniforms." Subsequently Egle and others were investigated and interrogated. One investigation concluded that Egle was "a very dangerous element to remain in the community" and his church "a pro-German nest" hatching out "pro-Germanism under the cloak of conscientious objection." But authorities took no official action.[55]

Three states away, in June 1918, the Western Federal District Court of Pennsylvania ordered the seizure of the Mennonite tract *Nonresistance*. The tract's publisher, the "old" Mennonites' official publishing house at Scottdale, Pennsylvania, was in the court's district. The two-page tract merely restated traditional Mennonite beliefs. But the court's warrant charged that it had been used "in connection with and as a means" of committing felonies under the statutes of the United States.

According to the warrant the users had done so by "unlawfully, knowingly and willfully conveying false reports and statements with intent to interfere with the operation and success of military and naval forces"; by causing "insubordination and disloyalty, mutiny, and refusal of duty"; by "obstructing and attempting to obstruct the recruiting and enlistment service"; and by "willfully uttering, printing and writing and publishing language to incite, provoke and encourage resistance to the U.S."

In early August, under the warrant, authorities seized 150 copies of the tract but took no further action against the Mennonite Publishing House. Nevertheless, the procedure was enough to cause Aaron Loucks, the Scottdale Mennonite who was so important as a camp visitor and a lobbyist for Mennonites in the camps, to fear legal action against himself. Loucks sought advice from Roger Baldwin, head of the American Civil Liberties Bureau, and appealed to the Department of Justice. To Loucks's relief a Justice Department official said nothing would happen if the Publishing House agreed not to distribute more leaflets or tracts setting forth the church's position on war.[56]

Nonetheless, soon thereafter U.S. Attorney Edwin S. Wertz of Cleveland, Ohio, tried to indict 181 Mennonite bishops and deacons. In August 1917 they had met at the conference at the Yellow Creek church near Goshen, Indiana, and signed a statement on military service. Wertz considered the statement a violation of the Espionage Act. In Iowa, Mennonite bishops were called before a federal agent in

Washington, D.C., to explain their endorsement of the document, but the Justice Department preferred not to pursue the matter. This was because federal authorities had decided that Mennonites and other conscientious objectors would be allowed to do farm work. Furthermore, no evidence had been uncovered to prove that Mennonites had attempted to make converts to their position or urged members who wanted to fight to change their minds.[57]

The only Mennonite to be arrested and fined for his utterances against conscription was Archibald T. Yoder of West Liberty, Ohio— the same person who resigned from the school board. His troubles did not stop with his resignation. In May 1918 he was arrested by a U.S. marshal and taken before U.S. Commissioner John E. West in Bellefontaine for having tried to persuade a local citizen, Arthur Hanger, not to enlist in the armed forces. Allegedly Yoder had uttered various unpatriotic statements, including one to Hanger to the effect that if he enlisted he stood a chance of being sent to hell by a German bullet.

On May 17 Yoder was released on a $15,000 bond. He was scheduled to be tried in November in Federal District Court in Cincinnati. On December 20 Yoder was indicted by a grand jury for having "feloniously obstructed and attempt to obstruct the recruiting and enlistment service." However, on March 3, 1919, the court decided not to prosecute. Its grounds were that Hanger was not a member of the armed forces at the time Yoder tried to persuade him. The court found further that Yoder's "advice" had not resulted in any injury to enlistment or recruitment.[58]

Mennonites suffered similar open hostility at Fairview, Michigan. Prior to the war Mennonites had been respected and appreciated there, although some residents envied Mennonites, who were rather active in Democratic politics, for their success in securing various elected positions in Comins Township. Now Mennonite attitudes and actions aroused anger. Local people took umbrage at Mennonite reluctance to buy bonds and contribute to the Red Cross. Even more, they resented conscientious objection in response to the draft.

In the Fairview congregation, only one young man served as noncombatant and one in regular military service while four refused to do either. We do not know if the local draft board discriminated against Mennonites, but there is evidence that at least one of its members, Sheriff Charles Farrington, showed "bitter prejudice" against them. He is even alleged to have suggested on one occasion that all of the conscientious objectors be sent to war or put in a row and shot down. William F. McNeely, a local gamewarden with political ambitions and chairman of the Oscoda County American Defense Society, was also hostile. "The Mennonites don't fight and they should not hold public office," he stated on various occasions.[59]

Much of the anti-Mennonite agitation was organized by the so-called Republican Ring, which included McNeely and his colleague John Speck. In March 1918, shortly before a Comins Township election, posters were distributed warning local voters that a vote for a conscientious objector was a vote for the Kaiser. In addition McNeely circulated an open letter to "the American Voter of Comins Township" in which he denounced Mennonites in the most vituperative terms. They were "known sympathizers" of the German emperor, he charged, and he urged the voters in this "bitterly crucial hour when the shaft of death" was poised for a blow at "our blood-bought liberty" not to select men for office who professed Americanism but gave "a lie to their claim by a halting, vacillating, will-o'-the-wisp patriotism that has the official o.k. of the Kaiser."

McNeely also accused Mennonites of gloating over German atrocities such as the sinking of the *Lusitania*, expressing pleasure over German military victories, and being unwilling to do anything for the war effort. The nation, he asserted, could not afford to have in her midst such "copperheads" who used their "poisonous fangs" at every opportunity to destroy the people's morale.

The sharp-penned politician especially lambasted a particular member of the Fairview Mennonite congregation who, he charged, had unsuccessfully tried to escape the draft by quickly marrying. According to McNeely the congregation had defended this slacker, trying by every means possible to secure his release. Finally McNeely urged every true American to register a vote against "these traitors" because a voting conscientious objector was a "hypocrite and a traitor and must be dealt with as such."[60]

On election day, April 1, 1918, many voters felt intimidated and either stayed away from the polls or voted for non-incumbents. As a result the Republican Ring won a resounding victory. But the victors were not satisfied and decided to burn down the Mennonites' meeting-place, located in the heart of Fairview, perhaps hoping that such an act would drive this "unpatriotic" segment of the population out of the county altogether. The plot had the support of various notable citizens including the editor of the local paper, the county clerk, and others.

During the night of April 4, McNeely and Speck set fire to the small wooden structure, which burned quickly.[61] Although the Mennonites did not institute legal action, other citizens did—prevailing upon

Circuit Judge Albert L. Widdis, a Democrat, to conduct a grand jury investigation.

In April, 1920 Judge Widdis and his prosecuting attorney, Herman Dehnke, questioned many persons. Few were willing to expose the truth. So Widdis decided to launch a new investigation and this time gathered a considerable amount of evidence. However, at that juncture various local politicians rushed to Lansing where they persuaded the attorney general to try to remove Widdis. Although the attorney general failed in that attempt, during the next two years legal action against him made it difficult if not impossible for Widdis to launch a new investigation.

Finally the Michigan Supreme Court vindicated Widdis, but by then the beleaguered judge took no new action in the arson case. Local Mennonites, who in 1919 built a new facility, showed the arsonists no malice. Eventually McNeely, Speck, and the Mennonites maintained friendly relations. Had Widdis succeeded in prosecuting the two men to the letter of the law[62] the case might not have ended with such good feeling.

Thus by 1918 or even earlier public opinion in many communities had become quite critical of and hostile toward Mennonites. In Protection, Kansas, a barber went so far as to put up a sign saying, "Dogs and Mennonites stay out."[63] Some government authorities shared these views. In June, 1918 Lieutenant Colonel W. Churchill, a member of the Military Intelligence Division of the War Department, alleged that there was "absolutely no question or doubt about the fact" that Mennonite anti-war and pacifist views had done much harm. He urged that they be "silenced at once."[64]

In Iowa the Henry County Council of Defense agreed that there was a "well-organized conspiracy operating through the German Mennonite churches to obstruct the draft and the war." But government authorities in Washington and in most states were not persuaded. They felt, as one intelligence report concluded, that in spite of their opposition to the war or their reluctance to support it as one might wish, Mennonites were a "most desirable class of citizens." According to that report they were "harmless in their activities," and because of their small number they would not, if left to themselves, become a "pronounced danger" in the war effort.[65]

Unfortunately, Mennonites made few efforts to explain their position toward war. Perhaps they preferred to suffer in silence or felt that any attempt to explain principles of nonviolence might provoke more than enlighten. In one incident bishop Simon Gingerich learned the latter. He and Pastor Daniel Graber met with the local Council of Defense and other citizens but did not succeed in explaining the Mennonite position to their listeners' satisfaction.

Newspapers also were reluctant or unwilling to explain the Mennonite position. Perhaps Jacob G. Ewert, professor at Tabor College, coeditor of *Vorwärts* and active as a draft counselor, was fortunate when in June 1918 *The Topeka Daily Capital* published a letter from him explaining that Mennonites were not disloyal but instead were against war in general. Wrote he, "The inviolate sacredness of all human life is one of the foremost ideals that Christ has brought into this world."[66]

Silas M. Grubb, editor of the GC paper *The Mennonite*, was more inclined to compromise with various wartime demands, but sometimes he also reaffirmed Mennonite loyalty. Like most Mennonites he denied being pro-German. It was not sympathy with Germany that made Mennonites pacifist, he explained; that belief was born long before the United States became a nation. In August 1917 he even dared to write that "a slacker in the kingdom" was "infinitely more contemptible" than one in worldly things.[67]

The *Gospel Herald* made an equally spirited defense of the Mennonite position, also denying emphatically that Mennonites were pro-German and cowards. It even argued that it took more courage "to stand for nonresistance than it does to quietly consent to noncombatant service or actual fighting. . . ."[68]

Goshen College President John (J. E.) Hartzler expressed much the same by contending "the most loyal and valuable citizen under the American flag is the honest, sincere, and genuine Christian who lives the teachings of him who is the Prince of Peace." Every person in the Mennonite church, Hartzler admonished, could render a greater and more noble service to God and to the human family than the man who enlists in military service. It might not be a difficult thing to die for a country but it took "great faith and courage to live for God and our country."[69]

The most elaborate defense came in a short essay by Gerhart Dalke, an MB author at Hillsboro, Kansas. Entitled "*A Defense of the Mennonites Against Recent Attacks Made upon Them,*" the essay reminded readers of Mennonite relief efforts, of their loyalty, and of their traditional opposition to war. According to Dalke, Mennonites believed that world peace could only be attained by international law based upon the Bible. "Love alone can establish world peace between nations," he concluded.[70]

In at least one instance Mennonites tried to defend themselves by resorting to violence. The altercation occurred in July 1918, in Butterfield, Minnesota. One morning a local citizen told two Mennonite cousins named Peter and Bernard Rempel, who were talking in German near a local hotel window, to "cut out" their German talk or move. Apparently, Peter Rempel, who claimed to have good patriotic credentials because two of his sons served in the U.S. Army, felt provoked.

Soon he and another Mennonite, John Rempel, were in a physical fight with his antagonist and an associate. During the fight John Rempel tried to reach for a revolver he carried in his pocket but was unable to do so. The men were finally separated but John and Peter Rempel were found guilty by a lower court. However, in June 1919 the Minnesota Supreme Court reversed the lower court decision. The grounds—nobody had proved that John Rempel had actually pointed his gun at anyone.[71]

Despite that reversal, the larger truth is that during the Great War many if not most American Mennonites found the various patriotic demands to be very difficult. They considered themselves to be productive and law-abiding citizens. They felt grieved that their neighbors and friends considered them less than patriotic. Many made compromises of one kind or another, but often with an uneasy conscience. Some of those compromises had to do with buying Thrift Stamps and Liberty Bonds. What did Jesus' puzzling words about paying the tax to Caesar mean in the context of this war?

4

Render unto Caesar the Things That Are Caesar's?

Aside from such matters as military conscription and honoring the flag, probably nothing caused more conflicts between Mennonites and their neighbors than questions of buying Liberty Bonds and contributing to the Red Cross, local war chests, and the YMCA. With much public support, the American Red Cross solicited contributions from citizens to support its humanitarian work. In fact, however, both the Red Cross and the YMCA soon became so tied to the war effort that they were cogs in the military machine. Some citizens became aware of the militarization of such organizations and were reluctant to contribute to this organization. But much of the public considered that kind of reaction unpatriotic. Reluctance to contribute triggered much public hostility.

Before the U.S. formally entered the war, many American Mennonites had donated to the American Red Cross. Quite a few Mennonites, especially in Kansas, had also contributed to its German counterpart. For instance, in September 1917 the General Conference Mennonite Church reported a total of $4,793.59 in contributions to the American Red Cross and $4,185.74 to the German Red Cross.[1]

After April 1917 Mennonites became divided over the issue. Many, especially those who belonged to more nonconformist branches, were less inclined to contribute than those who were more "liberal." In keeping with GC polity, the GC Mennonites' general conference did not take an official position on the issue, preferring to let each congregation decide it.

But Silas M. Grubb, editor of *The Mennonite*, probably spoke for many of the GC branch when he declared that as a pacifist he could not fold his hands when millions were in misery. Furthermore, he pointed out, if Mennonites wanted to be absolute pacifists they should not dig coal, pay taxes, or do anything else that might support the war. Even if one did not want to take up arms, one could at least be a good Samaritan and contribute to the Red Cross and the YMCA, and purchase Liberty Bonds.[2]

Grubb could have added that raising grain in war time, much of which would be used to feed the huge armies at the front, might also be objectionable. The editor pointed out an obvious truth—it was impossible not to contribute to or aid the total war effort. No position would ever be totally consistent, and there would be some questions on which each person would have to decide where to draw the line and how much to expose oneself to public rebuke and ridicule.

Various congregations agreed to contribute certain amounts per family to the Red Cross. Perhaps eventually a few of the contributors learned more of the true role of the Red Cross and had second thoughts. In September of 1918 Susan Ringelman, a sister of Henry Krehbiel, who had supported the Red Cross, wondered if it really was right to contribute to it. She had heard a Chautauqua speaker tell an audience there was nothing like the Red Cross "to bring the fighting spirit back into a discouraged and ready-to-quit soldier."[3]

In the large "old" Mennonite branch, as well as some smaller ones such as the Holdeman, there was more reluctance to contribute. Many might have contributed at first. Even as late as June 1918, the "old" Mennonite leader Aaron Loucks concluded that one could give to the Red Cross provided the donation was contributed to the right Red Cross branch. But by that time local solicitors were running into considerable Mennonite resistance. No doubt Simon Gingerich spoke for many of his church when he concluded the Red Cross and the YMCA indirectly encouraged militarism—plus other evils such as pool playing, theater going, etc. These, said Gingerich, were evils that his church could not tolerate.[4]

Local "patriotic" committees often pressured the reluctant, even to the point of threats. In May 1918 Aaron Dick of Mountain Lake, Minnesota, declined to make a Red Cross donation of $15; he soon received a letter from D. U. Weld, a member of the Cottonwood County Public Safety Association. Dick had better pay, the letter said, or be summoned to appear before the committee. Dick soon paid.[5]

In many instances public reaction was even less pleasant. To cite one of many examples, in the same month of Dick's troubles, Jacob B. Stehman, a member of the "old" Mennonites' Bethel congregation at Garden City, Missouri, was tarred and feathered by a party of about fifty men when he too refused. The vigilantes threatened his minister with the same treatment if the church would not host a political meeting. The congregation gave $1,200, contributed garments to a relief fund, and no harm came.

As in many communities, the local paper, *The Garden City Views*, lamented "beyond expression of words that anything of this sort should have to be resorted to in this community." But it suggested that every American would approve the tarring and feathering. The editor wrote that the Red Cross was an agency of God that cared for the sick and wounded, and men and women who refused to give to it were "too dirty to associate with the lowest beasts" that roamed the earth. He was just glad that not many persons needed the kind of treatment Stehman had received.[6]

In July additional trouble arose when Mennonites were reluctant or adamant about buying Liberty Bonds and Thrift Stamps. At Garden City there was sentiment for a "lynching bee." It did not quite happen, but for a short time authorities put the local bishop, Joseph C. Driver, in prison. They also struck an agreement with their local Mennonites. By its terms the "old" Mennonite Sycamore Grove and Bethel congregations expressed their "loyalty to the U.S. government, [and] their love for America." Concretely, they promised to deposit $1,500 each month with a local bank, for the benefit of the American Red Cross. In return, the authorities agreed to ask local citizens to recognize Mennonite beliefs, especially with regard to war. Other authorities made a similar agreement with the "old" Mount Zion Mennonite congregation near Versailles, Missouri. In that case, the Mennonites agreed to make three monthly contributions of $500 each to the Red Cross.[7]

Among others mistreated for refusal to contribute to the Red Cross or some other cause was Samuel (S. E.) Allgyer, an "old" Mennonite bishop in the Champaign County, Ohio, area. After the armistice of 1918, Allgyer was "visited" by a mob of about fifty men, which included State Representative Clyde Hooley, who was of Mennonite extraction. The men demanded a $100 contribution to the Salvation Army. Allgyer refused, saying he had already given $10 to this organization. The men grabbed him and cut off his hair with a pair of horse clippers. Later Hooley apologized for his participation in the affair.[8]

Few persons suffered more at the hands of self-styled patriots over the issue of "voluntary" contributions than did Niles Slabaugh, pastor of the MC Howard-Miami Mennonite congregation near Kokomo, Indiana. Superpatriots in Miami County had been busy organizing themselves for the war effort and had formed the so-called Loyal Citizens Vigilance Committee which at one time had some 2,500 members, including many prominent citizens. Members pledged to make the county "100 percent loyal" and to force anyone with a "yellow streak to get in line." (Before the Gulf War in 1991, yellow implied cowardice.)

In early May, 1918 some twenty local patriots staged "a little celebration" against an alleged pro-German citizen by giving him a "beautiful hand painting" in yellow. Furthermore, the committee was active in "persuading" all citizens to contribute to the Red Cross and a local war chest. Slabaugh and his brother-in-law Joseph B. Martin and probably others refused.[9]

On July 29 the two men were taken from their homes to meet a large and angry crowd in Peru, the seat of Miami County. Here the two men were grilled and intimidated. Although Martin finally agreed to contribute, Slabaugh refused. He told his tormentors he did not believe in killing human beings but believed in prayer as a means of winning the war and bringing the boys back home.

After the meeting, the vigilantes took Slabaugh to a dark alley. There they shook him by the neck and called him a "damn s.o.b., a dirty cur," and not a human being. However, they finally did let him go. The next day *The Peru Republican* added its scorn by arguing the county was no place for Slabaugh to live unless he changed his attitude toward the United States.

A few weeks later the guardians of patriotism tried one more time. In the evening of August 14, a group of "100 percent loyal" citizens took Slabaugh away from his home, shaved his head, and painted it yellow. Whether Slabaugh then agreed to contribute, we do not know. We do know that some of his tormentors later apologized to him.[10]

Many more controversies arose over the issue of Liberty Bonds and Thrift Stamps. As one way to finance the war effort, the government asked for the public to subscribe to so-called Liberty Loans and to buy Thrift Stamps. The bonds were especially important sources of revenue. Already in April 1917 the federal government asked the public to subscribe to a $2 billion loan, to be followed in September by another one of $3 billion. The Third and Fourth Loans were issued in April and July 1918 respectively, the April one for $3 billion and the July one for $6 billion. The Fifth or Victory Loan was issued in March 1919, for $4.5 billion. The average interest on these loans was about 4 percent.

Although the loans were to be voluntary, considerable pressure and intimidation were used to "persuade" citizens to contribute. In the

Government poster urging citizens to purchase Liberty Bonds.
Courtesy, Peter Ropp, Normal, Ill.

fall of 1917 Secretary of the Treasury William G. McAdoo set the tone. He told a crowd that a person who refused to subscribe or who took the attitude of letting the other fellow do it was a friend of Germany. He said a man who could not lend his government $1.25 per week at the rate of four percent interest was not "entitled to be an American citizen."[11]

The Treasury Department assigned a quota to each of the twelve Federal Reserve Districts, which divided their amounts among the various states. States divided their quotas among the counties. In each county, city, and town, local and precinct committees were organized that often consisted of individuals who also served on "patriotic" bodies, such as the above-named Miami Local Citizens' Vigilance Committee. Furthermore, many local newspapers, citizens' organizations, and clubs were called upon to assist.

Over time the entire system was so well organized that few could escape scrutiny and pressure. Those unwilling or reluctant to contribute were often threatened by their employers with loss of employment, summoned before special self-appointed "courts," placed on "slackers" lists, harassed, or in some cases physically abused. For instance, in Harvey County, Kansas (which included Newton) the county's War Council composed a special "Blue Book" listing names and contributions of all citizens. The names of those who had not contributed were referred to "several strong vigilance committees."[12]

Members of such committees reminded slackers that on their return the boys now in France would want to know who had helped them win the war.[13] Citizens around Inola, Oklahoma, were informed of whose names were on a list of contributors and reminded that it was important to ferret out anyone who was not 100 percent American.[14] Thus in many communities Liberty Loans ceased really to be voluntary. The results were impressive; the loans were always oversubscribed and brought the federal treasury a total of some $24 billion—about $6 billion more than anticipated. Many individuals gave amounts ranging from $50 to $1,500, with the average at $445. For many Americans the forced Liberty Loans became real hardships. Often individuals had to borrow to buy the Bonds.[15]

Citizens found themselves under similar pressure to purchase War Savings Certificates. The federal government saw the certificates as a means to tap people of lower incomes and even children. Such people could pay for them gradually by buying so-called Thrift Stamps. Post offices and banks sold stamps for as low as twenty-five cents and buyers affixed them to cards. Four dollars' worth of stamps could purchase a War Savings Certificate which carried 4 percent interest.

To sell as many stamps as possible, the federal government successfully encouraged local communities to form committees for the job. In all, in the period 1917-1920, the government sold about $1 billion worth of stamps. Obviously most citizens were under considerable pressure to contribute via Liberty Loans and Thrift Stamps—in addition to the heavy pressure to give to the Red Cross, the YMCA, and local war chests.[16]

U.S. Mennonites had not been confronted very often with the issue of war taxes. Many had resisted such taxes during Revolutionary War, and when an eastern Pennsylvania bishop named Christian Funk and some followers favored paying a certain tax, the issue set off a split in the Franconia Conference.[17] During the Civil War Mennonites seem scarcely to have resisted special war taxes and fees. In Europe Mennonites had seldom if ever objected to payment of taxes, even when they knew the money went for military purposes. In the sixteenth and seventeenth centuries, Dutch Mennonites even made special financial contributions to war efforts. In the Russian empire, Mennonites contributed money freely and rather generously to various war efforts between 1812 and 1917.[18]

In 1917 and 1918, in order to finance its military preparedness program and later the war effort, the federal government considerably increased income, excise, estate, and other taxes. During that period, federal revenues increased from $869 million to about $3.7 billion.[19] Mennonites did not object to such tax increases, although they knew most of the additional revenues went for war. They gave to Caesar what they believed was Caesar's. But they did object to or had serious reservations about what they perceived to be direct war taxes.

As had been true in the case of Red Cross and other contributions, the General Conference church was more inclined to advise its members to purchase Liberty Bonds and Thrift Stamps. Perhaps Editor Grubb reflected the attitude of many GC Mennonites when he informed his readers that failure to support the war would prolong the conflict and cause more suffering. Buying bonds was one way of supporting the government and could be compared with raising wheat.

As good citizens, Grubb argued, we must render unto Caesar and give the government what already belongs to it as Dutch Mennonites had done in the sixteenthth and seventeenth centuries. Did it become Mennonites, he asked, to change or improve upon a course laid out by our Lord?[20]

The influential General Conference leader and educator, President Samuel Mosiman of Bluffton College, enthusiastically supported Grubb's views. So did *Der Herold* at Newton, Kansas, and the *The Berne Witness* at Berne, Indiana—two papers published by GC Mennonite editors for Mennonites which frequently advertised Liberty Bonds. At Hillsboro, Kansas, *Vorwärts* also advertised the bonds in its pages, but in the paper's German section its editors revealed their real views, which were critical.[21]

In general, church leaders were reluctant to give advice. For fear of violating the Sedition Act of 1918—one section of which forbade dissemination of false information on the sale of war bonds—they became careful about what they said publicly. The effect was to leave the matter to each individual's conscience and judgment. "Old" Mennonite leaders such as J. S. Hartzler, Sanford (S. C.) Yoder, and Goshen College president John (J. E.) Hartzler expressed this sentiment. According to J. E. Hartzler, Mennonites should avoid all appearance of protesting against civil authority, follow as nearly as possible Romans 13:7 (render taxes and honor to whom they were due), and render unto Caesar the things that are Caesar's. Furthermore, he took the rather odd position that individuals' money was really government property, loaned to citizens for their convenience. If the authorities demanded its return, he contended, one could do no better than "to let the government have it."[22]

Early in 1918 Aaron Loucks suggested that Mennonites could best express their patriotism by purchasing Farm Loan Bonds under the Federal Farm Loan Act. Such bonds, he pointed out, could provide capital for agricultural development. They were in "no sense a war measure" and would be the "simplest way of lending to meet the problems of the government and at the same time receiving adequate security for our funds invested."[23] It does not seem that many Mennonites invested in such bonds. Moreover Loucks and other Mennonite leaders favored the so-called Crooks plan, discussed below.

Pressure to buy Liberty Bonds soon reached considerable proportions. The cases of Mennonites being interrogated by their neighbors on the local committees, neighbors who knew much about their wealth and incomes, were many. So were cases of personal abuse or defacement of church buildings.

In the summer of 1918, local superpatriots at Harrisburg, Oregon, padlocked the double doors of a Conservative Amish Mennonite meetinghouse, painted a wide yellow stripe around the building, and attached a sign above the doors which said, "This church is closed for the duration of the war." However, members broke the lock and continued to hold services.[24] In October 1918 superpatriots from Manheim, Pennsylvania, visited the home of Joseph A. Boll, pastor of the MC Erb Mennonite congregation, and doused it with yellow paint for his refusal to buy bonds.[25]

In May 1918 local citizens went to the Conestoga Amish Mennonite meetinghouse located near Morgantown, Pennsylvania, and "decorated" it with a flag for the congregation's refusal to do its patriotic duty.[26] More serious was the physical abuse. Police had to protect Joel Habegger of the Christian Amish Mennonite Church at Berne, Indiana, from an angry mob after he refused to buy bonds.[27]

Ray Weldy, an employee at the American Coating Mills in Elkhart, Indiana, was painted yellow and dismissed from his job for his recalcitrance.[28] John H. Stutzman of Milford, Nebraska, was fined in court for the same reason.[29] Laban Swartzendruber, a student at the Greenwood High School at Greenwood, Delaware, was punished for refusing to write an essay supporting the purchase of Liberty Bonds. His punishment: standing an entire day under the flag.[30]

But the worst fate befell Walter and George Cooprider, Daniel A. Diener and his son Charles, and John Schrag. The Coopriders belonged to the MC West Liberty Mennonite Church near Inman, Kansas. During the night of April 22, 1918, a mob of about twenty masked men, many from respectable families, went to Walter's house. They intended to tar and feather the man for refusing to buy bonds. Because Walter was not in good health the mob agreed to substitute George, the Coopriders' son, instead.

That same night the mob drove to the eastern edge of McPherson County where they visited the homes of the Dieners, pastors of the Spring Valley "old" Mennonite congregation near Canton. Here they tarred and feathered the elder Diener for his opposition to war bonds and his son for taking down a flag placed on the church building.

On June 3 the mob returned to the elder Diener's home and forced him to make a contribution to the Red Cross. One week later the two men were tarred and feathered again and the word "slacker" daubed in yellow on their homes. After these incidents both Dieners agreed to buy. The mob was now satisfied and boasted, "We sure made them come across"—although later some of its members apologized to the Coopriders.[31]

On November 11, 1918, John Schrag of Burrton, Kansas, was almost lynched by an angry and frenzied mob. Again the context was heavy community resentment against the Mennonites for their attitude toward war bonds. On November 11, 1918, a crowd celebrating the armistice decided to take their resentment out on Schrag, a wealthy local resident. Although Schrag had not bought any war bonds, he had contributed to the Red Cross and the Salvation Army. On Armistice Day the president of the Burrton State Bank invited Schrag to attend the downtown festivities. Schrag hesitated yet agreed to go.

But in Burrton a mob surrounded him, demanding that he buy bonds and salute and carry a flag in a parade. Saying the flag "stood for war," he refused to salute it when his tormentors thrust it into his hands, and then he dropped it. The crowd grew angry, slapped him, and poured a can of yellow paint over his head. Schrag did not resist but turned the other cheek. A witness commented later that "he exemplified the life of Christ more than I ever saw in my life."

Next, they put a rope around his neck and marched him down to

city hall threatening to hang him. However, the undersheriff prevented the lynching and transferred the beleaguered man to Newton and
later Wichita for safekeeping. After this incident many Mennonites
took their money out of the Burrton banks and traded in other places.
Their action considerably hurt the town's economy, and healing the
wounds took many years. John Schrag never fully recovered from the
ordeal; he vowed he would never trust "American" people again."[32]

Nobody can be sure there were not factors other than simple refusal to buy bonds and stamps. Some victims may in fact have been iras-
cible. Certainly some Mennonites were far from diplomatic. But when
their tormenters painted churches yellow—as happened in still more
cases at Birch Tree, Missouri; Fisher, Hopedale, Flanagan, and
Metamora, Illinois; Harrisburg, Oregon; Parnell, Iowa; Wakarusa and
Goshen, Indiana; and West Liberty, Sugarcreek, and Orrville,
Ohio—the slogans they left were likely to be as they were on the "old"
Mennonite church building at Metamora, Illinois. On one side were the
words "WE ARE SLACKERS" and on the other, "WE BUY NO
BONDS."[33]

Nor is it easy to determine how many Mennonites bought or did
not buy Liberty Bonds and Thrift Stamps. Many who purchased them
preferred not to talk about the matter. Often such persons did not re-
deem the bonds but donated them to some cause or a Mennonite college or mission. Much of the $100,000 raised in the immediate postwar
years by the Western District Conference for Bethel College consisted
of Liberty Bonds. Hesston College built a new administration building
largely with money from Liberty Bonds which individuals had bought
during the war and later donated.[34]

The evidence is clear that many if not most Mennonites bought
some bonds and stamps. Perhaps General Conference Mennonites
were more inclined to buy than were most other Mennonites, but many
others did buy, even members of the Old Order Amish. Some bought
because they sincerely wanted to be patriotic and responsible as citizens. But perhaps many more gave because they feared their neighbors
or the self-styled, self-appointed patriots who served on local committees.

Among generous if not eager purchasers were many Mennonites
in and around Berne, Indiana. Peter P. Schroeder of the Berne Mennonite Church assisted in the Thrift Stamp sales, while John F. Lehman, a
prominent Mennonite businessman and church leader, headed an advisory committee for the last or so-called Victory Liberty Loan campaign. Members of Berne's GC congregation even placed their war sav-

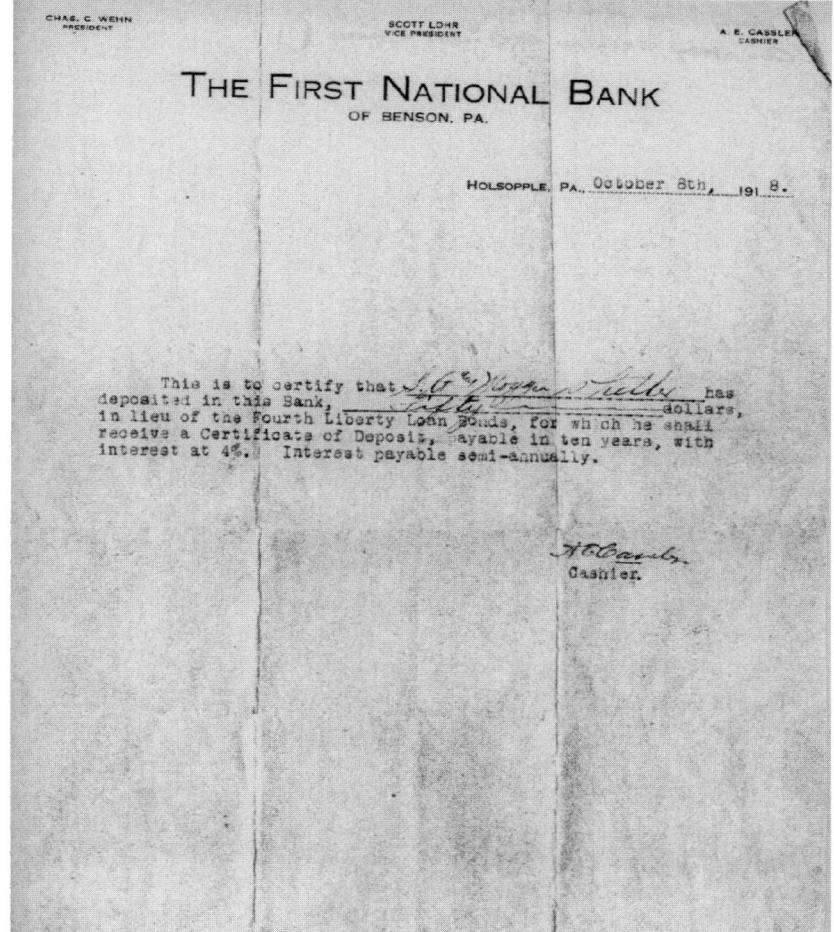

Liberty Loan contribution by Mennonites S. G. and Maggie Shetler.
Courtesy, Archives of the Mennonite Church.

ings stamps and bonds in the church's collection plates. Yet despite such support, anti-Mennonite sentiment persisted in Berne. Conscientious objectors were considered *personae non grata.* In June 1918 fire destroyed several Mennonite-owned businesses. Apparently Mennonites could not necessarily buy community approval or tolerance.[35]

The GCs' Bluffton and Bethel Colleges were other sites of enthusiasm for War Bond and Thrift Stamp drives. In the Bluffton area President Mosiman provided much of the leadership. In March of 1918, in what the Bluffton College paper, *The Witmarsum*, reported as a "stirring" address, Mosiman responded to a charge that "whenever you find a conscientious objector, you will find a German spy nearby." Said he, "Our men have bought Liberty Bonds and are going to buy more." Mennonites opposed war, he remarked, but they realized this war stood for "liberty, justice, and brotherhood."[36]

One week later *The Witmarsum* proudly announced that women living it the college's Ropp Hall had purchased Thrift Stamp books and $50 worth of Liberty Loans.[37] At about the same time Bethel College faculty and students participated in a Liberty Loan parade in Newton, and the college paper urged the purchase of bonds, stamps and contributions to the Red Cross to maintain the good morale of the army and win "the fight for democracy."[38]

In April 1918 members of the Eicher Emmanuel and Wayland congregations in Iowa were urged by their church paper, *The Pastor's Assistant*, to forget their individual differences for a while and contribute to the Liberty Loan drive. Probably these two congregations filled their quotas quite easily.[39] In April 1918 the local paper in the Turkey Creek Township area of McPherson County, Kansas, an area heavily populated with General Conference Mennonites, was happy to announce how "splendidly" the Liberty Bond quota had been subscribed.[40] Similarly, easy compliance was secured among Mennonites in South Dakota, most of whom (with the exception of the Hutterites and a few other congregations) belonged to the General Conference.[41]

Even among "old" Mennonite churches, cooperation was sometimes surprisingly easy. For instance, the Fairview Mennonite Church near Albany, Oregon, responded to all government requests for loans or war relief of any kind and some members even served on the local Council of Defense and Liberty Loan committees.[42] Their neighbors must have found them 100 percent American.

Most Mennonites in Lancaster County, Pennsylvania, bought Liberty Bonds. One leader, Israel B. Good, purchased at least $10,000 worth. Good even offered advice for selling the bonds, telling one salesman that with Mennonites it would be good to say that the money would go for soldiers' food and clothing.[43] A similar kind of logic swayed members of the East Bend Mennonite congregation at Fisher, Illinois. There members agreed to buy bonds on grounds that some of the money went to noncombatant uses.[44]

In other cases church officials and others yielded only after considerable pressure and threats. Such was the case with the agreement

Bishop Gingerich of Iowa and local and federal officials reached in February 1918. The authorities looked upon the agreement as a "penalty" imposed upon Gingerich for having caused a "disturbance" among the citizens of Wayland and vicinity." By its terms Gingerich's church not only agreed to display the flag but also to purchase $200 worth of Thrift Stamps and at least $5,000 in Liberty Bonds.[45]

A far more interesting agreement was the Crooks plan. It was reached in May 1918 between Amish Mennonites in Fulton County, Ohio, and the Eastern Amish Mennonite Conference on one side—and W. L. Crooks, representative of the Federal Reserve Bank of Cleveland, Ohio, on the other. Assisting the Amish Mennonites were the "old" Mennonite leaders Aaron Loucks and S. E. Allgyer.

Under the Crooks plan, Mennonites would deposit sums of money with certain local banks for the purchase of certificates of deposit. The amounts to be deposited would be determined over time. The crucial points for the Mennonites were that those deposits were not to be used for war bonds but for local ventures, nor would Liberty Bonds continue to be solicited from the Amish Mennonites. For the community, the Mennonite deposits freed other bank funds for uses Mennonites preferred not to support.

In the 1990s some people might well call such a plan "money laundering" and see it as not fully consistent with Mennonite principles. But apparently neither Loucks, his "old" Mennonite Military Problems Committee, nor various district-conference representatives saw serious difficulties with the plan. In fact, they immediately decided to negotiate similar agreements elsewhere.[46]

However, Crooks could not convince federal authorities in Washington to promise to quit soliciting Mennonites, so the plan collapsed.[47] Thereafter Fulton County Mennonites did give to bond and Thrift Stamp drives, with German Township alone contributing $18,000—$1,000 above its quota—in the fall of 1918. Obviously solicitors exerted considerable pressure. Local committees gave them a mandate to go to "those long-whiskered fellows and ask them to buy, and if they refuse to take them by their whiskers and shake it out of them." The solicitors took these suggestions seriously and even had to be calmed down and dissuaded by local Liberty Loan officials from using violence. This proved difficult because the local Patriotic League had worked the people up to a "fever heat" and many Mennonites were being watched "at the point of a gun" to make them buy stamps.[48]

Similar situations prevailed in other regions. In May 1918 the Franconia Conference, one of the large "old" Mennonite conferences of eastern Pennsylvania, agreed to purchase Farm Loan Bonds, but apparently few members did so. Later in the summer Franconia adopted something like the Crooks plan but apparently that plan also never went into operation.[49]

In Nebraska, in January 1918, Mennonites in Seward County asked for exemption from buying war savings bonds because they did not want "to aid and abet war in any form." About two months later, a Mennonite delegation from five counties met with the State Council. After "quite a discussion," the Mennonites agreed to carry their equitable share of the financial burdens. When a few weeks later some members of the Mennonite Brethren congregation at Henderson still refused to buy stamps and bonds, local bank officials persuaded them to comply.

The authorities in Seward County also had difficulties with Mennonite housewives who refused to sign pledge cards issued by the U.S. Food Administration by which citizens promised to do their share to conserve food. It is unlikely that Mennonite women were wasting food, but they objected that the wording on the cards gave too much support to the war effort and did not sign until the phrasing had been changed.[50]

At Morrison, Illinois, Mennonites made their own agreement with local patriots. The patriots agreed not to paint the church building yellow if the Mennonites promised to buy bonds. Both sides kept their promises.[51] Finally congregations and members in various places were exempted from buying bonds or stamps if they agreed to give or could show they had given to the Red Cross, the YMCA, a local war chest, or sometimes even to Mennonite relief. Such was the case in the agreements reached with the MC Sycamore Grove, Bethel, and Mount Zion congregations in Missouri.

But it was not always so easy. In at least two instances, local citizens seized property belonging to Mennonites who had been unwilling to buy Liberty Bonds. At Protection, Kansas, in October 1918, "patriots" confiscated four Jersey cows and one heifer, selling them at public auction for $297.50, after their owner Daniel S. Troyer had not contributed to the bond drive. Of the proceeds, $250 was deposited in the local bank and used to purchase a bond that drive organizers then delivered to Troyer.

The local paper, *The Protection Post*, lamented the need for "such a procedure" but agreed that the community could not tolerate a slacker. Its editor argued that anyone who made a personal gain by the war and yet would not contribute to its successful prosecution was no better than a war profiteer. Furthermore, the paper denounced those who enjoyed the rights of citizenship but were unwilling to help defend those rights with dollars. Such individuals, the paper warned, could expect "no leniency."[52]

At Jamesville, South Dakota, a Hutterite colony had a similar experience. In the 1870s some Hutterites had settled in South Dakota and a few in Montana. By 1917 South Dakota had fifteen colonies with a total of some 1,700 persons. Hutterites were prospering, and their prosperity often aroused the envy of neighbors. The war brought much grief to the Hutterites as some fifty of their young men, many of them married, were conscripted for military service. As indicated previously, it seems that because of the Hutterites' attitude toward the war, local draft boards refused to exempt their married men as they might have exempted others. Furthermore, Hutterites were not quick to contribute to the Red Cross and or to purchase Liberty Bonds. Indeed, they agonized much over the issue.[53]

By the summer of 1918, feelings between some Hutterite colonies and their neighbors had become quite tense. In August 1918 Attorney A. I. Wyman of Yankton, South Dakota, complained about the Hutterites' lack of patriotism and disinterest in public affairs. To Wyman these nonconforming, nonresistant communitarians were undesirable citizens and a "menace" to the community. Surely Wyman spoke for many of his fellow citizens.

The Hutterites finally offered $10,000 toward war relief if the money would go for humanitarian purposes. But the South Dakota Council of Defense demanded 5 percent of the proceeds of possible future land sales, an amount to be invested in Liberty Bonds and contributed to the Red Cross. The Hutterites agreed. They contributed some $25,000 to the purchase of bonds, $4,000 to the Red Cross, and $1,000 to the expenses of the State Council of Defense.[54]

But the Yankton County Council of Defense wanted more and assessed the Bon Homme Colony for $12,000. The colony refused, on grounds that it had already purchased some $5,000 in Liberty Bonds and contributed $512.85 to the Red Cross. So in early May 1918, the Yankton County Council of Defense dispatched a "squad of good citizens" to Hutterite pastures. There they seized one thousand sheep and one hundred head of cattle. On May 15 the local Liberty Loan Committee sold the animals at public auction for $16,000, although the Hutterites put the value at $40,000 or more.

With the proceeds the Committee tried to buy Liberty Bonds, but local federal officials, perhaps having some qualms about the ethics or the legality of the plan, refused to accept the proceeds. So the money was placed in a Yankton bank in the colony's name. At first the Hutterites also refused to accept the money. But later, having had enough of South Dakota, the colony used it to help buy land in Canada.[55]

The story did not end with Bon Homme. Either shortly before or after that colony's troubles a number of "patriots" invaded the Elm Spring Colony near Alexander, South Dakota, and badly beat up two of its members. And back at Bon Homme, someone broke into the grist mill and tried to adulterate the flour by placing glass in flour sacks. In June 1918 someone stole eighty-two gallons of wine from the Jamesville colony. The thief was found, but no charges were filed. Later, using the Prohibition Act, local officials raided the Bon Homme Colony and confiscated its wine. Despite the law, on Armistice Day some celebrants distributed the wine at the county seat.[56]

In the meantime, in May 1918, the State Council of Defense brought suit against the Hutterite colonies of Bon Homme County, asking for their dissolution. The Council argued that the colonies had transacted business while claiming to be a religious corporation, that their leaders had undue influence over the members, and that they had refused to supply men and money for defense. The case reached the South Dakota State Supreme Court, and in 1919 the court ruled against the Hutterites. However, already before that ruling, the first Hutterites had left South Dakota in hopes of finding a more hospitable environment in Canada.

The Liberty Bond question brought legal grief also to the Amish. Manasses E. Bontrager was a bishop of the Old Order Amish near Dodge City, Kansas. Samuel H. Miller was an Amish Mennonite and editor of *The Weekly Budget. The Budget*, published at Sugarcreek, Ohio, since 1890, was popular among Amish communities across the United States, especially for its large amounts of local and family news. During the war it frequently advertised for Liberty Bond drives, and the editor did not criticize the U.S. effort.

However, in May 1918, while Miller was absent from the office, the paper received a letter from Bontrager. On May 15 the paper's printer, apparently treating the letter as routine, set the type and published it. In it the bishop lamented that many Mennonites had purchased Liberty Bonds. He worried over what might become of "our nonresistant faith if our young brethren in camp would yield." He urged readers to profit by the example of these men who would rather die for Jesus than betray Him. Caesar might protect our property and we pay our taxes, Bontrager pointed out, but our intellectual and physical powers do not belong to him. Humans could not serve two masters. More pointedly, all who took up the sword and did not repent would perish.[57]

Someone reported *The Budget* version of the letter to federal authorities. Ever-zealous Cleveland district attorney Edwin S. Wertz decided to take legal action. Likely Wertz had political aspirations and seized upon the incident to further his career (later in the year he would try something even more ambitious against the Mennonites). Now he brought action against both Miller and Bontrager. Technically, the court could not very well prosecute the two men for having obstructed the selling of war bonds when the sale was officially voluntary. So the authorities turned to a section of the Espionage Act of 1917 which forbade the making of false statements or reports with the intent of interfering in the war effort. Maximum penalty for such a violation could be a $10,000 fine or imprisonment for twenty years or both.

In July 1918 Miller and Bontrager were indicted by the federal district court in Cleveland. Some people urged them to hire a good attorney. But the two men decided instead to defend themselves and to rely on the Lord and the prayers of God's people. On August 5, they each were fined $500 plus court costs. In court Bontrager admitted his error and said he wished that Germany might be beaten. Miller, and no doubt Bontrager also, found the whole affair to be the "most unpleasant experience" he had ever had. But he was happy to note the Lord had helped him.[58]

"Old" Mennonites Rhine W. Benner and Lewis J. Heatwole had somewhat similar legal problems. Benner was a Mennonite mission worker at Job, West Virginia, for the Virginia district "old" Mennonite conference. Heatwole, of Dale Enterprise, Virginia, was bishop of the conference's Middle District. In July 1918 Benner asked Heatwole for advice about buying bonds and stamps. On July 15 Heatwole conveyed an earlier recommendation by a committee of the "old" Mennonites' general conference which advised not to contribute anything that would be used to run the war machine. Heatwole urged the mission worker to be as true to the faith as were the brethren in the camps. Benner passed the same advice along to some fifteen members of his church.

A letter with the advice found its way to the U.S. Attorney Stuart W. Walker in Martinsburg, West Virginia, who decided on legal action. On July 17 authorities arrested Benner and jailed him in Elkins but a few days later released him on bond. Heatwole was not jailed, but he was indicted and ordered to appear in court in Martinsburg. Court officials advised him to plead guilty, but he refused, saying he would rather be put in "irons and chains." It was not an easy decision: he said the decision to plead not guilty caused him "extreme anguish."

The trial took place on September 18; the court found each man guilty of violating the part of the Sedition Act of 1918 which forbade obstruction of the sale of war bonds. They each could have received a $10,000 fine and/or a ten-year sentence. But thanks to "vigorous effort" by some of their brethren and their attorney, and with the permission of the Justice Department, the fines were only $1,000 each plus court costs. The Middle District decided to pay the fines and had no difficulty raising the money. Later, in March 1919, Heatwole tried to obtain clemency to remove "the stigma of humiliation and reproach" from his name. The Department of Justice refused.[59]

Again it is impossible to know how much Mennonites spent for Liberty Bonds. In addition to the scattered figures already mentioned, there are a few more. By October 1918 various churches in Indiana and Illinois contributed $200,100 for the purchase of bonds and $70,014 for Thrift Stamps. These contributions were in addition to $9,358 for the Red Cross and $8,118 for the YMCA.[60] In September 1918 president Mosiman of Bluffton College concluded that General Conference Mennonites had given mostly to the Red Cross, while others gave to the Mennonite Relief Commission for War Sufferers (MRCWS—an "old" Mennonite agency), and to the American Friends Service Committee.[61]

Mennonite relief growing out of World War I is another topic, to be discussed later. Clearly many Mennonites would have preferred to donate through their own churches' relief organizations rather than through government-sponsored schemes to raise money for the war. Some local and Liberty Loan officials let them do so. But surely no amount of money donated to Mennonite relief would have prevented public criticism of Mennonites. Their neighbors had too many grievances against them, resenting above all their refusal or reluctance to become soldiers for their country. Nor did those Mennonites in the home communities bear the whole brunt of anti-Mennonite sentiment. Young Mennonites who were drafted and sent to military camps faced more serious ordeals.

5

"Soldiers" of Uncle Sam

In September 1917 many American homes witnessed much sadness and grief when thousands of young men departed for military camps. Mennonite, Amish, and Hutterite homes shared in this outpouring of anguish, which was intensified by parental concern about their sons' exposure to the outside world. Many Mennonite parents must have felt their sons were like lambs being led away to dwell among wolves.

Congregations held special services for the draftees the day or evening before their departure, followed by tearful farewells at home or at the local train station. By the time they boarded the train with their bags and Bibles, many men felt as if they had attended a funeral and were, as one draftee later wrote, all "rocked emotionally."[1] Sometimes the draftee suffered further because he felt he had to refuse a flag thrust into his hands by a patriotic citizen, or because patriots expressed disgust as Mennonite men sang hymns in German before they boarded.[2]

Once on the train the Mennonites might find the journey to camp equally trying as other draftees used profanity, drank, and smoked. Hutterites sometimes found themselves ridiculed and humiliated by having their beards cut.[3] Through it all, Mennonites did not have the assurance that many of their fellow soldiers had—the feeling that they were serving their nation and the world in a great, righteous, exciting venture. They might believe, however, that it was God's will that they go to a military camp, have their faith tested, and try to live the life of nonresistant Christians.

Very few Mennonite registrants failed to report for duty. Those who did could not hold out long. Two Mennonites from McPherson County, Kansas, notified the local draft board that they were refusing induction; authorities promptly arrested them and sent them to Camp Funston in the same state.[4] David Schwartz, an Amish registrant from

Order of Induction into Military Service of the United States.

THE PRESIDENT OF THE UNITED STATES,

To *John T.* (Christian name.) *Neufeld* (Surname.)

Order Number *1527* Serial Number *607*

Greeting: *Having submitted yourself to a local board composed of your neighbors for the purpose of determining the place and time in which you can best serve the United States in the present emergency, you are hereby notified that you have now been selected for immediate military service.*

You will, therefore, report to the local board named below

at _____ McPherson, Kan. _____ (Place of reporting.), at *9 a.* m., (Hour of reporting.)

on the *24* day of *June*, 19*18*, for military duty.

From and after the day and hour just named you will be a soldier in the military service of the United States.

_____

Member of Local Board for __McPherson, Kan.__

Report to Local Board for _____ LOCAL BOARD for the County of McPherson, State of Kans. McPherson, Kansas.

Date __JUN 17 1918__

Form 1028. P.M.G.O. (See Sec. 157, S. S. R.)   3—6435

Induction Notice for John T. Neufeld.
Courtesy, Illinois Mennonite Historical and Genealogical Society, Metamora, Ill.

near Berne, Indiana, also refused to go, but then surrendered to the sheriff who took him to Camp Zachary Taylor, Kentucky.[5]

Draftees were dispatched to some thirty national army camps or cantonments throughout the nation. Almost every camp received some conscientious objectors but a few camps had many more than their shares—especially the camps known as Funston, in Kansas; Dodge, in Iowa; Zachary Taylor, in Kentucky; Sherman, in Ohio; Cody, in New Mexico; McArthur and Travis, in Texas; Pike, in Arkansas; Lee, in Virginia; Wheeler, in Georgia; Meade, in Maryland; and Lewis, in Washington.

In almost every camp conscientious objectors suffered abuse and ridicule, but at some the treatment was particularly bad. Among the worst were Funston, Dodge, Cody, McArthur, Greenleaf in Georgia, and Wheeler. Meade, Sherman, and Taylor were among the best. New draft calls came in 1918, even as late as September. The later draftees arrived better prepared than the first ones; they had heard enough to know what conscientious objectors faced.

Who was the average Mennonite conscientious objector who arrived in camp in September 1917 or later in 1918? What did he look like? Most of the men were farmers or farm workers with relatively little education beyond perhaps sixth grade. Few, perhaps not more than twenty, had college degrees. Probably the best-educated of Mennonite draftees was Jacob C. Meyer of Wayne County, Ohio, who in addition to a B.A. degree from Goshen College held master's degrees from Indiana University and Harvard.[6]

The average Mennonite's rural background and limited education help explain a lack of knowledge of current affairs or limited understanding of the war's significance. Many times military authorities (and later the members of the Board of Inquiry, appointed in 1918 to question conscientious objectors) were dismayed at the narrowness of such conscientious objectors' knowledge. Men seemed not even to know the names of current political leaders, even the president.

Harlan Stone, a member of this Board of Inquiry, was appalled over Mennonite and Dunkard conscientious objectors' "dense ignorance of what was going on in the world and their stolid indifference to those moral and political questions which were so profoundly stirring the minds and hearts of their fellow countrymen." [7] A colleague on the board, Major Walter G. Kellogg, agreed and concluded that he never realized there were so many American citizens who were so "intellectually inferior" and unworthy to assume the burdens and responsibilities of citizenship. He doubted if 50 percent of the Mennonites he examined should have been admitted into the army because of their "ignorance and stupidity." [8]

In fact, persons such as Stone and Kellogg may have seen the conscientious objectors somewhat narrowly themselves. They were men of the progressive era, a time when many leaders put what would later seem to be a naive faith in secular reforms, in the nation-state and government as agents for rooting out human evil, and in grandiose and naive slogans such as a "war to end all wars." Surely their visions—and even Woodrow Wilson's—were not broad enough to understand and accommodate groups with very different outlooks and worldviews, such as the Mennonites.

That Mennonites were indifferent or ignorant concerning the world's affairs did not mean that they or other conscientious objectors were intellectually inferior. One rather comprehensive intelligence test conducted among some one thousand conscientious objectors even showed these men scored higher than other draftees. Furthermore, contrary to what camps' psychologists often alleged, the results indicated that there was no reason to conclude that the men had cho-

Mennonite Church Membership Certificate of Philemon L. Frey, Amish Mennonite Church, Archbold, Ohio.

sen to be conscientious objectors because of "low mentality." The report of that comprehensive test concluded that some of the conscientious objectors were indeed "keen thinkers." [9]

Upon their arrival in camp, many conscientious objectors submitted their church membership certificates plus documents showing that their local draft boards recognized their noncombatant status. However, many camp officials ignored such papers and refused to accept them. The camp officers' principal objective was to persuade the men to become regular soldiers. If that failed, the goal was to persuade the Mennonites at least to serve the military effort as noncombatants by donning the uniform, agreeing to drill, and performing some kind of work.

Although the government did not define noncombatant service until March 1918, there was soon a general assumption that anyone who agreed to accept the uniform, to drill, and to perform certain tasks filled the role. With some exceptions most officers and many regular troops were hostile to if not contemptuous of conscientious objectors who could not go that far. In the atmosphere of the camp, such men were "slackers, yellow bellies, or yellow backs" rather than persons of high scruples.

General Leonard Wood, commander of Camp Funston, referred to conscientious objectors as "scoundrels." He suggested they be organized into labor battalions and sent to France or interned and treated as enemy aliens.[10] In this regard he and most military authorities accurately reflected public hostility as well. So their task as they saw it was to do everything possible to "persuade" conscientious objectors to see the error of their unpatriotic ways.

Usually a person who agreed to be a noncombatant was not harassed any further. However, most Mennonite draftees and also many Quakers, members of the Church of the Brethren, Molokans (members of a small Russian religious sect), and political objectors, such as the Socialists, refused to become noncombatants. It was especially these draftees, whose consciences did not allow them to serve the war effort even as noncombatants, who most provoked the military. Even in 1918, after the War Department had handed down more specific orders for fair treatment of conscientious objectors, military authorities continued the efforts to make "good" soldiers or noncombatants of these men. A considerable amount of physical and mental abuse continued through the entire war.

At the outset military authorities had few if any guidelines for treatment of conscientious objectors. When the authorities did receive instructions, they might not comply. Not until September 25, 1917, were they instructed to allow "selected" Mennonite draftees not to wear the uniform, because the question of "raiment" was one of the "tenets of their faith." [11] Even then, and throughout the war, many camp officials ignored that order.

On October 10 of the same year, military commanders were instructed to segregate conscientious objectors from the regular men. [12] In most military camps this order too was never enforced; often, camp officers simply did not inform the conscientious objectors that there were to be segregated units. At the same time, camp commanders were ordered to appoint instructors who would treat conscientious objectors with "tact and consideration." [13] Military authorities hoped fair treatment of the men would persuade many if not most of them to become combatants or at least noncombatants.

This order too was often ignored. And indeed, many times authorities were quite successful in "converting" or "persuading" the men. Of the 21,000 conscientious objectors conscripted during World War I, only about four thousand held firm to their beliefs and refused to yield. Of those about 1,700 agreed to become noncombatants. Yet the military was not satisfied. Officers wanted to convert the remaining 2,300 also, even though in the entire war they constituted only a tiny fraction of almost three million U.S. conscripts. [14]

At least until the summer of 1918, when some conscientious objectors rejected decisions of the Board of Inquiry, the principal sources of conflict between conscientious objectors who rejected noncombatant status and their military superiors were three: refusals to wear the uniform, to perform service, and to drill. Upon arrival in camp, most conscientious objectors received instructions to do one or all three of these directives.

Symbolically or practically all three requirements violated, or might violate, their faith. However, often the men's church leaders had given only vague instructions in such matters. The men had to determine for themselves the extent to which they might cooperate and obey. Many refused all three orders, except perhaps to cook for themselves and clean their own quarters.

Most military authorities did not meet such refusal with "tact and consideration." Perhaps the most benign initial response to Mennonite noncooperation occurred in Camp Meade, where already in September 1917 conscientious objectors were segregated from the rest. There they experienced relatively little trouble, although even at Camp Meade there was at least one case of physical abuse when a Quaker,

Henry Stabler, was brutally beaten.

In late September Secretary of War Baker visited Meade, spoke to the conscientious objectors, and left them impressed that he had sympathy for them. However, they were wrong. Baker did not have much appreciation for their stand. He himself described those same men as "well-disposed, simple-minded young people" who were imprisoned by their narrow environment and had no comprehension of the world outside of their own rural and peculiar community. He even felt that of those with whom he had talked only two seemed "quite normal mentally."

Whatever Baker's attitude, at Camp Meade the conscientious objectors performed only basic housekeeping tasks, then hiked to keep physically fit. In the summer of 1918, most of them received farm furloughs. To them, as draftee Isaac Baer wrote later, Camp Meade "was an island of peace in a sea of war."[15]

Other camps were not such havens. In most places the conscientious objectors who refused the three demands had to endure a considerable amount of mental and physical abuse. What motivated most Mennonite men to refuse to conform and to comply with military orders and to become "good" soldiers or noncombatants? The answers are not easy. Conscientious objectors have often been noted for their sturdy nonconformity and individualism. Some of them have opposed war because of a stubborn independence and fierce resistance to any kind of authority, discipline, and conformity. And indeed Mennonite draftees opposed military service because of unwillingness to conform.

But Mennonite nonconformity is communal and based on New Testament values, not individual autonomy. In World War I many Mennonites resisted military service because they feared that if they agreed to be combatants or even serve as noncombatants they faced disapproval and rejection from parents and church. Others resisted because they had fully internalized the traditional Mennonite peace position. Mennonite nurturing taught them at home and church that Christians were not to wage war. To be sure, in many cases their parents, teachers, and pastors did not always explain the biblical reasons for this Mennonite principle very adequately. And their teaching often did not help them explain very well what to do specifically, if an "enemy" invaded one's homeland or if faced with some other specific "evil."

Nonetheless, for most Mennonite draftees opposition to war was a part of their upbringing, and resisting militarization was practically an automatic reflex. Perhaps a few also acted from humanitarian motives or, more rationally, had concluded that war was a stupid, barbarian, wasteful, and senseless way of resolving conflict. Whatever the case, much of the contemporary testimony makes clear that many, indeed probably most, of the men were motivated by sincere religious convictions. Their willingness to suffer and to endure is eloquent testimony to the depth and sincerity of their beliefs. As Gustave Gaeddert from Camp Funston wrote in October 1917, "So we are awaiting the mercy of our heavenly Father for he has promised us that he will not ask more of us as we can do or endure. So we trust in God to help us in our churches."[16]

Perhaps it is easy to understand why the men did not want to wear military uniforms and to drill but less easy to understand their refusal to work. Mennonite conscientious objectors were not men who shunned work; indeed almost to a man they dreaded idleness. However, they realized or soon understood that even a small amount of work such as chopping wood or sweeping floors, no matter how innocent it might appear, would or could draw them further into the military net. The first small compromises would make it more difficult to maintain the purity of their position. As Ezra Deter wrote to his parents in July 1918, "A person has got to refuse any work at all or he is a goner."[17] Or in the words of draftee Allen B. Christophel, the "further you went with the military officials the further they demanded one to go. The further I went the less reason I could give for stopping—so I concluded the best place to stop was at the beginning."[18]

At Camp Zachary Taylor, Payson Miller voiced the same objections. He wrote in June 1918 that he was "daily becoming more convinced" that a Christian could not have any part at all in the military organization—"not even to the extent of raking grass seed at the hospital." The "most cowardly thing" a fellow could do, Miller had concluded, was to accept noncombatant service.[19] Editor Daniel Kauffman of the *Gospel Herald* supported these men with an argument that a draftee who had accepted noncombatant service in a hospital was just as "valuable in the work of overcoming the enemy as the man who carries the rifle." Nonresistant people, the editor admonished, must have no part of this work no matter what their task might be, combatant or noncombatant.[20]

Some of the motivation was more direct and practical. Many men soon realized that willingness to work would delay their transfer to the barracks set apart for conscientious objectors. One who learned that lesson was George S. Klassen at Camp Funston, who had agreed to wash dishes. Being a valuable worker, he was not transferred to the conscientious objector unit; in fact he was even selected to go overseas.

At that point Klassen refused to wash any more dishes and staged a kind of sit-down strike. Although threatened with court-martial, Klassen refused to budge and was eventually transferred.[21]

However, rendering some kind of service did not necessarily mean agreeing to become a real noncombatant. For instance, Jacob C. Meyer accepted kitchen and clerical work in Camp Jackson. As a defense he pointed to 2 Thessalonians 3:10, which admonishes that those who do not work should not eat. That principle, he said, seemed more appropriate than a conference resolution drafted by an inexperienced person. Meyer had no further difficulties and was later allowed to do overseas work in France for the American Friends Service Committee.[22] He was hardly a noncombatant contributor to militarism.

Many conscientious objectors made the decision not to render service, to drill, or to don the uniform only after much anguish and doubt. When in May 1918 Edward Waltner and several other Mennonite draftees in Camp Cody were asked to "volunteer" to drill and to care for sick animals, the men spent much time in struggle and prayer. On the one hand, Waltner wrote, there was the "voice, the fear of man, the glorious opportunities for advancement, the honor of the world, the safty [sic] of the loved ones at home." On the other hand was a higher voice which said, "If any man will come after me, let him deny himself, take up his cross, and follow me."

Because no one volunteered to care for the animals, twenty men were selected, but they refused to obey the order. A few weeks later Waltner and others were court-martialed.[23] To the military commanders the refusal to perform some of the most menial tasks such as sweeping floors or even swatting flies seemed absurd. They could or would not put themselves in the conscientious objectors' frame of mind.

The wearing of the military uniform and performing drill were equally important matters, although it seems that most men were more able to resist the latter than to ward off other impositions. Soon after their arrival in camp, many conscientious objectors were forced to put on uniforms. Many but not all refused. Refusal carried a high price—having one's own clothes forcibly removed or worse.

Moreover some men claimed to see no problem, saying that to wear such attire did not make them soldiers. As one draftee put it, the uniform "had nothing to do with Chirsheanity [sic]."[24] In many instances the men resisted wearing the full uniform but did don army overalls. Or they put on the uniform then later, if they still had their civilian clothes, put those back on. In one instance a Mennonite draftee was even told to return his uniform because the camp had a shortage.[25]

Camp Funston, Kansas.
Courtesy, Mennonite Library and Archives.

Camp Lee.
Courtesy, Mrs. Anna Rohren, Wadsworth, Ohio.

So in general a mere agreement to wear the uniform did not mean that the draftee had become a noncombatant. One could see many conscientious objectors in army attire.

Going one more step, men often agreed to render some service such as kitchen work, gardening, cleaning, and the like. Often, however, after some weeks or months such men changed their minds. Either they found their duties expanding, or they concluded they had compromised too much. In Camp Funston in the fall of 1917, many if not most Mennonite conscientious objectors (unlike the Hutterites) agreed to haul garbage. Initially the men probably agreed with Gustave Gaeddert, one of their number, that this kind of work was "harmless" and "truly constructive" even if the larger system of which it was a part was "destructive."

For a brief time even General Wood seemed pleased with the attitude of the conscientious objectors in his camp and reported that the men were doing "excellent work"—due, he said, to officers' "tact and firmness." However, trouble arose when some of the men refused to work on Sundays or to haul ammunition. That brought them some brutal beatings. Apparently camp officials pounced hard on draftees who initially agreed to work but later quit. They felt such behavior was inconsistent if not hypocritical.[26]

At Camp Travis, Johannes Klaassen and others worked in the store, kitchen, and barns. However, by Christmas 1917 Klaassen decided "after much personal soul searching" to quit when he and other draftees concluded they were aiding the war effort.[27] Lee R. Swartzendruber of Wayland, Iowa, reached a similar conclusion in Camp Forrest, Georgia, where he had initially agreed to work. But in mid-September he refused to render any more service. Testimony during an eventual court-martialing revealed Swartzendruber worked for a few days because he felt he owed the government something for having fed, housed, and clothed him. But after a while he concluded his service freed someone else to fight at the front.[28]

Fear of becoming too ensnared in the military net also motivated men to discontinue drilling. Rudy Yoder, for instance, who had agreed to drill in Camp Zachary Taylor, quit on realizing his service was all part of "legalized training for war."[29] Later in the war many men refused to cooperate when they rejected the Board of Inquiry's classification or assignment.

Military authorities used various means to "persuade" conscientious objectors to comply. They appealed to the draftees' patriotism or apparent lack of it, abused them verbally, and exerted psychological

Mennonite COs, Camp Funston, Kansas.
Courtesy, Mennonite Library and Archives.

Mennonite COs, Camp Funston, Kansas.
Courtesy, Mennonite Library and Archives.

pressure. If all else failed, they inflicted physical pain. Verbal, psychological, and physical abuse began at the time the first men arrived at camp and did not end until the conscientious objectors were discharged in early 1919.

It is difficult to determine if the abuse abated or became worse as time went on; but it seems to have been most widespread and intense in the summer and fall of 1918. During that time the military was given a freer hand to abuse conscientious objectors. Furthermore, the draftees of 1918 might have been better prepared and therefore more recalcitrant than those who went to the camps like innocent sheep in the fall of 1917. In any case, the military was successful in its efforts to coerce the men into complying with its objectives. As indicated, only some four thousand conscientious objectors held firm to their beliefs.

The psychological pressures on the men in camps were both positive and negative. William Handrich of Fairview, Michigan, who was assigned to Camp Custer in his own state, described the positive kind. One day in early 1918, several thousand men in full battle array marched by his barracks; the ground shook, and the building trembled. Here, Handrich wrote later, "was power, might, force! The military band played striking music that made your blood tingle! Ah, there was glory, power, honor!"[30]

As for the negative, probably all conscientious objectors, but especially those who refused to become noncombatants, endured some mental abuse which consisted of name calling, cursing, and ridicule. In September 1918, in Camp Greenleaf, John Witmer and Harvey Blosser (the only two conscientious objectors in that cantonment at that time) were taken to a public square and forced to read their Bibles over a period of several days while hundreds of men jeered.[31]

And then there was outright physical abuse, in many forms and in virtually every camp. Much of this abuse would not have occurred if camp commanders had followed by the adjutant general's instructions of July 30, 1918, and if the War Department had enforced its own stated policies. The July 30 orders exempted bona fide conscientious objectors from wearing the uniform, rendering service, or bearing arms, and said they were to be housed in separate detention barracks.[32] But camp officials ignored these instructions, allowed widespread abuse, and encouraged court-martialing the recalcitrants. The secretary of war, although he made some attempts, did not do enough to make camps officials comply with his department's policies. He did even less to punish the guilty.

One could compile many cases of physical abuse, but a few of the

Mennonite COs, Camp Funston, Kansas.
Courtesy, Mennonite Library and Archives.

Mennonite COs, Camp Funston, Kansas.
Courtesy, Mennonite Library and Archives.

Amish COs, Camp Funston, Kansas.
Courtesy, Mennonite Library and Archives.

Central Illinois Mennonite COs, Camp Wheeler, Georgia.
Courtesy, Howard Stutzman, Carlock, Illinois.

COs in Detention Camp #1, Camp Funston, Kansas.
Courtesy, Mennonite Library and Archives.

Mennonite COs in Camp Travis, Texas. X is Johannes Klaassen.
Courtesy, Mrs. Esther Bergen, Winnipeg, Manitoba.

worst tell the story. The full story includes cases of Socialists, Molokans, Quakers, and others being treated as badly as Mennonites. Moreover, many Mennonites and other conscientious objectors did not experience physical abuse. Yet the abuse was frequent. Common forms were the hot and cold shower, dunking, beating, kicking, lashing, wounding with bayonets and imprisonment in the guard house. There were also various instances of men being forced to drill with rifles strapped to their backs. In some cases a draftee's civilian clothes were torn off in an attempt to force him into uniform.[33]

An especially cruel torture was mock executions, either by simulating a firing squad or by hanging. In the fall of 1917 and again in the summer of 1918, a few conscientious objectors were almost killed in mock hangings—indeed might have been had not camp officers intervened in time. Another abuse was to threaten men with being buried alive; some were forced to dig their own graves.[34] In an exceptionally cruel torture, at Camp Greenleaf a conscientious objector was thrown into a cesspool and "baptized" with a shovel of excrement over his head. Shortly afterward Emanuel Swartzendruber was lowered head first into the cesspool.[35]

At Camp Dodge in the summer of 1918 several conscientious objectors, including at least one Mennonite, were put into the guardhouse for their refusal of the three standard demands (to work, to wear the uniform, and to drill). Besides being locked up, these men were subjected to sadistic treatment consisting of the cold water treatment, scrubbing parts of their bodies with a hair brush, and "exercises." The "exercises" consisted of holding a spoon at arm's length for several minutes, waddling around the room in full squat position, standing on one foot for one hour with the other foot tied to the hip, and transferring water by spoon from one bucket to another. Yet in spite of these and other humiliations, the men expressed no desire to avenge themselves.[36]

At Camp Lee in Virginia, most conscientious objectors were segregated, with a lieutenant named Lawrence F. Cramblet in charge of them. For some time they experienced little harassment and seemed particularly pleased with their treatment. They exercised regularly but wore no uniforms and rendered no service. However, on July 16, 1918, about twelve to fourteen of them were ordered to haul poles and to build a fence. When they refused Lieutenant George B. Kennedy and some noncommissioned officers forced the men to run for about two hours while beating, kicking, and knocking some of them down. Afterward the men were subjected to the cold shower treatment and one

Mennonite COs Orie Rupp, Harvey Hartzler, Philemon Frey, and ?, singing hymns.
Courtesy, Archives of the Mennonite Church.

Lieutenant Lawrence Cramlet, Camp Lee, Virginia.
Courtesy, Elam R. Hernley, Scottdale, Pennsylvania.

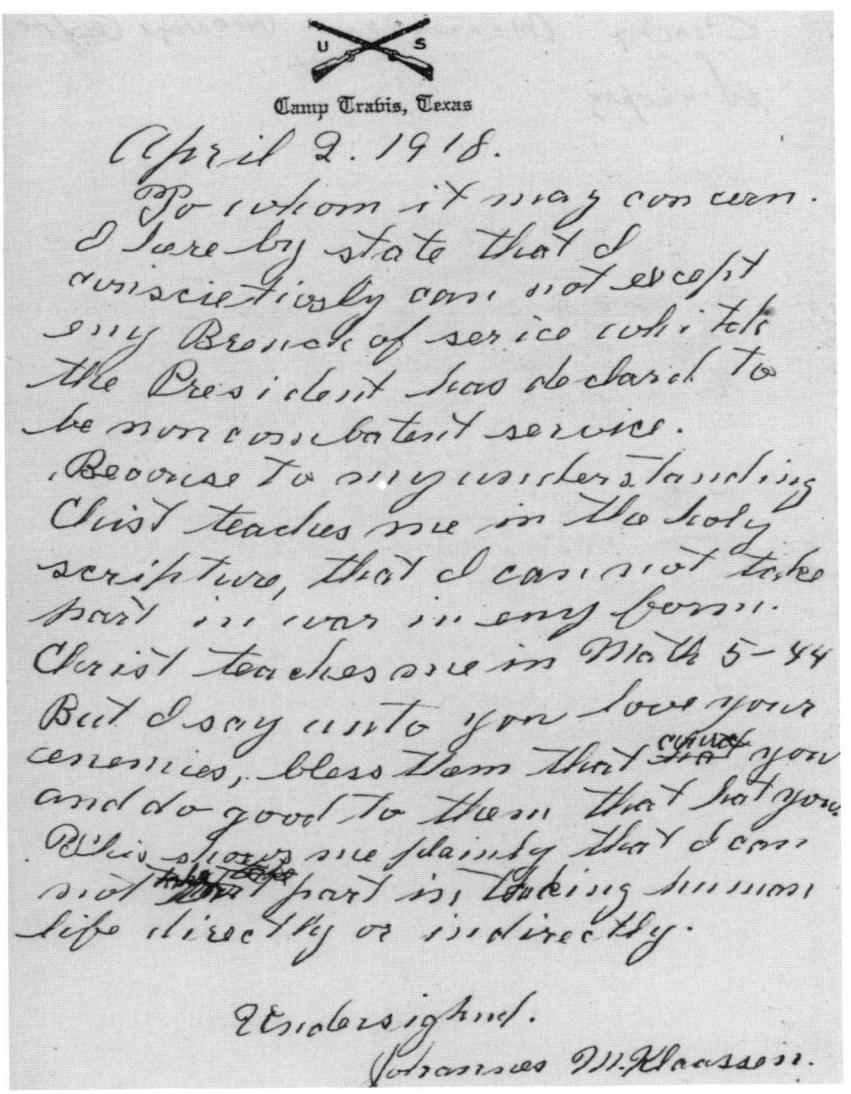

Camp Travis, Texas

April 2. 1918.

To whom it may concern.
I hereby state that I
conscientiously can not except
any Branch of service which
the President has declared to
be non combatent service.

Because to my understanding
Christ teaches me in the holy
scripture, that I can not take
part in war in any form.
Christ teaches me in Math 5-44
But I say unto you love your
enemies, bless them that curse you
and do good to them that hate you
This shows me plainly that I can
not take part in taking human
life directly or indirectly.

Undersigned.
Johannes W. Klaassen.

Draftee Johannes Klaassen in Camp Travis, Texas, informing military authorities he cannot perform any kind of military service.
Courtesy, Mennonite Heritage Centre, Winnipeg, Manitoba.

was scrubbed with lye. The torture was so cruel one man later testified that he would "sooner face the firing squad than go through more of the same kind of treatment."[37] In fact this incident became one of the few cases of camp brutality the authorities saw fit to investigate. It actually led to a court-martial of Lieutenant Kennedy.

A few individuals were especially singled out for brutal treatment. Among them was George Miller from Milford, Nebraska, who was stationed in Camp Dodge. In August 1918 his corporal beat him and broke his nose for Miller's refusal to do kitchen work. Later he was put under a cold shower, dunked under water, scrubbed with a hard brush, and deprived of his clothing and bedding. Afterward, according to Sanford C. Yoder who visited the camp as a minister, parts of Miller's body looked like raw meat. It took several weeks for his wounds to heal and eight months before he could breathe again through his nose.[38]

Another victim of military brutality was John Bergen of Hooker, Oklahoma. In September 1918 Bergen was severely beaten by a sergeant in Camp Greenleaf, Georgia, for his refusal to set up his tent and clean up after a storm because he considered such work military service. Bergen's jaw was broken and he spent two months in the hospital to recuperate.[39]

Walter D. Ford of Waynesboro, Virginia, was sent to Camp Humphreys in his home state. Here he was knocked down and struck with bayonets until he "was blood [sic] from head to foot." He cried to God to forgive his torturers for not knowing what they were doing—but his tormentors replied they did know what they were doing: trying to make Ford work. Ford took comfort in Jesus' promise that we will not be tempted and tried above which we are able to bear. Never before in his life, Ford wrote later, had Jesus' words seemed sweeter or truer.[40]

Few if any were more brutally treated than John H. Smeltzer of Wakarusa, Indiana. For his refusal to work in Camp Zachary Taylor, Smeltzer was thrown in the guard house, hit in the face, knocked unconscious, and kicked in the back. He also was jabbed in the hip by a bayonet, strung up by his thumbs, given the cold and hot water treatment, put to bed with seventeen woolen blankets on top of him, and dragged around the camp. Finally Smeltzer agreed to work a little but later recanted because "his conscience condemned him for making this promise." On June 20 he was court-martialed and sentenced to five years in prison.[41]

Hutterites were especially singled out, but less as individuals than as a group. Perhaps that was natural, since they were communal and made their decisions as a group. In addition beards, distinctive dress, and lack of social experience beyond their colonies made them stand out even more than did most Mennonites. In any case, even before their induction the draft boards in South Dakota (where many of them lived) showed them almost no leniency. For instance, the boards refused the exemptions to Hutterite fathers and other married men that the boards were granting to non-Hutterites.

Some fifty-four Hutterites were drafted during World War I, many of whom had children. More uniformly than Mennonites, Hutterites objected to undergoing physical examinations, were offended by foul language, and refused to render service. Their stance often led to exceptionally bad treatment. In Camp Funston their heads and beards were shaven; they were dunked, beaten, rolled through the mud; they were deprived of their Bibles and other religious literature; and they submitted to many other indignities.[42]

In the fall of 1917, Reverend Joseph Kleinsasser of the Milltown Colony in South Dakota even hired a local lawyer, F. D. Wicks, to plead the draftees' case with camp authorities. In the spring of the following year, Kleinsasser requested Frederick P. Keppel, assistant secretary of war in charge of all matters pertaining to conscientious objectors, to let the Hutterite men do farm work. His argument was pragmatic—there simply was "no wisdom in taking Hutterite men away from their families and farms" and allowing them to remain idle; the policy profited the government nothing. "Ain't the U.S. in need of many farms?" he asked. "Have they no use for grain or meat?"[43]

In November 1917 some thirteen Hutterites in Camp Funston offered the commanding officer, Lieutenant W. Paul Jones, some money for securing their release. Everything in camp and the little work they were doing was against their religion, they said. They could not conscientiously do any work whatsoever in connection with military service. Furthermore, they were all married men with children. The idea of payments to officers probably did not originate with the draftees but instead with three of their ministers—Jacob Hofer, John J. Wipf, and J. P. Entz, of Alexandria, South Dakota.

Wipf had already given some $120 to Jones for allowing worship services and being "so good to the boys." Now he promised Jones $1,000 if he could secure the men's release. Was this not outright bribery? Perhaps it was, but Wipf also informed Jones that all of this had to be "lawful." In January 1918, Hofer made a similar offer to Jones's successor, Lieutenant C. C. Ray. It is not clear to what extent the third minister, J. B. Entz, was involved, but apparently he supported Wipf's offer. Perhaps the Hutterites really believed that such a release could be secured legally, but they should have known that lieutenants did not have power to release any draftees.[44]

In any case, somehow other officers or perhaps even Jones and Ray themselves reported the bribery attempt to the legal authorities. As a result in January 1918, the three ministers were indicted and brought into court. The charges were that they had "unlawfully, feloniously, willfully, and corruptedly" promised to give a large sum of money to Jones and Ray with the intent to influence the officers; and that they had tried "to make opportunity for a commission of a fraud" in the securing and discharging from military service the draftees Paul Entz, Peter S. Entz, Joseph Waldner, and others.

The trial was not held until October 1919, in Federal District Court at Leavenworth, Kansas. The three defendants pleaded *nolo contendere* (no contest), and the trial ended in a hung jury. U.S. Attorney Fred Robertson feared a new trial would produce the same result since the ministers, dressed in their "very simple garb," had impressed the jury as being honest and conscientious. Furthermore, the principal witness for the government had come across as unsavory; in Robertson's words, the witness was "surrounded with a set of circumstances and a personal demeanor which at once places the government at a disadvantage." The U.S. attorney general allowed Robertson to dispose of the case as he saw fit. On June 7, 1920, the Federal District Court, then meeting in Kansas City, Missouri, fined Hofer and Wipf each $100 and acquitted Entz.[45]

If Hofer and Wipf were guilty of attempting to bribe, authorities in different military camps and in Washington were guilty of doing little to stop or even investigate physical abuses. Baker and Keppel could have done much more to warn military officials to abide by the War Department's instructions, and to listen to and investigate complaints. But they chose not to do much. Investigations of physical abuse often concluded the charges were not proven. For instance, in the case of Daniel Miller in Camp Cody, the adjutant general admitted this draftee had been the subject of a "practical joke," which consisted of giving him a cold bath and the placing of a rope around his neck. However, he concluded there was no evidence Miller had "actually been hanged by the neck."[46]

Captain Eugene C. Brisben of the provost marshall's office at Camp Funston also concluded that "anyone with half a mind" could readily determine the allegations of abuse were false—that it was "ridiculous" to believe that any officer or enlisted man might be foolish enough to incriminate himself by violating strict regulations laid down by the War department.[47] Walter G. Kellogg, a member of the Board of Inquiry (a federal committee established in 1918 to determine the sincerity of conscientious objectors), also dismissed the charges. He referred to them as "good-natured hazing" undertaken in the spirit of fun. Rather than condemn, Kellogg praised the army for preventing abuse by maintaining good discipline.[48]

Despite that attitude of "see, hear, and speak no evil," a few investigations did result in legal action against military personnel. In Camp Dodge the man who so badly mistreated George Miller, Corporal Poindexter, was court-martialed, sentenced to ninety days, and reduced in rank. However, he was soon released and reinstated.[49] Lieutenant Kennedy was court-martialed for his brutal treatment of conscientious objectors in Camp Lee. In that case a Mennonite named Elam R. Hernley, one of Kennedy's victims, managed to smuggle a letter to Loucks in which he reported the events of July 16. Loucks informed Secretary Baker, and Baker ordered the court-martial.

Some of the men were reluctant to testify against Kennedy because they did not want to avenge themselves, but they did testify at Kennedy's trial. On the other side, military personnel testified to refute the charges. On October 10, 1918, Kennedy was acquitted on grounds that the testimony was conflicting and inconclusive.[50] In December 1918 the War Department dismissed two officers in Camp Funston for their "unduly severe disciplinary measures" against conscientious objectors and in the next month it reprimanded a few others.[51]

No doubt there would have been more court-martialing if conscientious objectors had been willing to press charges. But as Menno Diener of Arthur, Illinois, said later, "We felt that we could not conscientiously testify against them for it would be helping to punish them and cause ill feelings between resisting and nonresistance." Diener thought that such a course would lead to "a poor light of Christianity in our church and backyard."[52]

Although many military men were cruel to the conscientious objectors, others tried to be kind and considerate. In Camp Sherman in Ohio, the men had a real friend and protector in Captain Robert J. Hough, the officer in charge of the conscientious objector detachment. Yet Hough was not uncritical of Mennonites and doubted the sincerity of some. With the typical tendency to confuse the sectarian outlook with low intelligence, he felt that some Mennonites, and especially the Amish, were men of "low mentality." He also found them ignorant in most worldly matters, which was much nearer the mark but of course reflected not only naïveté but the fact that Mennonites and Amish had their own ideas about what matters were important.

To Hough's credit, he respected conscientious objectors despite such judgments. He later helped to settle a serious conflict between civic leaders and some of his men on farm furloughs in Ohio.[53] In the same camp on at least one occasion, a Colonel Pond was so moved by the testimony of James Gnagey and other Mennonite men "that tears could not be restrained." Pond left that interview with a Bible from one of the boys under his arm and a copy of the *Gospel Herald* in his pocket.[54]

In some instances military personnel apologized for the abuse heaped upon the men. There were even instances of reconciliation, forgiveness, and expressions of admiration for the conscientious objectors. John Kropf of Harrisburg, Oregon, and other Mennonites at Camp Lewis became very fond of an exceptionally kind sergeant, whom they gave farewell gifts upon his discharge.[55] In fact they also gave farewell gifts to another sergeant who had been very hateful—whereupon that man broke down and tearfully confessed he was ashamed for the mistreatment he had meted out.[56] However, conciliatory gestures did not always bring repentance. When an Amish minister visiting Camp Dodge tried to shake the hand of a captain, the officer slapped the Amishman so hard he knocked off the man's glasses.[57]

To respond to the abuses, and to minister to the many needs of men in camp, Mennonites established special committees. But the committees did not begin their work until after the first men had arrived in camp. In November 1917, Henry P. Krehbiel, member of the CGs' Western District Exemption Committee, received a letter from a draftee in Camp Travis, Texas. The draftee begged for help and advice. "I do not know," the draftee wrote, "why in the world the committee or the conference does not ever let us know what to do." How should he act, so as to be true to the teachings of the Bible?[58] He raised his questions just as various committees were being formed.

During the rest of the war, the committees' individual ministers would render the men valuable services. In addition to its Western District's pioneer committee, the GC church's overall general conference established an Exemption Committee. Its members were Peter Jansen of Jansen, Nebraska; Maxwell H. Kratz of Philadelphia; Bethel College President John W. Kliewer; Peter H. Richert of Goessel, Kansas; John Lehman of Berne, Indiana; Bluffton College President Samuel K. Mosiman; and Henry P. Krehbiel of Newton, Kansas.[59] Meanwhile in August of 1917 the "old" Mennonite Church had appointed its Military Problems Committee.

In addition to those three, other Mennonite groups and conferences appointed committees. Among Amish Mennonites and "old" Mennonites (who in the World War I decade were rapidly merging into one denomination), several district conferences appointed a "Committee of Ten"—the Western Amish Mennonite and the "old" Mennonite conferences of Missouri-Iowa and Kansas-Nebraska. That was in December 1917; the committee included Daniel H. Bender and Sanford C. Yoder, two men who would give exceptional help and counsel to draftees in the camps. The Eastern Amish Mennonite Conference, the GCs' Eastern District and Northern District conferences, and the "old" Mennonites' Lancaster and Indiana-Michigan conferences each appointed similar committees.[60]

Often home congregations also helped sustain the men, as pastors or other church leaders visited, worshiped, and counseled with them. For instance among the MBs, one such leader was Henry W. Lohrenz, president of Tabor College, who did much for his brothers in camp.[61] Another MB who was exceptionally helpful was Jacob G. Ewert, writer, editor, and professor at Lohrenz's college. Despite severe physical handicaps, Ewert counseled many men on draft matters.

However, not all the counselors and pastors counseled firmness; rather often some of them suggested compromise with the military authorities. The men frequently resented such advice, feeling that their pastors really did not understand their difficult position. Some home congregations also urged a more accommodating attitude, evoking similar reactions.[62] Moreover, quite a few draftees in camps located far from Mennonite communities had few if any visitors—even though they needed the visits more than the others.

Of all these committees, the most important were the Exemption Committee of the GCs' general conference, the GC Western District's Exemption Committee, and the "old" Mennonites' Military Problems Committees. In the early summer of 1917, the Exemption Committee of the GCs' general conference printed and distributed draft information and tried without success to persuade Washington officials to grant Mennonite men exemption from all forms of military service. In September of that year, it recommended that draftees accept only service designed to support and to save life. They were not to participate in any work that would result in personal injury.

At that time or somewhat later, most of that committee's members believed that the men should not refuse all work. Committee members also visited military camps but most likely only saw and interceded on behalf of men in Funston and Travis.[63] Much more active and important

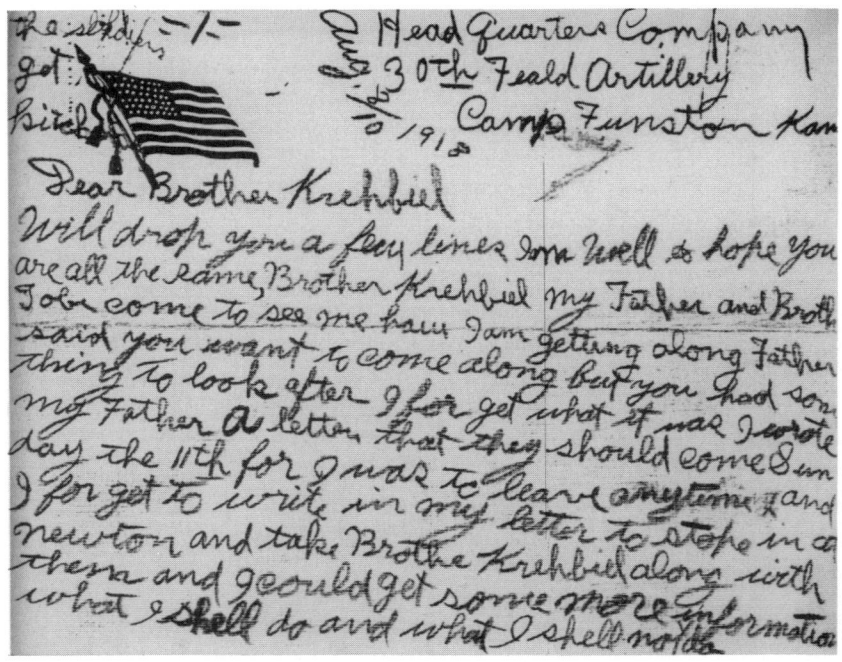

Plea for help from Draftee Jacob Base to Henry P. Krehbiel.
Courtesy, Mennonite Library and Archives.

was the Western District Exemption Committee. Its members also visited and cared for draftees in Camps Funston and Travis, where most of the men from their own district conference were staying. In these camps committee members listened to the men, conducted worship services, occasionally interceded with camp authorities, and tried to formulate guidelines for the three key questions of work, drill, and the wearing of uniforms.

Because the issue of what work to do was the most pressing, the Western District Conference, at its committee's urging, took up the matter. On October 25, 1917, the conference resolved that the men could render any service outside the military establishment which helped to support and save life. The conference rejected any work that resulted in personal injury or loss of life to others. The committee concluded the work currently assigned to the men in Camp Funston and Camp Travis "virtually constituted military service." Therefore, the

Henry P. Krehbiel.
Courtesy, Mennonite Life.

Aaron Loucks.
Courtesy, Mennonite Publishing House.

men should accept it only under protest.[64]

When GC committees or conferences advised men to do some work, they were at odds with the "old" Mennonites' Military Problems Committee. That committee was one of the most influential and active and has left detailed records.[65] While Jonas (J. S.) Hartzler handled all the committee's very extensive correspondence—as many as thirty to fifty letters a day—Aaron Loucks assumed the arduous burden of visiting the men in camp. Loucks traveled thousands of miles to counsel draftees and to intercede with military authorities. According to Hartzler, his colleague's task was often "nerve-racking [*sic*]" without respite. Even at home, Hartzler observed, Loucks could not rest because he too was faced with much correspondence and was constantly having to plan his next trip. Loucks was a strong man, Hartzler believed, but he often came home with his "stomach and nervous system all out of working order."[66]

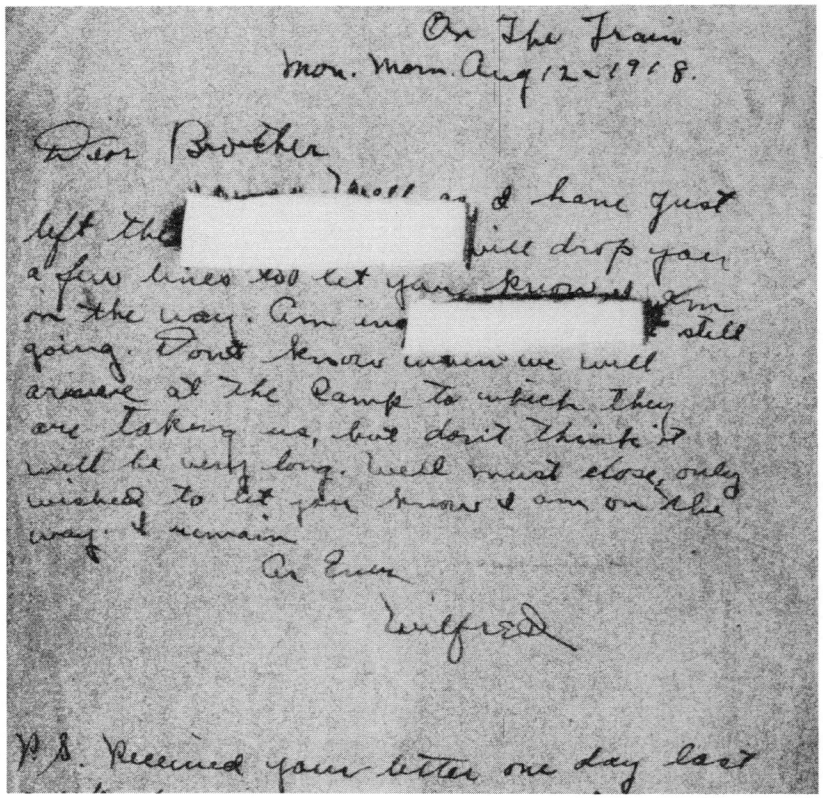

Wilfred Gingerich's censored letter to War Problems Committee.
Courtesy, Archives Mennonite Church.

On the issue of what work to accept in camps, Loucks regretted the General Conference advice. He informed Krehbiel that his committee could not recommend that the men cooperate even that far with camp authorities. Loucks hoped they would soon be segregated from regular soldiers as they had been at Camp Meade. Believing that noncooperation had worked in the men's favor at Camps Zachary Taylor and Sherman, Loucks argued that he had reason to believe a firm position of noncooperation would bring better treatment in the end.[67]

Krehbiel disagreed. He feared that Loucks's position and decision produced a "disconcerting effect." Moreover, he considered that, even inside the camps, some lines of work that were "useful" and "purely humanitarian" were all right, as long as the work was not "part of the military establishment."[68] How Krehbiel could imply that work inside the camp might not be "part of the military establishment" is rather puzzling. And indeed in late January, the Western District's committee advised the men in Camp Travis it would be preferable to choose a detention camp rather than to accept work declared to be noncombatant under military jurisdiction. In that, it took a position more like that of the "old" Mennonites.[69]

The issue of service was a major one at a meeting of twenty-two delegates representing eight Mennonite denominations and held at Goshen, Indiana, on January 9 and 10, 1918. At that meeting, the conferees seemed to agree that, to be consistent with Mennonites' creed and principles, any service rendered to the government under the Selective Service Act could not be under military direction or administration. A resolution to that effect was adopted. Addressing President Wilson, the conferees reaffirmed their loyalty to their "beloved country." However, they informed Wilson quite directly that their young men could accept neither combatant nor noncombatant service. Instead, they preferred agricultural work.

Despite that meeting, the various Mennonite groups and their special committees charged with the responsibility of looking after the welfare of the draftees never cooperated much. The delegates in Goshen did establish a few committees, but there is no evidence they accomplished much or performed any major tasks. Yet they did agree to authorize Loucks to represent all Mennonites in case joint action was needed.[70]

At the outset one of Loucks's most difficult tasks was to solve some serious problems in Camp Dodge, Iowa. In the usual ways, camp officials were trying to force some thirty conscientious objectors, most of them Mennonite, to wear uniforms and to render service. The commander of the camp was General Edward H. Plummer, an ex-Quaker. To Sanford C. Yoder, Plummer seemed "very cordial and sincere." But as commander he refused to segregate the conscientious objectors from the rest of the camp.

The men were receiving conflicting advice from various visiting ministers and so were confused and uncertain. Most of the men refused to drill and to wear the uniform; they also refused to render service except for some kitchen work. Eventually they were transferred to the remount depot and put under a harsh disciplinarian, Captain Brooks P. Sparks. He made them work, drill, and wear the uniform; but after a few weeks, six of the men decided that they had to refuse and were placed in the guardhouse. Two of the imprisoned men were Eli Salzman and Albert Freyenberger from Wayland, Iowa. Word of their uncooperative behavior got back to their community and aroused considerable resentment against Mennonites there.[71]

As discussed above, the two General Conference Mennonite churches in the Wayland area were among the most patriotic of all Mennonite churches across the nation in World War I. However, many local citizens were suspicious of the Sugar Creek "old" Mennonite church, whose bishop was Simon Gingerich. As will be recalled, the Henry County Council of Defense was especially active in enforcing patriotic conformity. Its members and other local "patriots" were angry over the Mennonites' stand on military service and their refusal to display the flag. So they warned Gingerich not to go to Camp Dodge to advise draftees. In late February they pressured the bishop and two local pastors, Daniel Graber and Sebastian Gerig, into signing an agreement promising to advise the draftees in Camp Dodge to put on their uniforms and obey their officers.

The day after Gingerich signed the agreement he tried to repudiate it, telling the superpatriot Dr. Stone that his signature had been coerced. But Stone would have none of it. "Ah, we have it now," he told the bishop triumphantly. "Nothing can be retracted." To General Plummer, Stone exulted that "we have been able to break down the noncombatant attitude in this community completely, so that I have forced a signed statement for publication from them." Stone even hoped the agreement would "discomfit that walking delegate of theirs from Pennsylvania, Loucks," if Loucks tried to "undo the work" and "to bring a split in their entire organization."[72]

Shortly thereafter, camp officials informed the men of the agreement and ordered them to wear the uniform. After several men refused, their officers threatened them with execution. A few days later Loucks and Sanford Yoder arrived at camp where the former spoke to officials and fourteen of the men. Loucks was careful not to tell the men that they should not be soldiers, but he informed them of their rights and told them to stand by their faith and trust in God if they really believed in their church's position. He also assured them that the church would deal charitably, not harshly, with them.

Apparently, Loucks' words had a positive effect. Most of the men decided to leave the remount depot and to take off their uniforms. Roy Buchanan, one of the six incarcerated men, probably spoke for others when he wrote later that the men had been very thankful for Loucks's explanation. But he also wished they could have had all this information earlier, before going to camp. Thereafter, the situation in Camp Dodge did improve. Several men were excused from drill and various forms of service and allowed to take off the uniform. The six in the guardhouse were released. Yet that was not the end of the troubles at Camp Dodge.[73]

A major frustration was that President Wilson did not define noncombatant service until March 20, 1918, almost a year after the U.S. entered the war. The delay was a problem not only for draftees and church leaders; the confusion that resulted often left military authorities embarrassed and frustrated over their inability to solve their problems with conscientious objectors. Behind the delay were probably two causes. First, Secretary Baker preferred to postpone the definition as long as possible to provide camp authorities more time to "persuade" conscientious objectors to do the "right patriotic thing" and become soldiers. Second, the president wanted a legal, civilian alternative for those who could not accept noncombatant duty.

As early as January 1918, President Wilson suggested the possibility of allowing conscientious objectors to do civilian work and promised to have Baker propose such a measure. Most likely the idea that emerged—farm furloughs—originated with Baker. Congressman Griest, who represented the district which included Lancaster, Pennsylvania, may have helped put forward the suggestion. Griest received the idea from Israel B. Good , an influential member of the Lancaster Conference committee assisting the draftees.[74]

In any case, Baker had a Farm Furlough Bill introduced into Congress. However, the bill's sponsors never made clear to Congress that the major purpose was to provide a way out for conscientious objectors. Instead Congress operated with the impression that the intention was to grant the furloughs to regular soldiers to relieve industrial and agricultural labor shortages. On March 8, 1918, Congress accepted the measure without much debate.[75]

Secretary Baker appointed R. C. McCrea of Columbia University to administer the program and requested the three historic peace churches to appoint a commission of nine to advise him. The two presidents of GC-related colleges, Mosiman and Kliewer, agreed to appoint Silas M. Grubb, editor of *The Mennonite*, and Maxwell Kratz, the Mennonite lawyer from Philadelphia.[76] Apparently, however, this committee was never formed. Nor did anyone give systematic information to church leaders on how the new law could provide immediate relief. And several months passed before federal officials really began to implement the Farm Furlough Act.

Because of the government's hesitation or delay in implementing the Furlough Act, Mennonites responded only to the president's executive order of March 20. This order defined noncombatancy as service in the Medical or Quartermaster General Corps or the Corps of Engineers—three integral parts of the military establishment. On the other hand, the decree ordered anew the segregation of those who refused noncombatant service and forbade the infliction of "punitive hardship of any kind." However, the men were warned and reminded they were subject to military discipline and possible court-martial if they failed or refused to comply with lawful orders. Such discipline applied even if they refused "by reason of religious or other conscientious scruples."[77]

Apparently the government had made some concessions to conscientious objectors but at the same time had provided camp commanders with new authority to bring them under military discipline. Behind the government's equivocation there was, most likely, fear of public opinion. This became obvious when in late April the War Department allowed military authorities to begin court-martialing conscientious objectors who refused to accept noncombatant service and did so defiantly and with questionable sincerity.[78] From conscientious objectors' point of view, perhaps the only encouraging development at this time was the appointment in April 1918 of Frederick P. Keppel as third assistant secretary of war. A former dean of Columbia College, Keppel was put in charge of all affairs pertaining to conscientious objectors.

Surely Keppel was not as hostile to conscientious objectors as many federal and military authorities were. Yet he wished most of them had followed the example of the one-time conscientious objector Alvin York, who had changed his mind and become a war hero. Conscientious objectors, Keppel believed, should be given opportunities to think for themselves, by which he apparently meant that they should be freed from the churches' and families' influence so they might listen more to the government. He was quite sure that if a certain officer had not recognized York's sincerity and desire to do his duty, "a man of his temperament might easily have found his way into Leavenworth, instead of becoming a hero."[79]

With Keppel in charge of all matters pertaining to conscientious objectors the government could and would pay more attention to this problem. But, as events would show, Keppel did little if anything to stop or investigate abuses, to discourage military officials from court-martialing conscientious objectors, or to instruct them to segregate the latter more quickly from the regular soldiers.

The Mennonite response to the official definition of noncombatant service varied. Although Loucks and the Military Problems Committee still rejected noncombatant service, they now moved a bit toward Krehbiel's position and urged the men to render some service. The "old" Mennonites' committee as well as similar committees was becoming more cautious, because its members feared possible prosecution under the Espionage Act and the Sedition Act.

Federal authorities watched Loucks especially closely after his successful intervention in Camp Dodge. In March A. P. Sherwood, special agent of the U.S. attorney's office in Ottumwa, Iowa, investigated Loucks and recommended legal action against him for possible violations of the Espionage Act. However, the attorney general did not think Loucks had violated the president's order of March 20.[80]

In May the Henry County Council of Defense drew up eighteen charges and twenty-five complaints against the Mennonites, some of which were specifically directed against Loucks. They accused him of having "constantly assumed" a most "dictatorial and insulting attitude" toward army officers, and of having persuaded men who were willing to serve to choose other alternatives. Subsequently the Iowa Council of National Defense and the U.S. attorney in Ottumwa, Iowa, urged an investigation of Loucks, whom they identified quite ridiculously as the "president of the Mennonite Church," that "German agent," and an "oily hypocrite." The government, they said, should fight him without gloves. It also recommended an investigation of the Mennonite Publishing House because of its "insidious literature."[81]

In July 1918 Loucks's situation became more precarious when he was accused of having alluded from the pulpit to some local businessmen selling Thrift Stamps as a "bunch of cigarette suckers standing in the Public Square, gambling in war savings stamps." Later either local or federal authorities forced Loucks to retract these comments. Through it all, Loucks was somewhat intimidated.

The Department of Justice launched an investigation of Loucks and the Mennonite Brethren in Christ paper the *Gospel Banner*. According to Keppel, federal authorities "put the fear of God in him."[82] Loucks did not cease his activities, but he and Hartzler became much more cautious in their advice to the men. For instance, in September 1918, the latter wrote to one draftee, "Again you are well aware that for me to advise would be a serious thing."[83]

The two men even evinced some sympathy for military officers, conceding that at least some of them had been unjustly blamed for cruelty when they were "simply trying to do their duty. Uncle Sam meant to treat the boys right," Loucks and Hartzler alleged. They urged the men not to challenge and humiliate officers openly when commanded to perform certain tasks. For instance the men should not say, "I will not," but be more diplomatic and explain "mildly," in a private conversation, why they could not.

By refusing all kinds of work such as cleaning up around the barracks, cooking, and the like, some men, they believed, were bringing trials upon themselves unnecessarily. They did not consider the men compromised if they signed up for noncombatant work or if it was made clear that whatever work they did was under protest. Even putting on a uniform would not necessarily be disastrous, Loucks and Hartzler now reasoned, because in some cases men were forced to wear it but later allowed to take it off. Finally Loucks and Hartzler still assumed that draftees might have to suffer. But suffering for Christ, they explained, would be an opportunity to glorify God more than they could possibly do at home or anywhere else.[84]

Leaders of the General Conference Mennonite Church were still more inclined to accept noncombatant work. In *The Mennonite* Silas M. Grubb even scorned those who refused to serve in a military hospital.[85] The Exemption Committee of the General Conference Church, which seems to have met rarely in 1918, urged men in camps to accept some work and to wear the uniform. Committee member Unruh reminded draftee Ben Saur in Camp Funston that Christ had never refused to serve the suffering and that it had been the Lord's mission to do good and save lives.[86]

Peter Jansen, who as a Nebraska politician was deeply immersed in American political culture, was most gratified with the president's executive order of March 20 and recommended the men accept work in the Medical Corps. He could not see how it would be against "the conscientious scruples of anyone to help alleviate suffering" and to perform a Samaritan service. Nor did Jansen see any problem with wearing the uniform. This was, he argued, simply a requirement brought about by "the exigency of war"—a demand that could have no effect upon one's conscience.[87]

The two college presidents Mosiman and Kliewer thought much the same. The former reminded some men that they were soldiers and, like everyone else in time of war, owed the country some service. He warned against the "beast" of German militarism which he had seen during his stay in Germany and urged the men not to engage in "hairsplitting" over the wearing of "the uniform and such things." He believed that on the whole the men had received "splendid treatment."[88]

The Western District Exemption Committee had been unable to reach a consensus on the issue of service, but most of its members believed the men should do some work provided it did not mean actually bearing arms. Nor did they agree about the wearing of uniforms. Meeting on April 10, 1918, the committee did not protest or express dismay over the president's order of March 20. Instead they simply recommended that each draftee decide according to his own conscience on what work he would accept.[89] This decision meant a reversal of the committee's earlier recommendation of the previous October.

About one month later the committee met with representatives of the Mennonite Brethren, Krimmer Mennonite Brethren, and Holdeman Mennonites. This time the committee and the delegates rejected the kind of service the president's statement had specified, and informed Secretary Baker accordingly. Interestingly, an earlier Mennonite Brethren meeting at Ebenfels, Kansas, reluctantly recommended noncombatant work provided it could be done without "restraint of conscience."[90]

However, Krehbiel, probably the most influential member of the Western District Committee, later commended two draftees named Otto Regier and Jacob Richert for having accepted service in the Medical Corps. According to Krehbiel, the two men had adhered to the principles of Jesus Christ "in the exercise of love and goodwill."[91] He praised them even though he wrote his sister at about the same time that those who had accepted noncombatant work had done so contrary to the advice of his committee.[92]

In the weeks and months following, people such as Loucks and Krehbiel had to counsel the men with "great circumspection," because federal agents were most likely watching them as committee members.[93] As Krehbiel and Wedel told a draftee named Harry Graber, "We can give you very little support. You have to have your own views of pacifism because the pressure is too great on us. They can hold us for treason if we advise you to stand firm."[94]

Even visiting the men in camp to look after their spiritual needs became more difficult. For instance, in Camp Travis committee members were allowed only to preach and not to have private conversations with the men.[95] In July two members of the committee, Krehbiel and Unruh, went to Washington, D.C., to discuss the situation with Keppel. Keppel reminded the two men that noncombatants were part of the military and that although they did not have to bear arms they had to drill. Furthermore, Keppel did not think it was possible for those refusing all three types of noncombatant services to do civilian work in camp without being considered part of the military.[96]

By early summer the federal government was finally ready to implement the Farm Furlough Act. Now a new fate might await those conscientious objectors who refused to accept noncombatant status.

6

"Absolutists" and Soldiers

Over time three basic categories of Mennonite draftees emerge, in addition to some men who did not quite fit those classifications. First, there were absolutists who refused any kind of service, at least any beyond very minor work such as cleaning their own quarters. Being adamant, many of them were brutally treated, court-martialed, or both. Second, there were those who took the middle road and signed up to serve as noncombatants in the Engineering, Medical, or Quartermaster Corps, as President Wilson specified in March 1918. Third were the outright combatants.

Draftees in the second and third categories were, of course, real soldiers of Uncle Sam. But there were quite a few who never agreed to be soldiers but who were not quite absolutists, either. These were men who more or less compromised and worked, for instance, in camp kitchens or bakeries or laundries. Although they did some noncombatant work, they did not sign as noncombatants and were never so in a formal sense. A number of such men, but by no means all, had second thoughts; refused work they had earlier accepted; became near-absolutists; and suffered harassment, hazings, and court-martialing.

Finding an acceptable solution for the small group of absolutists proved difficult. By summer of 1918 most of these men were kept in separate detention barracks, where they hoped that under the Farm Furlough Act they might be released to do useful work. But the government, not knowing how to select the men, hesitated to apply the new law.

Finally on June 1, 1918, after months of temporizing, the War Department established a so-called Board of Inquiry. Consisting of three men, the Board had the difficult assignment of questioning all conscientious objectors who had refused to serve as noncombatants. A man whom the board found to be sincere might apply for a farm furlough or ask to go overseas to work with the American Friends Service Committee. Those who failed the board's test would be classified either as non-combatants or combatants.[1]

The three individuals appointed to the Board of Inquiry were Major Richard C. Stoddard, who was later replaced by Major W. G. Kellogg; Harlan F. Stone, dean of the University of Columbia Law School; and Julian W. Mack, a member of a U.S. Circuit Court of Appeals.[2]

Of the four who served, Kellogg was probably the least sympathetic. He did not fully agree with former president Theodore Roosevelt—who had suggested that the U.S. send its conscientious objectors to France. There, Roosevelt thought, association with soldiers would have the "missionary effect" of winning them away from their "base creed" and raising them to "worthy levels in an atmosphere of self-sacrifice and of service and struggle for great ideals." But despite some differences with Roosevelt, Kellogg did suggest that the government should dispatch most of the men overseas to perform farm work or other labor. The absolutists, he thought, must be placed in separate camps and if possible deported or disenfranchised.[3]

Kellogg found it difficult to understand why conscientious objectors would not work in military hospitals and give aid and comfort to the men in uniform. As previously indicated, far from being impressed by Mennonite conscientious objectors, Kellogg found them woefully lacking in understanding or knowledge of the world and, he wrote, almost "bovine" in their appearance. However, after the war Kellogg

COs waiting their turn before hearing of Board of Inquiry, Camp Dodge, Iowa. Courtesy, Mennonite Library and Archives.

conceded that most conscientious objectors had been generally sincere, not shirkers or cowards as he had previously believed. As for Major Stoddard, he impressed one Mennonite, Ezra Deter, as a stern man, but also a "fine and considerate" person who was ready to praise conscientious objectors for their stand and their grit.[4]

Early in June the board began its difficult task, starting with 144 conscientious objectors in Camp Meade. However, many months would pass before the board completed its work, and in fact it never did question and classify some of the men. Probing and determining each conscientious objector's sincerity was not an easy task, and the board may have made many errors.

One way it tried to prove the conscientious objector's insincerity was by asking him if he smoked, drank, or ran around with "wild women." Some board members showed their contempt for the men by scolding them for belonging to some "nut society" or by telling them they did not deserve to live in the United States. Of course, the board often posed the hoary "what if" questions. For instance, a member asked Homer Schlegel what he would do if a "big nigger" came along and tried to rape his mother. Isaac Baer was "intensely questioned" for thirty-five minutes at Camp Meade by Major Stoddard who "twisted" and tried to entangle him in every way possible. They were "brainy men," Baer wrote later, and there was no one to help him but the Holy Spirit, who he said guarded him during the questioning.[5]

In general, if a conscientious objector had joined his church before April 6, 1917, and seemed sincere, the board recommended him for a farm furlough. By the time the war ended, the panel had heard 2,100 cases. Of these, it recommended 1,500 for farm furloughs, 390 for noncombatant service, 122 for regular military duty, and 88 for overseas relief work.[6] Although the Board of Inquiry worked diligently, many weeks passed before most men were heard and reassigned. Many did not receive hearings until the end of July or early August, and, of course, some men never had hearings. Furthermore many men encountered obstacles in camp and were not allowed to leave.

When news of the farm furlough system became known, many farmers requested that military commanders release the men. Mennonite congregations and the various conference committees assisted in processing applications. It seems, however, that Loucks, Hartzler, and camp commanders did most of the administrative work.[7] Conscientious objectors were elated over the opportunity to do something useful and perform the kind of labor most of them knew best. Although regulations stipulated a man had to work on a farm at least fifty miles from his

418 8-8-18 200 Camp Sherman Print

I   Frey, Philemon P.   No.   1871011.

Conscientious Objectors Detachment, Camp Sherman, Ohio, pursuant to the letter of the
Adjutant General of the Army, July 30th, 1918, do hereby make application for furlough to
engage in agricultural service without pay from the Government.   If granted such furlough,
I hereby agree to retain for my personal use from any pay, reward, commission or other
emolument which may be received by me for such service, either directly or indirectly from
any person, firm or corporation, a sum no greater than the pay of a private in the military
service of the United States, plus an amount reasonably necessary for my subsistence, in the
community in which I may hereafter be employed.   And I hereby agree that I will contribute
to the American Red Cross, any and all such pay, rewards, commissions or other emoluments
which I may receive for such service, over and above the pay of a private plus an amount
reasonably necessary for my subsistence, as aforesaid, such sum to be turned over to the
American Red Cross in any manner that the Secretary of war may hereafter provide.

Philemon Frey

Witness:

R. J. Hough
Capt. Inf. R.C.

Farm Furlough Application of Philemon L. Frey, Camp Sherman, Ohio.
Courtesy, Archives Mennonite Church.

home, many in fact worked on Mennonite farms quite close to home.

It was also agreed that if a man earned more than $30 per month
he would donate the excess to the Red Cross.[8] However, not all applications for farm furloughs were granted, and commanders could think of
all sorts of excuses for not letting the men leave. Perhaps the basic reason was their determination not to make life too easy for conscientious
objectors. Thus many men who had been recommended by the Board
of Inquiry for a farm furlough remained in camp until late 1918 or early
1919.[9] During that time abuse and court-martialing conscientious objectors continued unabated.

Not every community welcomed the furloughed men. In mid-
September in Fulton County, Ohio, members of the League of American Patriots came to see Bishop E. L. Frey and demanded the expul-
sion of some twenty conscientious objectors. Frey wired Captain
Hough, the man who commanded the conscientious objector detachment at Camp Sherman. Hough promptly left for the county's seat,
Wauseon, where he met with a group of citizens. He assured them that

COs doing farm furlough work on Seward Stock Farm (Petersburg, Virginia). Courtesy, Mrs. Anna Rohren, Wadsworth, Ohio.

COs doing farm furlough work at Interview Farm, Odebolt, Iowa.
Courtesy, Mennonite Library and Archives.

the men were under full civil and military protection and warned everyone not to touch them. That ended the difficulties.[10]

At about the same time some fifty carloads of citizens of West Liberty, Ohio, and vicinity were reported to have gone to Springfield to see Congressman Simeon D. Fess. Their purpose: to protest the "intolerable" presence of conscientious objectors on farms in their community. Furthermore, they complained about the Mennonites, who they claimed, refused to assist in the prosecution of the war but did not hesitate to take wartime prices for their farm products. Fess sympathized with the complaints, and stated his contempt for those hiding behind the "amendments" to the Selective Service Act—that is, the Farm Furlough Act. He offered to try to repeal the "amendments." Later in the month, Bishop Samuel E. Allgyer, Captain Hough, and others met with citizens of West Liberty and nearby Urbana. They succeeded in calming the waters.[11]

The situation in some Iowa communities was just as bad. Bishop Sanford Yoder chose six men in Camp Dodge to work on two farms near Kalona but "a wave of opposition spread over the county" and some two hundred local citizens gathered and told the employers to remove them. The farmers complied, and the men went back to camp.[12] Later some of these men and several others were assigned to the Adams Ranch in Oldebolt, Iowa, where they stayed until the end of the year with no further difficulties.[13] Seven conscientious objectors employed at the State Sanatorium in Iowa City also were returned to camp. However, at Independence, Iowa, Gustave Gaeddert and others worked peacefully on a farm belonging to a state mental hospital.[14]

By early October Loucks, Krehbiel, and Keppel concluded that the farm furlough had not been a success in the Middle West. They suggested something else must be done for the men. Furthermore, they were concerned about the men's fate once the harvest season was over. They correctly feared the men would again be idle in camp. In fact this had already happened to some men.[15]

For some time other alternatives had been suggested. In July, 1917 the Western and Northern District Conferences of the GC branch, the Mennonite Brethren, and the Krimmer Mennonite Brethren had proposed putting the men to work at irrigating, draining, and farming public land.[16] In October of that year a committee of the "old" Mennonites' Lancaster Conference had suggested that its church buy or lease land on which to employ conscientious objectors. In early October 1918, J. S. Hartzler suggested to McCrea, administrator of the furlough program, that Mennonite men be allowed to farm part of the Pima Indian Reservation in Arizona. Apparently the official's reaction was positive, but by late October, as the war was almost over, he thought it better not to launch new ventures.[17]

An attractive idea was to allow conscientious objectors to work in so-called reconstruction hospitals where disabled soldiers would be rehabilitated for civilian life. Some Mennonites already had been working in mental hospitals. Several conscientious objectors from Camp Lee were furloughed to work in a state institution at Williamsburg, Virginia.[18] As early as April 1918, Gustave Gaeddert suggested Mennonites themselves build a hospital for recuperating soldiers.[19]

Allen H. Erb, secretary of an "old" Mennonite sanitarium in La Junta, Colorado, was willing to care for soldiers afflicted by tuberculosis. Caring for such men, Erb felt, would give Mennonites "an excellent chance . . . to do something for our government that would not violate our principle of nonresistance." His board did not support the idea.[20] But the GCs' Western District Conference did agree, saying that such rehabilitation work was "in line with the teaching of Christ to do good and to save life" and that it did not violate Mennonite creed or conscience.[21] Henry Krehbiel explored the idea further and finally suggested the idea of Mennonite-run reconstruction hospitals to Keppel and McCrea. But McCrea rejected the idea because he doubted that army authorities would agree.[22]

An "old" Mennonite ministers' conference at Scottdale, Pennsylvania, approved of service in army reconstruction hospitals provided the men did not have to wear uniforms. But Orie B. Gerig, who was about to be dispatched to France for an assignment with the American Friends Service Committee, vehemently protested that idea. Such a compromise, he argued, would "seriously threaten the very foundation of the principle we as a church have chosen to preserve." He thought that if Mennonites allowed their young men to enter army reconstruction, it would become "next to impossible" to persuade them to join Friends Reconstruction.

Furthermore, Gerig warned against a policy of compromise as pursued by the Church of the Brethren—who, he believed, had lost its identity as a peace group. To Gerig there was no honorable position in a half-way stand such as army reconstruction, a kind of service in which men would be "soldiers of Uncle Sam," something they did not wish to be.[23] However, the real concern of Sanford C. Yoder and others was that some men might go ahead and accept hospital reconstruction work or some other service "against the express attitude of the church."[24] Fortunately this question became academic, since the end of the war brought the discharge of most men by the end of 1918 or early 1919.

In late November 1918, a few weeks after Armistice Day, federal authorities decided to discharge the men on farm furloughs and conscientious objectors still in camp who had refused noncombatant service and had been found by the Board of Inquiry to be sincere. Men who had not yet appeared before the Board of Inquiry were to be examined by its members Mack and Stone; the men would be discharged if found sincere. Finally, Mack and Stone would examine many court-martialed conscientious objectors in Fort Leavenworth. Such men might well have been skeptical about examination by those two, for they had lost faith in the board's objectivity. But Henry Krehbiel, who in December 1918 witnessed Mack and Stone question some two hundred men, felt confident their cases were "perfectly safe in their hands."[25] It is difficult to determine if the two men judged each case correctly, but clearly some men were disappointed with their classifications.

An issue that may have complicated the release of many men was the problem of military pay. During their stay in camp, many conscientious objectors refused such pay. As a result some congregations and conferences supported the men in camp with monthly allowances.[26] However, in December and January many camp officials would not grant these men discharges, unless they first signed the payroll. To speed their discharges many agreed to sign and later donated the money to relief or returned it to the U.S. Treasury as "conscience money."

By late February 1919, the U.S. Treasury had received some $4,319 in refunds. The Franconia Conference even raised some $3,700 to reimburse the men. But not much was known about such refunds or donations to relief. Public criticism, already inflamed over the early release of conscientious objectors, was further angered over the apparent "greed" of these individuals who refused service and therefore, according to the critics, deserved no pay.[27]

In January and February 1919 the government released most conscientious objectors who had rejected noncombatancy, and many Mennonites who had been sent to Fort Leavenworth federal prison were released following their court-martialing. Others were to be discharged during the same year. Upon discharge most conscientious objectors who had chosen the absolutist rather than a noncombatant position received a blue discharge paper—signifying dishonorable discharge. In many cases a blue discharge would have blocked a conscientious objector from re-enlisting even if he had wished to. It is doubtful any conscientious objector ever considered such an option.[28]

When they left the camps, many men did not enjoy a kind farewell. When Benjamin Ebersole and other conscientious objectors picked up their discharge papers and pay at Camp Meade, they had to walk through a large crowd of soldiers who had returned from overseas and were obviously hostile to them. "I am sure," Ebersole commented later, "if our officers would not have been there, we might have been torn to pieces." Later a few soldiers refused to ride with them on the train.[29]

Upon arriving home most of the men seem to have had little difficulty blending in, especially if the community had many Mennonites. But there too, they sometimes were met with hostility. Cornelius Voth encountered "angry sentiments" in his home community in Oklahoma. When he moved to his former hometown in Kansas he met similar feelings, especially from old school friends. He felt like "an alien in an alien land," and often trembled inwardly lest he be asked about his "glorious war experiences." Later the actions of some prominent members of the local American Legion forced Voth to resign as a high school teacher.[30]

Joseph J. Wagner of Metamora, Illinois, who had experienced considerable mental abuse in Camp Fort Thomas, Kentucky, later complained bitterly over the lack of interest in him by his church. He also felt ostracized by his employer and fellow employees for his wartime stand. Because of such feelings, Wagner left his community permanently and went to Chicago.[31] Undoubtedly many others were similarly ostracized.

Although few Mennonites became war casualties, the war did take its toll even among those who refused any kind of service. Some men in camp and others on furlough succumbed to various diseases or died in 1918 from the so-called Spanish flu. That dreadful epidemic took the lives of thousands of U.S. civilians and soldiers, both at home and overseas. It is difficult to estimate the total number of Mennonite absolutists who succumbed to this dreadful disease, but the total might have been as high as twenty-five. Most of them died in late 1918. Some died after they had been in camp for only a few weeks or months. A few of those who died left families behind. Some bodies were shipped home in army uniforms. One Mennonite conscientious objector from Indiana was declared dead in Camp Zachary Taylor, Kentucky, but when his parents brought his body home they noticed it was moving. He survived and lived for many years after this harrowing experience.[32]

In addition to mental and physical abuse, many conscientious objectors also faced courts-martial.[33] No Mennonite or other conscientious objectors were court-martialed prior to May 1918. Up to then camp officials were not sure they were allowed to court-martial conscientious objectors. Then in April 1918, new regulations removed all doubt. From the summer of 1918 through January 1919, many, including quite a few Mennonites, were tried. The most common charge was refusal to obey a military order to render service, to wear the uniform, or to drill. Sometimes a conscientious objector had refused to render service after he had initially agreed to work or to serve as a noncombatant and then changed his mind.

Specifically, most men were charged with violation of articles 64, 65, and 96 of the Articles of War. These articles, which like most other articles of war had not changed much since colonial days, subjected to court-martial any person charged with willfully disobeying the lawful command of a superior officer or any person accused of "disorders" or "neglects" or conduct that brought discredit upon military service. Finally, the court-martial manual stipulated that "disobedience to a command [that] involved a violation of the accused's religious scruples" was not a defense. Most conscientious objectors were tried by a so-called general court-martial which consisted of five to thirteen officers—most of whom were quite hostile toward conscientious objectors. The judge advocate served as the prosecutor.[34]

In most court-martial cases the legal counsel was not very competent. It was not until 1948 that defenders had to be members of the legal profession. Nor were the defending counselors very supportive of their clients. "Why should he exert himself to get us acquitted?" defendant Edward Waltner asked. Other officers even dubbed his counsel a conscientious objector. Waltner's counsel did not advise defendants nor did he tell them it would not be advantageous to take the witness stand. He told Waltner nothing about the right to object to irrelevant questions, which came often.

Defendants did have the right to choose civilian counselors, and at least eleven Mennonites did so. In eight courts-martial in Camp Funston, the defendants secured the legal assistance of F. D. Wicks of Scotland, South Dakota, who tried hard to represent his clients. However, he was unable to persuade the court to mete out justice. Most Mennonites were defended by military officers, few of whom were sympathetic toward conscientious objectors. A verdict required a simple majority unless there was a possibility of a death penalty. The court's decision was reviewed by the commanding general who could "disapprove" the verdict. In all, the World War I system of military justice toward conscientious objectors was rather harsh and produced many severe sentences. That harshness was in keeping with public opinion toward conscientious objectors. In truth, however, American military justice in World War I was harsh towards regular soldiers also.[35]

While the charge against most court-martialed Mennonites was refusal to obey orders, four of them were tried for failure to report for induction—an offense considered desertion. The first was David B. Hostetler of Reedsville, Pennsylvania, who had not appeared at Camp

Meade as ordered in April 1918. He received a sentence of five years in prison. Another was Oscar E. Hartman of Fulks Run, Virginia, who in May of 1918 had declined to report for duty at Camp Lee in his home state. Acting as some Mennonites had when drafted in Virginia during the Civil War, Hartman had hidden in a nearby wooded, mountainous area. But in June 1920, a year and a half after the end of the war, he had finally turned himself in. His ensuing sentence was light—three months.

The other two deserters were David and John B. Goertzen, cousins from Henderson, Nebraska, and members of the Mennonite Brethren church. In mid-September 1918, the Goertzens registered for the draft but received permission from their local draft board to go to Canada for thirty days in search of work there. In mid-October induction notices went out to them but they did not respond. They later claimed that they had been ill and living with relatives where they did not receive their mail. In 1920 they returned to Henderson, but in March of that year the local sheriff arrested them. Their court-martialing occurred two months later in Omaha.

The two Mennonites rested their case on not having received their induction notices and also on an argument that they had believed no one would be drafted after the armistice. But the prosecution argued the two men had not had good reason to leave the country. Work had been available in the United States; the men had simply sought an excuse to escape the draft. Finally, they were charged with not returning after the thirty-day period or as soon as they had recuperated from their illness.

The court found the two men guilty of desertion and sentenced David Goertzen, who was married and had one child, to two years of hard labor—a sentence later reduced to one year. His cousin received a three-year sentence but served only a year and eight months. In accordance with a law on the books since the Civil War, Hostetler, Hartman, and the two Goertzens also lost their citizenship. No legal evidence of regaining these men citizenships has come to light, but John Goertzen later claimed to have regained his in the 1930s.[36]

A total of 504 conscientious objectors were court-martialed in World War I, some 142 of them Mennonites. All but one of those Mennonites were U.S. citizens. In addition to being punished for the charges against them, Mennonites were often treated extra harshly because of their German ancestry. None was tried before May 1918, but many were court-martialed during the rest of that year. Military authorities apparently hoped that court-martialing so many would counterbalance the more lenient policy of late 1918. More than one half of the Mennonites' courts-martial were in May and June 1918. In the summer there was a lull, but another rush of courts-martial followed in the fall. The action continued with at least eight Mennonites court-martialed in December and January, and three who had refused induction were tried as late as 1920.

Some military camps were much more eager to court-martial conscientious objectors than were others. The largest number of Mennonite courts-martial took place at Camp Travis and Camp Funston where in each thirty-one Mennonites were tried for refusing to drill, wear uniforms, and/or other offenses. At Camp Zachary Taylor were twenty-eight; at Camp Cody sixteen. In other camps the number was fewer than five each, although the total added up to quite a few.[37]

Sentences varied from one to forty years. Authorities in Washington, D.C., knew that most sentences were absurdly severe but allowed them to stand because, as Keppel told Krehbiel, they wanted to give "backbone to the military morale." About half of the 138 Mennonite men for whom there are court-martial records received sentences of twenty-five years or more. Three men received very severe sentences —one for thirty years, one for thirty-five years, and one for forty years. Other sentences were less severe but still very harsh.

John O. Smeltzer of the Holdeman Mennonite Church near Wakarusa, Indiana, had the dubious honor of receiving the most severe sentence that survived the review of camp authorities. His ordeal may do more than statistics to tell us about military justice. Inducted in May, 1918, Smeltzer was sent to Camp Forrest in Georgia. There he refused to do kitchen work, and on June 20 was sentenced to forty years in prison. In the camp guardhouse, Smeltzer felt uncomfortable because he was imprisoned with soldiers who had committed various crimes. But he was especially anxious to be released because his wife was about to give birth to their first child.

In November Smeltzer's conviction was reviewed by Acting Judge Advocate General S. T. Ansell, who was somewhat disposed to be lenient in such cases. Ansell found no evidence of insincerity on Smeltzer's part and considered the order to perform kitchen work illegal because such duty was not included in the president's definition of March 20, 1918. Ironically, the courts-martial and their reviewers could have made similar findings about almost all military orders issued to conscientious objectors after the president had defined noncombatancy.

But Smeltzer was not released from prison until late December. In mid-February he was still languishing in camp, where, he complained, he was "not in the hands of Christians." Perhaps the military authorities in Camp Forrest were making a showcase of him and therefore keeping Smeltzer as long as possible. However, on February 25, 1919, he was finally released and even received an honorable discharge.[38]

In time, authorities reduced many Mennonites' sentences and even annulled one. This happened in February 1919, when the Camp Funston commander ordered the release of John J. Entz. A Hutterite from Hutchinson County, South Dakota, Entz had been sentenced to hard labor for life. But authorities released him on a technicality. Often camp commandants lowered the sentences, but in at least one case a commandant tried to raise one. In September 1918, at Camp McArthur, Chris E. Miller of Cass County, Missouri, was court-martialed for refusing to cut sticks for the kitchen stove, to drill, and to wear the uniform. Miller had a good defense counsel who apparently persuaded the court to be lenient; he received a sentence of only two years. To the camp commander, Colonel Charles F. Bates, the sentence seemed "entirely inadequate" and "subversive of the discipline of the camp." However, the court refused to change the sentence.[39]

Joseph H. Wurz and Joseph S. Walter, Mennonite draftees at Fort Dodge were each court-martialed twice. In September 1918 both were tried and sentenced for quitting work in the Medical Corps. Ansell then set aside their sentences on grounds that as conscientious objectors they should not have been forced to wear military uniforms. Nonetheless, in December Wurz and Walter were still in the stockade at Fort Leavenworth. In mid-January 1919 they were released and ordered to return to camp to be discharged. However, upon arriving at camp, the two men were ordered again to render service. When they refused they were promptly retried by a so-called summary court-martial and given three-month sentences. However, only a few days later, on January 24, they received their discharges, perhaps through the intervention of Professor Jacob Ewert of Tabor College.[40]

Most of the men were tried individually, but there were two collective trials. One such trial involved the well-known case (discussed below) of four Hutterites—Jacob Wipf, and the three brothers Michael, David, and Joseph Hofer of South Dakota—two of whom died in federal prison. The other was on June 7, 1918, in Camp Travis, Texas.

In the Camp Travis case, forty-one conscientious objectors were put on the dock together for refusing to wear uniforms and to drill. All but ten were Mennonites, most of them Oklahomans who had been in camp for about nine months. At first most had agreed to do some work in the kitchen, store, or barns, but then they had developed serious reservations about their decisions. According to one of them, Albert G. Voth, by December 1917 he had reasoned and had told his captain that the sole aim of the military establishment was death and destruction of the enemy. He preferred, he said, to approach his fellowman with love and good will and to render service in an "unabridged Christian spirit." By such logic Mennonites could not consent to do any work of a military nature and would rather endure punishment than do anything they believed was wrong.

At Christmastime, after "much personal soul-searching," the men decided to refuse to work. They concluded that "*anything* they do will aid the war effort." The GCs' Western District Exemption Committee supported them in their decision. Before and after Christmas, committee members visited the men, as did Voth's father, Henry R. Voth, well-known as a former missionary to the Hopi Indians. The elder Voth was of the opinion that the men should do something, but the men disagreed and told him that if they were to go further, they would be "more deeply sucked into it."

In April the men again refused, this time to do some gardening, and a month later they decided to refuse to wear uniforms. On May 20 about two hundred soldiers on horseback surrounded the conscientious objectors' barracks, and later they took the pacifists to a different area and camped them for four days in a broiling sun. On June 7 forty-one recalcitrants were collectively court-martialed and sentenced to life terms—sentences later changed to twenty-five years. Shortly after the sentencing, they were transferred to the military stockade of Fort Leavenworth federal prison.[41]

In a few cases Mennonites were tried individually, but at the same time and place for the same offense. For instance in May 1918, twenty-five Mennonites were court-martialed at Camp Zachary Taylor in Kentucky for having refused to perform yard work near the base hospital. With one exception all received the same sentence. In the same month seven Mennonites were court-martialed at Camp Cody in New Mexico for having refused to work in the stables of the Veterinary Corps Auxiliary Remount Depot. Their sentences ranged from ten to twenty years.

In December 1918 and January 1919, eight Mennonites were court-martialed at Camp Funston, Kansas, for disobeying orders to pave a road. During most of 1918, conscientious objectors in this camp had not been required to work; however, after the armistice of November 11, military authorities had decided to test the men and expose them as hypocrites. Camp officials had believed that with the possibility of an early release from military service, many conscientious objectors would now be willing to compromise and work. Therefore, they had ordered the men to pave a road in camp although, as was clearly shown during the trial, this work had been unnecessary.

At first most of the conscientious objectors had refused to obey the order. But after some time only eight men had held out. One of the defendants, John J. Entz, received a life sentence—but his was the sentence which the camp commander set aside on the basis of a technicality. The others received sentences varying from five to twenty years. Not only had the court tried the eight men for the same offense; for all eight, practically the same persons had made up the court.[42]

Of the Mennonites court-martialed, fifty-three belonged to the General Conference and thirty-six to the "old" Mennonite church. The larger number of General Conference Mennonites does not necessarily mean that GC men were more committed to nonresistance. Rather, the number of courts-martial varied from camp to camp according to the whims of the military authorities. Yet the large number of court-martialed GC Mennonites does demonstrate a deep commitment to conscientious objection. Indeed, in light of church leaders' advice to be more compromising, the draftees' commitment seemed at times greater than that of their elders. From other Mennonite groups, sixteen Mennonite Brethren, ten Old Order Amish, five Holdeman, eight Hutterites, and a scattering of others suffered courts-martial.[43]

In many courts-martial the judge advocates tried to test defendants' sincerity by raising questions about their biblical faith and their patriotism. A standard gambit was to ask what defendants would do if their sisters or mothers were attacked by a savage Hun, or what they would do if the country were invaded by the Germans. To those hoary questions, most defendants gave a standard reply—they would rely on God to assist them.

The court also tried, usually unsuccessfully, to make the defendant say President Wilson and others erred when they took the nation into war against Germany, and that such leaders were not good Christians. Many defendants had little difficulty rejecting the Old Testament's justification for war and no problem proving the consistency of Jesus' peace witness. During the trial of John J. Entz in January 1919, the judge advocate asked Entz whether the chasing of the money changers out of the temple did not prove that Jesus had supported war. Entz's simple reply: he had never heard that Jesus "had hurt anybody."

The defendants had much more difficulty when asked about the apparent contradiction between Mennonites' refusal to support the war effort by participating in combat and their willingness to raise grain and other foodstuffs—production which the government was loudly encouraging as part of the war effort. To that question, few defendants could give a good answer. Their usual response was simply that a farmer did not control the flow and price of a commodity once it had reached the market.[44]

On occasion the court sought to prove that the defendants were mentally and intellectually inferior. For instance, at Camp Cody during the trial of Jacob E. Tschetter, the camp psychologist testified that the defendant was of "sub-normal mentality" and "slightly below normal in intelligence." On the basis of this and other evidence, he tried to persuade the court that the man was a malingerer and insincere. Unfortunately, Tschetter's legal counselor made virtually no effort to rebut the psychologist's testimony.

It is true that occasional language problems and lack of worldly knowledge caused some Mennonite defendants to leave an impression of being ignorant, if not somewhat stupid. But overall, if the records of army intelligence tests in World War I show anything, they show that the native intelligence of Mennonites and that of other conscientious objectors was above the average for U.S. conscripts.[45]

It may well be that Quakers and political conscientious objectors were more articulate in their defenses than was the average Mennonite. But Mennonites' expressions of simple and trusting faith had their own eloquence and certainly testified to their commitment. Clearly, almost all the court-martialed Mennonites wanted deeply to serve God rather than man and believed firmly that Christianity was incompatible with war.

Typical of many of answers were those of Ray Metzler and Amos M. Showalter. Metzler, drafted in June 1918, was from Nappanee, Indiana. At Camp Zachary Taylor, he agreed to do noncombatant work in the Quartermaster Corps but some time later changed his mind. According to his testimony, he had asked God if by working he was still "going according to His [God's] will . . ," and God had answered in a way that made him feel guilty. So Metzler had requested to be released. "I believed as though I would rather face death than go ahead with what I had taken up," he informed the court. The court sentenced him to twenty years.[46]

Showalter was an "old" Mennonite from Rockingham County, Virginia, a member of the Bank congregation. After spending several years in Kansas and Missouri, in 1915 he had enrolled at Goshen College where he was graduated in 1917. He had applied to go to the American Friends Service Committee's relief unit in France, and in May of 1918 he had been accepted. Unfortunately, while waiting for his passport, he was drafted. Soon he was at Camp Funston, where he spent three weeks in the guardhouse.

Then in late August he was transferred to one of the base hospitals to work as a floorman or attendant. Showalter agreed to work for one day, but on August 29 he refused any more work. On October 24 he was court-martialed. His counselor, Captain Ralph E. Fleicher, made a fairly good effort to defend Showalter, using certain regulations laid down on July 30 to challenge the court's jurisdiction. But he was overruled. Furthermore, Fleicher pointed out, quite correctly, that Showalter had not "willfully" or insubordinately disobeyed the order but had done so with civil "manner, intent, [and] demeanor." Showalter insisted on testifying on his own behalf. When he did, he read and submitted a written statement telling his judges that he was not before them as a soldier but as a conscientious objector.[47]

Showalter also told of his grandparents' loyalty during the Civil War in Virginia and insisted he was willing to sacrifice everything for his country, provided such sacrifice did not interfere with the relation of his "soul to the spirit of his Creator." Disagreeing with his government's decision to go to war, he said he preferred to follow Jesus' instructions to love one's enemies, and to suffer abuse and injury and not seek recompense. Such teaching, he told the court, was "the mold in which my character was cast" and was a vital part of his religious life. To deny that would mean renouncing allegiance to Jesus Christ and forfeiting all "peaceful relation of his soul to its creator."

In response, Judge Advocate Lieutenant George Imbrie took Showalter to task and expressed dismay that the defendant was willing to go to France to work at reconstructing what had been damaged by "the barbarians who threaten our gates" and yet had refused to work in camp. Imbrie was appalled at Congress' decision to let "cowards" be excused from fighting for their wives and daughters and thus hide behind "the skirts of their women." He wanted to deal firmly with such cowards and pacifists. The court agreed and condemned Showalter to a life sentence. The camp commander changed it to twenty years. However, several months later, in January 1919, Showalter was released.[48]

Toward the end of 1918, some 135 court-martialed Mennonites were imprisoned in the stockade of the federal prison at Fort Leavenworth, Kansas. At that time about 350 religious objectors were jailed at Fort Leavenworth.[49] There they were forced to wear prison garb and at first were forbidden to mingle with other prisoners. Many—perhaps most—of them were called before a board of examiners who interrogated them about their beliefs. Jesse Brenneman, who held a college degree, was asked why he was a conscientious objector. Why did he wish to classify himself with "an ignorant, dull, and illiterate crowd" who held such "narrow-minded notions about religion"?[50] However, in general, prison officials preferred the conscientious objectors over other prisoners, because these earnest idealists were much more cooperative.

Life in military prison was harsh and often brutal. Men complained about the food, overcrowding, homosexuality, and occasional violence.[51] However, in many respects the stockade was a relief. Now they were liberated from military rule. Moreover, working conditions were quite tolerable. After a time most men were allowed to work under very loose guard, often outside the gates on the prison farm or elsewhere. The guards did not worry that these prisoners would run away because, as one said, "They are all right. You see they believe in the Bible. And they try to live the way the Bible tells them to live. That's why they don't need so many guards."[52] Johannes Klaassen, who had been court-martialed at Camp Travis, milked cows on the prison farm. He found his job "very easy."[53] John Neufeld wrote that he was "really enjoying" himself as much as he ever had.[54]

Some conscientious objectors refused to work in prison just as in camp; they soon found themselves in solitary confinement, manacled to the bars of their cells. Such was the sad fate of the four Hutterites—the three brothers David J., Joseph J., and Michael Hofer, and their brother-in-law Jacob J. Wipf. Each of the Hofer brothers was married and had children. They, together with an Andrew Wurtz, were drafted in May 1918 and sent to Camp Lewis in Washington. Already on the train to camp, some fellow-draftees humiliated the Hutterites by cutting their beards. In camp they refused to sign the so-called Enlistment and Assignment Cards by which a draftee agreed to follow all military commands, render any kind of service, wear the uniform, and drill.

They were beaten and all of them except Wurtz, who was separated from the others, were placed in the guardhouse. As for Wurtz, because he too refused to comply with military orders he was forced to wear the uniform, held under water, dragged over a wooden floor with a rope tied around his legs and splinters entering his body, and then thrown into a ditch. He finally agreed to do garden work and later worked on a nearby dairy farm.[55]

On June 10 the three Hofer brothers and Wipf were court-martialed and sentenced to twenty years of imprisonment.[56] The Hutterite minister Joseph Kleinsasser tried to persuade Keppel to intervene on behalf of the men by describing the kind of treatment the three had endured. "Now, dear Keppel," Kleinsasser wrote on July 14, "is there no reasonable way to find out a persons [*sic*] conviction, or stand, or religion?" Quite bluntly, he wondered if it were necessary to torture people in order to find out their religion and if the government, of which Keppel was a part, was not responsible for tolerating such outrages and to accept the "huns [*sic*] ways?"[57]

Kleinsasser's moving appeal had no effect. The three men were transferred to the federal prison on the island of Alcatraz. Here also they refused to cooperate. So the wardens stripped them of their outer clothing, confined them in their cells with their hands cross-chained to iron bars, and fed them little food and water. Within five days the four men were covered with boils and insect bites and had swollen arms. The ordeal in Alcatraz continued from mid-1918 until November, when they were transferred to the military prison at Fort Leavenworth.

During a night in November 1918, the men arrived at the railroad station. According to later allegations, the guards then drove them with bayonets to the prison, which was located about three hundred yards down the road. Further, according to the allegations, the men, who had been overheated in the railway cars, now caught colds when they were again stripped of their outer clothing. Military officials denied that the guards had acted so brutally and callously.

But on November 21, Joseph and Michael Hofer were transferred to the military hospital. David Hofer and Wipf, still refusing to work and wear uniforms, remained shackled for two weeks to the bars of their cells. Had he put on the uniform, Wipf stated later, he would have been a "hepocriss [*sic*]."[58] Wipf did manage to send telegrams to the wives of Joseph and Michael, warning them of their husbands' condition.

Unfortunately, the women were given train tickets to Fort Riley instead of to Leavenworth, and when they finally arrived at Leavenworth their husbands were almost dead. Joseph died at about 8:30 a.m. on November 29, 1918. As a final insult, authorities dressed his body in the military uniform which he had so persistently and valiantly rejected. Reverend Jacob (J. D.) Mininger, an "old" Mennonite minister and city missionary of Kansas City who often ministered to men in Fort Leavenworth, was at Joseph's side when he died. Mininger later testified that "if ever I saw a person die as a real Christian and pass from this life into a better world, it was Joseph Hofer."[59]

Michael Hofer told Mininger, "I wish it had been I instead." And on December 2, he died, with his brother David at his bedside. This time the brothers' father begged the authorities to dress the body in Hutterite clothes, and they relented.[60] Meanwhile, after Joseph's death, the men's pastor, John Wipf, was trying to secure the release of the men by pleading with Senator Edward S. Johnson of South Dakota to intervene with Secretary Baker. "I can't stand it no longer," Wipf wrote. "So for God [*sic*] sake, please help us and put a stop to it. Go and see Hon. Baker. secr of war. He can stop it, I know, please do your best, but at ones [*sic*]." [61]

Johnson may indeed have intervened. In any case, David Hofer was released a few days later and the chaining of prisoners discontinued. Wipf remained in prison, but, as he reassured his wife, Katharina, on December 8, 1918, he was holding fast to his covenant with God until death and counting on the reward or crown which God had promised to all who suffered for his sake. In April 1919, he too was released.[62]

The exact cause or causes of the two Hofers' deaths remain unclear. The Office of the Surgeon of the Disciplinary Barracks at Fort Leavenworth concluded that the cause was pneumonia.[63] It is possible that the men succumbed to the Spanish flu. But there is little doubt that brutality at Alcatraz and Fort Leavenworth played a part. It is true that prison officials were faced with an unusual and trying situation when the Hutterite men refused even to do prison work or wear a prison uniform. Court-martialed, incarcerated conscientious objectors usually cooperated in the prisons, even if they had not done so in situations that were more clearly military. They realized that the prison system would not allow noncooperation. Furthermore they believed that the work they rendered in prison did not contribute to the war effort.

The "old" Mennonite advisers Loucks and Hartzler understood such points. In October 1918, reasoning that there was a difference between a conscientious objector in camp and a person in military prison, one of them had urged the four Hutterites to go to work "at once."[64] But Hutterites made no such distinction. These four Hutterites were like another named Jacob Waldner, who has left us a camp diary. He held to the classic Anabaptist doctrine of two kingdoms in its most radical form—and in that view the world was one large realm of radical evil. With such a viewpoint there was little reason to distinguish between the world's military camps and its prisons. They were all part of the same system.[65]

On the other side, prison officials surely lacked the compassion, sensitivity, and plain decency to make some allowance for these four simple Hutterite farmers and treat them with some leniency. Joseph and Michael Hofer were victims of inhumane military and penal systems, and martyrs for their faith. They joined their ancestors of the sixteenth century who had died when they stood firm.

Later, in 1919, Professor Jacob Ewert was moved to compose a long poem, "The Martyrs of Alcatraz." Two of its stanzas read,

> Four bearded men there stand in chains
> With hand-cuffs fastened to the bars
> Their arms stretched up, in fevr'ish pain
> With bruises not yet changed to scars
> They barely reach the slimy floor
> With their bare feet, in underwear
> Their shiv'ring bodies weak and sore
> And yet their hearts are strong in prayer
>
> Thank God that these objectors four
> So gentle and so meek and odd
> Are not alone; but many more
> Have love to man and love to God
> That prompts them to keep Jesus' laws
> To love and bless, forgive and bear
> But not assist in warlike cause
> Tho hatred threatens everywhere[66]

The two Hofer brothers were not the only prisoners to die in Fort Leavenworth. At about the time they died, the Spanish influenza and other maladies caused other deaths among the prison population, including deaths of some Mennonites. Among them was Johannes Klaassen, who died in mid-October. His father, Michael Klaassen, former pastor of the Sichar Mennonite Church and later elder of the Herold Mennonite Church near Cordell, Oklahoma, had not been able to persuade the local draft board to grant his son an occupational deferment. Members of the local board disliked Mennonite conscientious objectors, and, according to the elder Klaassen, "looked for spite and savagery of war."

At one time Johannes considered escaping to Canada, but for a variety of reasons the family decided against that idea. Johannes was one of the thirty-one Mennonites court-martialed at Camp Travis. Of the total of forty-one in that trial, three others died in Fort Leavenworth prison during the flu epidemic. On October 16 Johannes' family received a telegram informing them that his condition was critical. His father arrived at Leavenworth on October 18. But by then the son had died. The elder Klaassen took the body home and upon opening the casket he found that the body was attired in a military uniform. "Oh, my son!" he cried in agony, "Why have they done this to you? . . . If you would not wear this uniform in life, you shall not wear it in death!" Much to the anger of local Cordell citizens, the family removed the uniform and dressed the body in civilian clothes. Later that year the Klaassen family and other Mennonites from the Cordell area left and moved to Canada.[67]

Mennonites in Fort Leavenworth prison were frequently visited by relatives and ministers. Prominent among the ministers was J. D. Mininger. Mininger was able to visit men in solitary confinement and conduct worship services with the others. Especially memorable was the Christmas service in 1918, attended by some 185 men. "Brother Mininger . . . never in this world will fully realize how great a service he rendered to us and our Master," one of the men wrote after the war.[68]

On January 10, 1919, amid public chagrin and anger, 113 court-martialed conscientious objectors, many of them Mennonites, were released. Their release came at about the same time as the discharge of many other absolutist conscientious objectors directly from the camps. Apparently Washington authorities were anxious to resolve the conscientious objector problem. Perhaps they even felt some guilt about the frequent mistreatment. But as for the public, the *Kansas City Star* surely spoke for most citizens when it described the release as "an insult to the uniform." Baker, the paper charged, had placed a "premium on cowardice" and rewarded "evasion of duty."[69] The Kansas House of Representatives also lambasted Baker's "iniquitous" release of these "slackers, cowards, and traitors, and dangerous civic nondescripts."[70]

But the government persisted and soon discharged the others. Although the men had been reasonably well treated in prison, release brought immense relief. As John Neufelt wrote in his diary in late January, "We marched through one gate with the sentry. Then the other outside gates were opened and we heard for the last time 'Forward march,' to which we have not heard the word 'halt' yet."[71] Albert Voth considered his release a "bewildering experience." Not until he rode home on the train did he regain "some semblance of being a private human being in his own right."[72]

In late January 1919, many of the ordinary prisoners in Fort Leavenworth prison quit working, complaining of overcrowding and other bad conditions. Probably there were few Mennonites and other reli-

Discharge Certificate of Chriss Graber.
Courtesy, Archives Mennonite Church.

gious conscientious objectors among the strikers. In any case, the incident was peacefully settled.[73]

Like many other discharged conscientious objectors, those who had gone to prison were not always welcomed home by their neighbors. Upon his return home to Berne, Indiana, Tilman Soldner heard people calling him a prison bird. A dentist, he also found the door of his office painted yellow, and some of his clients boycotted his practice. Especially "worldly" and "evangelical" church people, Soldner complained, held grudges against him and many members of his own Mennonite church had "no use" for him. One wonders how long the scars inflicted during the trial, imprisonment, and hostile homecoming remained with him and many others.[74]

Few draftees suffered more during World War I than these court-martialed conscientious objectors. But many of them believed their sacrifices were not in vain. George Miller, one of the most abused Mennonite conscientious objectors, rejoiced that God had found in him an instrument worthy to be tried for Christ's cause. He attributed his trials to the will of God and hoped their effect would be to teach others about Christ. "Returning good for evil will still have its effect upon a nation, church, and individual, if only put into practice," he concluded.[75]

Allen B. Christophel was court-martialed at Camp Zachary Taylor. Later he testified that he was thankful for having had the opportunity to let the world know he did not approve of such "heathenish and barbarian practices as the world was engaged in." [76] Such men had shown themselves to be faithful and obedient followers of the Prince of Peace. Their faith stories may serve and inspire many today, as the examples of the martyrs inspired generations of Anabaptists and their spiritual descendants.

The sacrifices of the men and their families also strengthened the Mennonite peace position and prepared a new generation for World War II and beyond. Finally, in the 1930s and 1940s, some of them and their spouses would become leaders in peace activities and in and around Civilian Public Service camps. Nor were the furloughed and court-martialed conscientious objectors the only absolutists or examples of faith. Many Mennonite young men along with parents and other family members left for Canada before or after their registration. Some two hundred Mennonites left in 1917. The next year five to six hundred went, plus about a thousand Hutterites. Many of the Canadian-bound were from Kansas, Oklahoma, Nebraska, and Minnesota. About two-thirds of the Herold Mennonite Church near Cordell, Oklahoma, left in 1918.[77] On the other hand, after the war many Mennonites and

Hutterites returned home, blended in, and encountered few difficulties.

Soldiers, Noncombatant and Combatant

Both before and after the U.S. entered World War I, many of the nation's Mennonites accepted noncombatant service. They were not the first Mennonites to accept some forms of military service short of bearing arms. After many Mennonites had emigrated from the Russian empire in the 1870s, the majority who stayed agreed to perform forestry service. That was more alternative service than noncombatancy, but during World War I many of them did medical work in the Russian army as well—which certainly was a form of noncombatancy.[78] We do not know if the Russian model—one of the most liberal and generous in any of the Allied countries in World War I—had any influence on American Mennonites. One might think this not to be the case since those Mennonites who left Russia in 1874 were not inclined to compromise the principle of nonresistance. However, many of their descendants served as American noncombatants in World War I.

As mentioned previously, in the 1700s, during the French and Indian War, some Pennsylvania Mennonites assisted the British army with teamster services. But those men did not become an official or integral part of a war machine. During the U.S. Civil War, some Mennonites were compelled to serve as noncombatants or even as combatants in the Confederate army. In World War I, many American Mennonites and others chose noncombatancy because service in any of the approved noncombatant branches of the military (Medical Corps, Quartermaster General Corps, and Corps of Engineering) was a patriotic option and compromise and usually but not always guaranteed one immunity from mental and physical abuse.

Not all conscientious objectors had the mental and religious qualities to withstand the enormous pressures put on absolutists in the camps. When Warren Gish (in Camp Columbus, Ohio) faced the threat of a twenty-five-year prison sentence if he would not do army work, he signed up for noncombatant service. Later he deeply regretted doing so and prayed for delivery. Army life "with its cussing, singing of popular songs, [and] dirty talking" made him as a Christian feel out of place. But his military superiors would not allow any backsliding and Gish was not ready to face a court-martial; so he continued.[79]

Gideon H. Amstutz, who agreed to serve as an orderly in the base hospital in Camp Jackson, felt similar remorse—and asked God and his Mennonite church to forgive him.[80] On the other hand, some bent to

Noncombatant Clarence Stutzman.
Courtesy, John Stutzman,
Bloomington, Illinois.

Noncombatant Aldus Logenbill
in cowboy attire in Camp Travis,
Texas. Courtesy, Davis Habegger,
Fort Wayne, Indiana.

pressure from home. Edwin Waltner told of a person in Camp Cody who had been considered one of the "staunchest"—but news from home told him that neighbors were mocking and despising his wife and other dear ones, so he yielded.[81]

For men with convictions against noncombatant service but not the strength to stand alone, an important factor was support or pressure from fellow draftees. If fellow Mennonites in camp denounced non-combatant service as simply an escape from severe testing, as "the most cowardly thing to do," or as a way to be "in the swim," their influence could easily be enough to help a wavering individual to stand firm. In such cases the man had to choose between being thought of and called a coward by military people or by fellow Mennonites. But in some camps, individual Mennonites were almost completely isolated from others of their kind, so they had no peer support.[82]

In some cases military superiors tricked men into noncombatant service. An officer might say that the requested work was of minor consequence, that it related only remotely to the military, or that the Board

*Neither an "absolutist"
nor a noncombatant.
Daniel Metzler as cook
in Camp Lee, Virginia.*
Courtesy, Elam Hernley,
Scottdale, Pennsylvania.

of Inquiry had designated such work. At Camp Cody officials repeatedly and successfully solicited "in a friendly way" for hospital work. Later the men discovered they were still very much a part of the military effort and could even be sent overseas.[83] Faced with the whole problem, J. S. Hartzler urged the men to use "great discression [*sic*]" in choosing noncombatant service. He warned them that accepting noncombatancy could help bring the entire church under the hand of the law.[84]

Quite often men changed their minds and tried to persuade their military superiors to let them withdraw from noncombatant status. Doing so, many asked for help from one of the church conference committees. Aaron Loucks received many such requests, but in those cases he was none too eager to respond. To have signed up for noncombatant service and then to call upon "that man Loucks" to undo the mistake seemed to him "most foolish." It seemed to him that those who did so were men of conscience but too little backbone; they had to suffer the consequences.[85]

Some noncombatants were indeed willing to suffer the consequences of withdrawing. They quit working and mustered the courage to face a court-martial. One such, in addition to Wurz, Walter, and Showalter, was Rolla Wenger. Wenger worked as an orderly in a base hospital at Camp Sherman. But then he was assigned to go overseas and refused. So he was court-martialed.[86] Wilfred Gingerich agreed to do noncombatant work at Camp Beauregard in North Carolina, firing the incinerator and doing kitchen work. But he too refused flatly to go overseas and regretted ever putting on the uniform. For some reason he was not sent overseas.[87]

There were also conscientious objectors who sincerely believed they could render some kind of Christian, humanitarian service by ministering to the sick and wounded. Among them was Lester Detrow of Leetonia, Ohio, who worked as an orderly in a base hospital at Camp Jackson, South Carolina. Detrow and seven other Mennonite conscientious objectors did not consider their work wrong and believed they could do a lot more good in camp than at home. To Detrow there was not much Christianity in a person "who did not beleive [sic] in helping the sick and wounded boys as much as we can." Most important, he believed he was right about his decision because of spiritual satisfaction he felt and "sweet communion" he had with God in prayer.

However, Detrow was concerned about his parents' attitude and about rejection by his church. In December 1918 he informed his mother that during a furlough at home he did not want to be seen in his uniform any more than necessary. Although he himself felt all right about his uniform, it would be "something for people to talk about."[88]

Finally, there were many Mennonites who considered it their patriotic duty to serve as noncombatants. To assist the government in its war effort was one way they could display their love of country. It would be a good testimony of Mennonite patriotism. Among them was David Janzen. In the 1850s during the Crimean War, his grandfather had assisted the Russian army by hauling soldiers and provisions. In the 1870s David's family left the Russian empire and settled in California. When David was drafted, his father told him, "Son, never forget you are a noncombatant, a Mennonite."

At Camp Lewis, Janzen had little difficulty accepting military authority because he always liked "a soldier's uniform" and felt a "fascination" for a soldier's life. Furthermore, as a noncombatant he would have pride and ego gratification. He looked with a degree of contempt on his fellow Mennonites, considering them sluggish, dull, and "ignorant of the mercies of our adopted land." He would have been happy if a company of Mennonite boys had gone overseas for work in field hospitals. In October 1918, Janzen left for France where he stayed until June 1919.[89]

Hospital work at home or in France was one kind of work Mennonite noncombatants performed. They also did camp maintenance, and several men cared for animals in so-called remount depots. Charles Kauffman of Fairview, Michigan, served as a messenger at the front in France, and A. C. Burky, serving in the Quartermaster Corps, taught officers' children at Camp Terry, New York.[90]

Apparently no Mennonite noncombatant was killed in action in France, but some did succumb at home or overseas to the Spanish flu or other diseases. Among them was John Brubaker at Camp Meade, who had been persuaded to accept noncombatant service before he had time to consider it carefully. At Meade he helped care for men with pneumonia; then, overworked, he himself died in April 1918. Some of his friends considered him a "conscientious martyr of Camp Meade."[91] Benedict J. Roth served in the Medical Corps in France, where he died in January 1919 shortly before he was scheduled to return home. He is buried in France. Later in his home town of Chenoa, Illinois, the American Legion named its Post 234 after him.[92]

In general, noncombatants were discharged later than were the absolutists. When they returned home, their congregations did not always welcome and accept them. Since they had become an integral part of the military system, many of them, like combatants, had to apologize for their decisions and ask for forbearance and forgiveness. We do not know how many refused; likely many left their Mennonite churches and joined other denominations.[93] Many noncombatants applied for soldiers' bonuses, instructed their families to request the federal government to pay for their burial expenses, and joined the American Legion. Perhaps some of them believed they had let their Mennonite light shine in the army and could continue to do so in the American Legion.[94]

A few Mennonites accepted full combatancy. Most did so voluntarily. Obviously their commitment to Mennonite nonresistance was not strong. No doubt most were eager to do "the right popular, patriotic thing" and support the nation in time of war. Perhaps their churches and their parents had neglected to preach and teach nonresistance. Some belonged to Mennonite communities in Iowa, Illinois, and Kansas, which consisted of descendants of Palatinate, Alsatian, or Swiss immigrants who had became less interested in traditional Mennonite peace concerns. For instance in September 1918, Henry Krehbiel complained about the desertion of the "Christ-taught doctrine of non-resistance by Kansas Mennonites of South German extraction."[95]

Similar erosion of the doctrine had occurred among Mennonites in the GC Eastern District, who had seceded from the Franconia Conference in the 1840s and had become quite acculturated by accepting American attitudes. Such Mennonites were the ones most easily swayed by superpatriotic appeals. The Eicher Emmanuel and Wayland GC Mennonite churches in southeastern Iowa are clear examples. Their support for the war effort was unswerving and their praise for those who rallied to the colors unstinting. Many if not most members were proud to be "100 percent Americans" and to show their loyalty by rendering military service.

In late 1918 ten members of these two churches were either in or on their way to France as soldiers; five were in the Navy. Of the Wayland congregation only one individual refused combatant or noncombatant service.[96] Jake C. Regier, president and manager of the Buhler Mill and Elevator Company in Buhler, Kansas, expressed similar Mennonite patriotism. In August 1918 he congratulated his brother, Emil, for deciding to become a "REAL American soldier" at Camp Funston. He was sure a "higher hand" had guided his brother and was proud he had not shown that "yellow streak" one found in 95 percent of the conscientious objectors in the army.[97]

Almost every group has its dissenters, especially in individualistic America. Some men came from Mennonite homes and churches where nonresistance had been taught but they were still swayed by patriotic fervor, a desire for adventure, or other motives. Among them was Calvin Weaver, son of a Pennsylvania Mennonite pastor who sneaked out through a bedroom window and enlisted against his parents' wishes. He was killed in combat.[98]

Some sons of Mennonites were so eager to become soldiers that they joined churches which had no history of a peace witness where no one would try to dissuade them or later berate them for their decisions.[99] Finally some became combatants when they yielded to pressures in camp. Such men obviously lacked the strength of conviction or were unable to endure much mental and physical abuse. In some cases they may have developed personal bonds and friendships that pulled them into combatancy.

While many Mennonite congregations found it difficult to permit their young men to serve as noncombatants, they found combatant service totally unacceptable. Defying the congregation and opting for combatant service could lead to exclusion from the communion service or even from the church community itself. But sometimes congregations were divided and did not know how to respond. Such was the case in the Salem Mennonite Church, a GC congregation near Dalton, Ohio. Here Clayton Welty, son of deacon Andrew Welty, enlisted in the Marine Corps. Welty was a Bluffton graduate and his decision to enlist was heartily endorsed by *The Witmarsum*, his alma mater's student paper, who considered his response to "democracy's call" a "noble one."[100]

In June 1918, Welty was wounded in the terrible battle near Chateau Thierry, France, and returned home. In March 1918, Pastor Adam W. Sommer announced to the congregation his decision to expel Welty because he had not abided by his church's constitution. Quite a few members disagreed with Sommers; they were also expelled. The congregation's firm stand angered many of the Mennonites' neighbors, and there were rumors that local patriots would burn down the church building.

The local sheriff investigated the matter and called the pastor and Sunday school superintendent into his office. Even federal agents arrived from Cleveland to investigate; the zealous United States Attorney Wertz in Cleveland favored prosecution. But cooler heads at the Justice Department disapproved, on grounds that the congregation had not prevented Welty from enlisting, and that a church had the right to decide the composition of its membership. In 1919 Sommer resigned his position, but Welty never returned to his congregation.[101]

Some Mennonite combatants died in camp or were killed in France. One of the first who died was Samuel Huser, a member of the Defenseless Mennonite congregation near Berne, Indiana. In May 1918 Huser succumbed to pneumonia at Camp Taylor; his home church hosted a military funeral.[102] In September of the same year Rollin Hershberger of Middlebury, Indiana, died in combat in France. His brother asked Bishop D. D. Miller to preach the funeral service in the Forks ("old") Mennonite church. Miller, a denominational leader, refused on grounds that he had a previous commitment to visit Camp Zachary Taylor. Subsequently, rumors had it that Miller refused to perform the service because Rollin Hershberger had died in combat. Miller denied that charge, and apparently his strong denials were enough to prevent any kind of mob action or federal investigation.[103]

Among Mennonite combatants who were killed or died in France were, for instance, Jacob Hofer, Edward Burghardt, Jonas Deetz, Peter Schantz, Clarence Yoder, Harvey Schrock, Jacob Stuckey, David Burkholder, and Ira Schantz. Burkholder had belonged to the Holdeman ("old") Mennonite Church near Wakarusa, Indiana. In camp he was so badly treated that he agreed to accept combatant service. He was killed in action on November 4, 1918.[104] Ira Schantz was a member of the Eicher Emmanuel Mennonite Church. He received his basic training at Camp Pike, Arkansas, and in September 1918 was shipped to France. During the voyage he became ill with the Spanish flu and died at age twenty-four, soon after he arrived. In 1926 his body was returned home and reinterred after an impressive service in his home church (which was attended by several ex-servicemen).[105]

Unfortunately we know little about Mennonite combatants of World War I or even World War II. They seem to have left virtually no records telling us at least something about their thoughts, feelings, experiences in battle, and reflections after their return. Perhaps after the war most of them left their Mennonite churches. Some might have been ashamed of their decision to fight and kill while others were not repentant. Whatever their sentiments, many did not feel comfortable returning to the Mennonite fold. However, in some cases ex-combatants were reaccepted after they confessed their errors before the congregation.[106]

⚬ ⚬ ⚬ ⚬ ⚬

The conditions in various military camps were such that many a young and inexperienced man yielded under various pressures or mental and physical abuse. However, over time the government did provide a generous alternative—the farm furloughs—although not every conscientious objector succeeded in availing himself of this option. Unfortunately, the government was often unwilling or unable to prevent or correct the camps' abuses. Too often the federal government was a victim of its own war propaganda, and its treatment of conscientious objectors is a case in point.

During the Second World War, Mennonites would be better prepared, although for many young men the moral choice would be more difficult than that of their fathers. Nazi Germany and Japanese imperialism seemed to be more real threats than the Kaiser. But in the interwar period, Mennonites developed considerable peace education and grounded many of their young people better in nonresistance. The government did not repeat its egregious errors of World War I. War propaganda was more restrained, and under the Selective Service Act of 1940, conscientious objectors were not required to go to military camps to be grilled and mistreated; they were not pressured so heavily to become noncombatants or combatants. Instead, in the CPS system, the government provided a generous civilian alternative.

For most Mennonites World War I was a difficult and trying time when their patriotism was questioned and found wanting. They had always considered themselves loyal and productive citizens, but now many of their neighbors felt they were not doing their patriotic "bit" for the war effort. In that crucible, many developed a new appreciation of what it meant to be members of the kingdom of God. Perhaps the Mennonite war experience was well summed up by Ida Kauffman of Fairview, North Dakota. "Living through those days," she has written, "gave me a fear of what non-Mennonites might do to my family. But it also gave me an understanding of what nonresistance really was."[107]

This copy for reference purposes only
Permission to reproduce must be secured from
THE ARCHIVES OF THE MENNONITE CHURCH,
1700 S. Main St., Goshen, Ind. 46526

Camp Sevier
S. C.
Nov. 11, 1918.

Dear folks at home:—

I have heard more singing & yelling today than I have for sometime. Everybody seems to be happy and rejoicing.
WORLD WAR STOPS! is the head line of the Atlanta Georgian Extra this evening. The report is that there will be some quick changes made in the different camps.
I received my overcoat and the pillow today also the card and letter that left Dalton Nov. 7.
I was glad for the pillow and I may dream about home tonight. The weather was not so nice today it was cloudy and cool.
I started to make another pillow top today I think I can finish it tomorrow.
Have you heard from Henry Latley? This is all for this time from your loving son and brother
Walter M.

Draftee Walter Martin informing his parents the war is over.
Courtesy, Archives Mennonite Church.

7

The Aftermath

The bitter war experiences left deep scars in various Mennonite communities that took many years to heal. Furthermore, because many Mennonites had experienced so unpleasant encounters with their neighbors and authorities, they reassessed and questioned their acculturation into the American mainstream. The war experience was partially responsible for a conservative reaction in the Mennonite church. On the other hand, Mennonites wanted to reach out to ease the needs of a suffering postwar world. In the past generation or two, they had already begun to reach out extensively with charitable work and missions. Now they became even more outward-looking.

Having been accused of not doing their part during the war, Mennonites were eager to respond to the tremendous social and economic needs of the postwar years. As historian James C. Juhnke has often pointed out, amidst other motives they seemed to feel an affinity for the nation and a need to feel that they were good citizens after all, despite the many epithets against them.[1]

Large parts of Europe, the Middle East, and the Soviet Union offered huge opportunities to extend aid to the war's many victims. North American Mennonites did not fail to respond. During the war they had discovered each other anew and had begun to cooperate as never before on matters such as the draft and relief. In the postwar era, they broadened such efforts. In 1920 their new cooperation reached a high point with the establishment of the Mennonite Central Committee (MCC). Mennonites had already donated funds to and done relief and reconstruction work for the American Friends Service Committee (AFSC), and during the war the "old" Mennonites had established their own Mennonite Relief Commission for War Sufferers (MRCWS).

The MRCWS was established in December 1917, in Elkhart, Indiana, with Loucks as president, Levi Mumaw as secretary, and George L. Bender as treasurer. Among other activities it agreed to support reconstruction work in France under the auspices of the AFSC. The MRCWS also agreed to assist The American Committee for Armenian and Syrian Relief and to raise at least $200,000. By April 1919 it had received $463,000 and was supporting some fifty relief workers in France plus about the same number elsewhere in Europe and in the Middle East.

The General Conference branch had had the Emergency Relief Commission since 1899, and the Mennonite Brethren had an organization known as United Orphanage War Relief. In January 1918 representatives of the three agencies met at Goshen, Indiana, to discuss ways of promoting relief efforts. What emerged was an agreement to carry on a vigorous campaign for relief of war sufferers, but to do it through the existing organizations.[2] After the war Mennonites still donated to the AFSC and to their own organizations, and they considerably expanded their relief work in France. They also initiated relief work in the Middle East by serving with The American Committee for Armenian and Syrian Relief. And in 1920 MCC began extending large-scale aid to Mennonites in the Soviet Union.

Early in 1919, The American Committee for American and Syrian Relief asked the MRCWS to assist in its relief efforts in the Middle East. In January 1919 delegates from several "old" Mennonite organizations—the MRCWS, the Eastern Mennonite Board of Missions and Charities, and the Lancaster and Franconia district conferences—accepted the offer. The delegates decided to send not only money but some workers. On January 25, 1919, seven men departed for the Middle East, accompanied by Loucks and another church leader, William Derstine. Eventually some thirty men and two women—Vesta Zook and Vinora Weaver—served in the region. In monetary contributions, North American Mennonites gave some $2.5 million to relief in the Middle East, the Soviet Union, and Europe.[3]

In western Europe, France was the main center of Mennonite relief activity. Many Mennonites in military camps and others shared the eager spirit of draftee Fred D. Augsburger. In July 1918 he told Loucks that he wanted to get into relief work. "I don't favor making money and living a selfish life while the world is bleeding. I think it is our duty to get out and help the suffering," he wrote. "We must help our brothers."[4]

One problem for volunteers like Augsburger was that, at that time, Mennonites did not have a reconstruction organization of their own. The best option available seemed to be the AFSC. The AFSC had been doing reconstruction in France since late 1917. Already in 1917 one Mennonite, John D. Zook of Urbana, Ohio, had been among the fifty-four volunteers the AFSC sent to that country. By the end of 1918 the number of Mennonite AFSC workers was still only nine; after the Armistice, the flow quickened and in 1919-1920 some fifty-four Mennonites served.[5]

Most of those who went were men who had been released in 1919 from military camps or from Fort Leavenworth prison. Despite harrowing experiences many had suffered there, all were anxious now to give a positive witness. Most of the volunteers who served were exceptionally progressive members of the "old" Mennonite church. Some, however, belonged to the General Conference or the Mennonite Brethren branches.

The main site of the Mennonites' AFSC work in France was Clermont-en-Argonne. This was a small village located in the western part of the Meuse Department, a region devastated since 1916 by the terrible battle of Verdun. The volunteers were also active in the village of Neuvilly, located a few miles from Cambrai in the Nord Department, as well as in Ornans, a village in west-central France. In those places they mostly built homes and gave agricultural assistance. Sometimes they also worked alongside German prisoners of war. In all the locations, the volunteers found the work most rewarding. Some, for instance Roy Buchanan, testified that it became one of the most meaningful experiences of their lives.[6]

But in France Mennonite volunteers did not always see eye-to-eye with their AFSC supervisors. They sometimes alleged that the supervisors knew less about the work than they did. Nor were they satisfied with the support from their own church. The financial assistance was rather generous, in the end totaling some $291,000, but they would have liked more moral support.[7]

Before he left for France one worker, the well-educated Jacob C. Meyer, urged that church leaders visit the unit. The MRCWS agreed and in May 1919, Bishop Samuel E. Allgyer and a more youthful Vernon Smucker did visit. They listened to, and discussed the volunteers' concerns, and strongly supported their call for far more ambitious Mennonite relief efforts in Europe and the Soviet Union. Allgyer appointed three relief workers to go to Central Europe and the Soviet Union to investigate the situation there—although the MRCWS was rather ambivalent about the relief efforts the trip implied, and in 1919 even resolved to disband.[8]

Postwar Soviet Union was wracked by civil war and other turmoil which brought millions, including most of the Mennonites in its territories, to the point of starvation. Europeans and Americans, Mennonites among them, began to hear urgent pleas for immediate and large-scale relief. The cries did not fall on totally deaf ears. Among Mennonites, those in Europe promptly provided aid. And in America, the Mennonites in July 1920 established a new and almost unprecedented inter-Mennonite organization, the Mennonite Central Committee (MCC). MCC's initial purpose was to render aid to needy co-religionists in the Soviet Union. Initially it had support from only three Mennonite groups—the "old" or MC Mennonites, the GC, and the MB—but eventually almost all other Mennonites joined.

In the early 1920s the new agency concentrated on relief to Soviet peoples and managed to send considerable amounts, albeit quite often through the American Relief Administration (a private organization headed by future president Herbert Hoover and enjoying widespread support from many churches and others in America). The first MCC relief team consisted of three men who arrived in September 1920 in Constantinople and later extended its work into the Crimea and the Ukraine.

Some time later one member of the relief team, Clayton Kratz, disappeared—almost certainly having died or been killed—amid civil strife in the Soviet Union's Ukraine. To most Mennonites he, rather than their young men who had died in the trenches in France, was a true martyr for a worthy cause. In any case MCC sent food which saved many lives, plus horses and tractors which helped farmers get back into production. Later in the 1920s, MCC concentrated more on helping thousands of Mennonite emigrate from the Soviet Union and its communism. Thereafter, MCC took up different kinds of challenges, notably those of working with other historic peace churches to design, win, and operate programs of government-approved civilian alternative service in World War II and afterward. Since the 1940s MCC has also carried out relief and development work in many parts of the world.[9]

From the beginning there has been irony in MCC's work. Through MCC's involvement with the American Relief Administration, Mennonites cooperated with agents of the other kingdom. And MCC's work in the larger world inevitably accelerated some processes of acculturation which many post-World War I Mennonites hoped instead to slow down or even stop.[10]

MCC was conceived and born out of World War I experiences and postwar needs and initiatives. The experiences included limited but genuine inter-Mennonite cooperation and the discovery of some common identity running through the complex Mennonite tapestry;

the strong desire of many Mennonites to do their patriotic "bit"; the eagerness of many Mennonite youths to carry out the gospel in practical ways; and the sense of moral obligation once again to assist fellow Mennonites in the Russian empire (as an earlier generation had done in the 1870s). It may be that inter-Mennonite cooperation would have evolved sooner or later without the Great War. But it was that war, that senseless and cruel conflict so much decried by most Mennonites, that helped launch the new inter-Mennonite venture. And that launching became one of the most important, most energizing, most exciting events in modern Mennonite history. Out of the incredible carnage of the Great War, some good did come. What irony, that the terrible war somehow made Mennonites its beneficiaries!

Many relief workers wanted Mennonites to be even more actively involved in relief and other humanitarian work as well as in addressing the world's social and economic needs. These Mennonites felt that during the war their church had failed to communicate a Christian concern for social and economic justice. Many, such as Jacob C. Meyer, reached such conclusions while in military camps or in prison. They wanted, in the words of relief worker Payson Miller, "to release the men powers [*sic*] of the Mennonite church."

Behind such remarks was a strong opinion, especially among some activist, progressive young people of the "old" Mennonite church (the very kind who dominated the unit in France) that their current church leaders were failing miserably to cultivate and retain the "potential power" of the church. Because of this, the activists argued, the church was losing many young people. Especially among "old" Mennonites, the complaints echoed conflicts which had little to do with relief. A new generation of youth, many with some college education, wanted a much larger share of leadership. A spirit of activism competed with older styles of humility and nonconformity as marks of valid Christianity. And in sum a more acculturated progressivism competed with tradition.

But within those important conflicts, there was a genuine theological concern. The relief workers and others for whom Meyer spoke believed that their church had failed through "misapprehension" of Christianity's real mission and message. Those in Meyer's camp thought that the Mennonite church was spending most of its time saving itself. Calling for what they said was a new kind of conservatism, they wanted to teach, not withdrawal from the world, but involvement and commitment to alleviate human suffering. Instead of isolating themselves, they wanted Mennonites to say, "I have come to you with

Christ as my shield and helper to bring to you the bread of life. He has promised never to leave nor forsake me, and with his help, I will show you what kind of a life he wishes us to live in all of our social and business relationships." In sum, they wanted a new, "practical" rendition of the gospel message.[11]

To be able to share and articulate such concerns, the Mennonite volunteers at Clermont-en-Argonne had been trying to organize themselves. In late March 1919, they decided to send questionnaires to different Mennonite congregations. In them they asked if the church should interest itself in an aggressive social and mission program and if young people should be trusted to establish some permanent organization which would work to that end. Then on June 20-22 they met in a large tent on top of a hill near Clermont-en-Argonne, a site of bitter fighting during the war. Attending the meeting were some sixty persons who included the MRCWS representatives Allgyer and Smucker; Pierre Sommer, O. R. Liechty, and C. J. Gerber from France; and, rare in that overwhelmingly male company, two women, one a Dutch Mennonite relief worker named Ada Cnoop Koopmans. One evening the group met in a tent as the sun was setting. By the light of several coal-oil lamps, they shared their wartime experiences. More formally, there

Mennonite COs leaving for France.
Courtesy, Mrs. Anna Rohren, Wadsworth, Ohio.

Mennonite relief workers, France, 1919.
Courtesy, Archives of Mennonite Church.

Two female relief workers in France. One is Ada Cnoop Koopmans.
Courtesy, Archives of the Mennonite Church.

were sermons and speeches and the drafting of a proposed constitution for a future so-called Young People's Conference.[12]

An address by Meyer conveyed much of what the conference was about. Meyer urged Mennonites to go forth with the message of the Master in the most effective way—by deed and life. He complained that young men in the Mennonite church were stifled and feeling much as the apostle Paul had when he was hindered by those not "in the work." Despite all obstacles, Paul had carried on. Meyer hoped the conference itself would be a means for his listeners to develop their convictions, go to work in the social order, and practice what Jesus had said in the Sermon on the Mount. Another volunteer, Orie B. Gerig, affirmed Meyers' sentiments and urged Mennonites further to promote social and economic justice.

As the sessions neared their end, the gathered group adopted a constitution for a new organization of the young generation of Mennonite activists. Proposals for the new organization's name were revealing. They included "The Mennonite Young People's Movement"; "The Mennonite Life Movement"; or "The Mennonite Open Forum Movement." The first name, emphasizing a new generation, won out. But the other two names, emphasizing vitality and freedom of ideas, also said something about the organizers' vision.

In any case, the constitution said that the new organization's purpose was to deepen the spiritual life of the Mennonite church, to study Mennonites' social responsibility as it had been experienced during the war, to promote Christian education, to provide relief and reconstruction, and to inspire young men and women to consecrate their lives to the conservation and extension of the principles of Jesus Christ. Finally, the constitution expressed the ideal of inter-Mennonite ecumenicity, which included promoting cooperation with Mennonites in Europe and the Soviet Union. Payson Miller was elected to be the new organization's moderator.[13]

The Young People's Conference, as the organization was finally called, held its first meeting in August 1920 at West Liberty, Ohio. There was a second meeting in July 1922 at Sterling, Illinois, and another which became the final one, in June 1923 at Middlebury, Indiana. By the time of the last meeting, the leadership especially of the "old" Mennonite church was in considerable confusion and disarray. This situation affected the Young People's Conference and contributed to its demise. For some time much of the organization's energy was channeled into *The Christian Exponent*, a publication that ran from 1924 to 1928 and espoused the Young People's Conference viewpoint and pro-

gram. *The Christian Exponent* folded in 1928. Lack of financial support
was a large factor, but that in turn suggested the whole movement's
fragility.[14]

The demise of the Young People's Conference and *The Christian
Exponent* must have come as a relief to many conservative and fundamentalist church leaders, who were fearful of a drift toward "popular"
religion and too much emphasis on social action. Such leaders preferred to emphasize sound doctrine, nonconformity, and authority of
church leadership. The conflict between the "radicals," as they were
sometimes called, and the church establishment was part of a larger debate on the meaning and impact of the war experience on the Mennonite world. It was a tragedy that the Mennonite churches did not provide far more opportunities for these young persons to lead and to use
their energies and their strong commitments.

Perhaps it was easier to reach out to a suffering world than to re-
appraise the war's impact on Mennonite acculturation versus nonconformity at home. In meetings at Fairview, Michigan; Burrton, Kansas;
Collinsville, Oklahoma; and elsewhere, Mennonites pondered their relationships with their neighbors, especially with the many who had de-
rided and humiliated them. In many communities it was difficult to re-
establish relationships of trust. Ill-feeling and suspicion lasted for decades.

In some instances Mennonites did not turn the other cheek and
quickly forgive patriotic neighbors. Near Peoria, Illinois, Mennonites
asked J. W. Kirkton, president of the Livingston County Soil and Crop
Improvement Association and a man who had been very critical of the
farm furlough system, to apologize for his wartime behavior. He refused. Some Mennonites then told him they would not help thresh his
grain.[15]

In South Dakota relations between Mennonites and non-
Mennonites were aggravated by attempts to oust the Hutterites from
that state. In 1919 the South Dakota Council of Defense initiated legal
action against the Hutterite colonies, seeking their dissolution. It
charged that under the guise of a religious body, the Hutterites were
acting like a corporation for economic gain. Of course, there were also
accusations that the Hutterites were unpatriotic and had refused to
contribute to the war effort. In fact, the critics asserted, the colonies
were a menace to the society and government of South Dakota.

The state itself took up the charges; in September 1919 Judge A.
E. Taylor of Beadle County ruled in favor of the state. The judge upheld the charges of doing secular business for profit while devoting lit-

tle of the ensuing income to religious worship and education. In the opinion of the judge, Hutterite colonies had violated a state law which set a limit of $50,000 on the value of property held by religious corporations. Furthermore, he found them guilty of not contributing to the defense of the United States and of using the German language.[16]

Having found the Hutterites guilty, the judge ordered the sale of their property in excess of $50,000. He also forbade the colonies from engaging in agriculture, stock raising, and other secular pursuits. Shortly after this decision, the secretary of the State Council of Defense boasted the court's ruling would "absolutely exterminate the Mennonites in South Dakota." The danger that this prediction might come true seemed all the greater in 1922, when the South Dakota Supreme Court upheld much of the lower court's ruling.

However, the higher court did not require the liquidation of Hutterite holdings. Hutterites might stay on as an unincorporated organization. But by that time most of South Dakota's Hutterite colonies had already left for Canada. The exodus continued until only the Bon Homme colony was left. By 1933 all Hutterites had emigrated, but three years later some returned. Many more moved to South Dakota in the years following.[17]

Because of unpleasant wartime experiences, many Mennonites reiterated a sharp distinction between the two kingdoms. As a result many grew less inclined to serve in local government or even to vote. The war was also partly responsible for the GCs' general conference decision in September 1917 to withdraw from the ecumenical Federal Council of Churches of Christ. Meeting at Reedley, California, the conference accepted a minority report that recommended withdrawal because other churches in the council had overwhelmingly supported the war effort. But with overtones of the modernist-fundamentalist debate growing hot in American Protestantism, the report also alleged that membership in the Federal Council meant association with the champions of the "dangerous theology."[18]

Mennonites' own versions of that acrimonious confrontation between modernism and fundamentalism caused many Mennonites to question even more the wisdom of close association with the "other kingdom." In the 1920s this debate deeply divided American Protestantism and also affected Mennonites. The Mennonite version of fundamentalism not only represented such ideas as biblical inerrancy and belief in the virgin birth, the resurrection, and so forth—but also a return to a strict separation of the two kingdoms, or nonconformity.

The "old" Mennonite church was especially torn by this division.

For instance, it was largely the cause of an exodus of many faculty members and a one-year closing of Goshen College in 1923-1924. For Mennonites, the modernist-fundamentalist debate in Protestantism and their own somewhat similar quarrels complicated the formulation of a coherent peace theology.[19] Fortunately, the strain between Mennonites and the other kingdom eased. That was because most Americans felt increasingly disillusioned with their nation's wartime venture. Albeit for reasons different from those that moved Mennonites, many Americans concluded that U.S. involvement in the Great War had been an egregious error. Certainly it had not fulfilled the Wilsonian promise of a new world order.

Although many Mennonites preferred as much nonconformity as possible, the war and immediate postwar era pulled in the other directly—hastening acculturation and contact with the other kingdom. For instance, the war accelerated the movement away from the German language. Especially for the so-called Russian Mennonites of Kansas, Nebraska, South Dakota, and elsewhere, it was the use of the German tongue that had set many Mennonites apart.

The war also stimulated cooperation with other denominations such as the Quakers and the Church of the Brethren, and with government officials. The entire postwar relief effort was a significant broadening experience for many Mennonites, as they reached out to a suffering world as well as to European Mennonites. In 1925, at Basel and Zurich in Switzerland, a new kind of Mennonite conference took place—the First Mennonite World Conference. Without question, Mennonite World Conference emerged from important contacts made during and immediately after the war.[20]

War experiences also made Mennonites more concerned with maintaining and reinterpreting their traditional peace testimony. Many of them concluded, rightly or wrongly, that much more educational work could and should have been done prior to World War I; they now tried to vitalize and reinterpret the idea of Christian love and nonresistance in light of new experiences. In 1919 Mennonites had a good opportunity to witness for peace by signing petitions against a proposal for peacetime universal military training. Along with many other Americans, thousands of Mennonites signed.[21]

Meanwhile the "old" Mennonite church continued its war Military Problems Committee—which from 1925 onward was named the Peace Problems Committee (PPC). With the able Orie O. Miller (eventually well-known for a long career as chief executive of MCC) as its secretary, the PPC carried on a variety of tasks. For instance, it was responsible for a number of important publications on Mennonite non-resistance and for organizing peace conferences at Goshen College in 1935 and 1939.

In the GC branch, a Peace Committee comparable to the PPC was appointed in 1926. Henry P. Krehbiel was the committee's leader. In 1936 an International Mennonite Peace Committee was established, and three years later, as World War II loomed, MCC appointed an inter-Mennonite committee for North America—the Mennonite Central Peace Committee. Mennonites also participated in a Conference of Pacifist Churches which met periodically between 1922 and 1931. In 1935 they took part in a meeting of the Historic Peace Churches (HPC) organized by Krehbiel at Newton, Kansas.

The HPC meeting helped lead to further cooperation and in 1940 to the drafting of a proposal presented to President Franklin D. Roosevelt for a civilian option for conscientious objectors. Much of this proposal was incorporated in the Selective Service Act of 1940—a measure that reintroduced military conscription.[22] At Goshen College, Guy F. Hershberger and others revived a Peace Society. And Hershberger began a course on "War, Peace and Nonresistance"—a vehicle by which he developed his thought until, in 1944, it culminated in a landmark book by that title.

Meanwhile, Hershberger gave a notable address at a 1935 conference, outlining different paths that conscientious objectors might take and proposing alternative service.[23] At about the same time others, including another highly thoughtful "old" Mennonite scholar named Edward Yoder (who served at Hesston and Goshen Colleges and the Mennonite Publishing House) published many pro-peace articles for Mennonite youth.[24] At Bethel College and among GCs, in addition to the work of Krehbiel and others, Professor Emmet L. Harshbarger provided much leadership in the area of peace education through writings and active membership in the Kansas Institute of International Relations.[25]

But Mennonites were reluctant to participate in many of the peace organizations and movements which operated in the United States between World Wars I and II. Perhaps they remembered that too many such organizations had compromised in 1917 and supported the war effort. Furthermore, the theology of many was too liberal for many Mennonites. Many of the organizations were quite secular, with a more pragmatic approach toward peace and war.

Despite the efforts of some thoughtful persons, as a whole Mennonites did not succeed in formulating a coherent peace theology or in reinterpreting their traditional peace concern in light of their World War I experiences. The fundamentalist-modernist controversy was partly responsible for this failure. A fundamentalist leader such as John H. Mosemann, Sr., a powerful bishop in the Lancaster "old" Mennonite conference, was quite sure that the modern peace movement was a "satanic delusion." He saw the movement as a mighty deceptive force intended to mislead the church of Christ and take her headlong into the clutches of "modernistic and liberalistic" leaders.

The fundamentalist leaders included George R. Brunk I, who in a hard-hitting publication he began in 1929 and named *The Sword and Trumpet*, rejected the Gandhian approach to war and violence and argued that nonresistance was not possible for unconverted nations.[26] Historian John Horsch wrote a book called *Die biblische Lehre von der Wehrlosigkeit* [The biblical teachings of nonresistance]. In this first major Mennonite study of nonresistance in the twentieth century, Horst rejected "pacifism" (which he thought quite different from biblical nonresistance) because it smacked too much of modernistic theology. He considered social betterment, education, international arbitration— all popular peace concerns in the interbellum period—ineffective and misguided without regeneration through Christ.[27] Ironically, some Protestant modernists such as the well-known Harry Emerson Fosdick held strong pacifists views which they did not surrender during World War II. Yet such modernists were anathema among Mennonites.

But while the fundamentalist views engendered controversy, Mennonites kept peace concerns alive. When the U.S. entered World War II, in 1941, they were better prepared than ever to meet the challenge. If many young men chose to accept military service in World War II it was not because churches had neglected peace concerns or failed to persuade the government to provide conscientious objectors with an acceptable civilian alternative.

During World War II about 46 percent of all conscripted Mennonite men chose either combatant or noncombatant service. Because we have no reliable statistics on the Mennonite response to the military draft in World War I, it is difficult to say if a higher percentage of Mennonites chose military service in the years 1940-1945 than in the period 1917-1918. In Kansas the percentages were about the same.[28] Yet it is safe to conclude that the wrenching experiences of 1917-1918 considerably strengthened traditional Mennonite nonresistance. The suffering and sacrifices of the Mennonites in and outside the military camps in World War I were not in vain. They were the foundation of the Mennonite peace witness of the next generations.

Appendix:

Some Statistics of Mennonite and Other Historic Peace Church Service in World War I

Of the original twenty-one thousand World War I conscientious objectors about four thousand persisted in their stand. It is generally assumed that about one-half or approximately two thousand of those were Mennonite.[1] Yet it is difficult if not impossible to determine exactly how many Mennonite men were drafted in World War I. Nor does it seem possible to provide reliable figures on the number of those who agreed to be noncombatants or combatants and those who chose the more absolutist stand. Most of the available figures such as camp and church records are incomplete. Perhaps the only reliable source of information would be the draftees' military records which are scattered through papers on some three million individuals, papers located in the National Personnel Records Center in St. Louis, Missouri.

However, aside from the formidable task of studying all the records, these materials are not very accessible because the researcher must have prior approval from the ex-servicemen or their descendants. Some reliable statistics for a few states or conferences were gathered around the end of the war, but they do not give us the total picture. Subsequent efforts to collect data proved to be very difficult. A questionnaire sent by the author a few years ago to all Mennonite communities in the United States brought only meager returns.

Professor Guy Hershberger, who in his long and distinguished academic career spent considerable time investigating the World War I Mennonite experience, concluded the total number of draftees must have been about two thousand.[2] However, data collected by him and others in the Archives of the Mennonite Church in Goshen, Indiana, show a total of 1,349 conscientious objectors.[3]

That list is incomplete because it does not include all noncombatants, Hutterites, or Amish draftees. We do know that the total number of Mennonite draftees in Kansas was 323.[4] In South Dakota a total of eighty-two Mennonite men were drafted:[5] in the Illinois and Franconia "old" Mennonite conferences, seventy-two and twenty-six respectively were called.[6] The percentage of draftees of the total Mennonite population in a given area varies. In Kansas it was probably about 1.3 percent while among Franconia Mennonites it was .25 percent. Even if the higher percentage figure were taken, no more than about one thousand (1.3 percent of about eighty thousand) Mennonites could have been drafted. We know this figure is too low. Perhaps the total number of Mennonite conscientious objectors including noncombatants was about 1,500.

How many of the draftees refused combatant and noncombatant service, and how many accepted one of those alternatives? The Mennonite response to military conscription varied and was different for various denominations. Perhaps typical of the "old" Mennonite Church response was the pattern of its Franconia Conference. Of twenty-one men who were drafted, sixteen, 76 percent, refused both combatant and noncombatant service; one individual, 4 percent, agreed to noncombatant service, and four, 19 percent, became regular soldiers.[7]

The response among General Conference Mennonites varied considerably. In five Kansas counties, sixty-three, 31.19 percent, chose the absolutist stance; 126, 62.37 percent, agreed to serve as noncombatants; and thirteen, 6.44 percent, went to war as "regulars." [8] Members of the Central Conference with congregations mainly in Illinois, whose background was a progressive kind of Amish and which later joined the General Conference, were much more willing to serve. Of the seventy men who were drafted only five, fewer than 7 percent, took the absolutist stand; twenty-seven, about 38 percent, agreed to become noncombatants; and thirty-eight, more than 54 percent, became combatants.[9]

Two other interesting examples of General Conference response to the draft are the Alexanderwohl, Kansas, and Berne, Indiana, Mennonite congregations. Of the former twenty-six, about 33 percent, chose absolutism; twelve, about 47 percent, became noncombatants; and two, or about 4 percent, took up regular service.[10] The remaining four left for Canada. Of the Berne, Indiana, GC congregation fifty-four men were drafted of whom perhaps seven, about 18 percent, refused both combatancy and noncombatancy; forty-one, 74 percent, became noncombatants; and six, about 11 percent, were regulars.[11]

Among the Mennonite Brethren, many were willing to serve as noncombatants. Of forty MB men in five Kansas counties twenty, 50 percent, served as noncombatants; but of the remaining twenty none served as regular soldiers. Of a total of 193 MB draftees across the U.S., twenty-four served as combatants.[12]

Of the Krimmer Mennonite Brethren in Kansas, fourteen of the fifteen drafted took the absolutist stand. However, nationwide 27 percent of KMB men served as noncombatants.[13] Perhaps a few Amishmen and Hutterites served as noncombatants; a few of the Amish (probably not yet church members) even served as regular soldiers.[14]

On the basis of the above-cited statistics, is it possible to compose a general Mennonite response to military conscription in World War I? Guy Hershberger concluded that 65 percent took the absolutist position, 32 percent agreed to perform noncombatant work, and only 3 percent were willing to serve as regulars.[15] J. S. Hartzler seemed to agree, writing that only "a very few, indeed, took regular service."[16] However, one is inclined to conclude that fewer men accepted noncombatant and more of them accepted regular military service than such writers thought. The number of those choosing regular service may have been as high as 10 percent.

How do Mennonite statistics compare with those of other historic peace churches? Unfortunately, statistics for Quakers and the Church of the Brethren are even less complete than those for Mennonites. In the nineteenth century, the Quaker peace position had eroded so that in World War I perhaps no more than 350 Quakers served as absolute conscientious objectors compared to some 2,300 who accepted full military service. Probably about 600 Quakers were noncombatants.[17]

In the Church of the Brethren, noncombatant service was a very acceptable option; of a total of 135 Brethren draftees, 119 chose that alternative. Apparently some Brethren ministers even pressured young men to serve as noncombatants or combatants.[18] One member of the Church of the Brethren was so unhappy with the compromising position of his church that he requested Loucks to help and advise him. If drafted, he did not want to serve as a noncombatant.[19]

Thus, in comparison with the other two main historic peace churches, Mennonites maintained their position well. Perhaps with more preparation, education, and organization they might have done even better.

Notes

Foreword
1. For a summary of the themes and literature on the Progressive era, see Arthur S. Link and Richard L. McCormick, *Progressivism* (Arlington Heights, Ill.: Harlan David-son, 1983). An essay by Allen F. Davis, "The Flowering of Progressivism," appeared first in *American Quarterly* (Fall 1967), 516-533, and was reprinted in *The Impact of World War I*, ed. by Arthur S. Link (New York: Harper & Row, 1969). The meaning of the war for American democracy is insightfully explained by Ronald Schaffer, *America in the Great War: The Rise of the War Welfare State* (New York: Oxford University Press, 1991). The authoritative work on military conscription in World War I is John Whiteclay Chambers II, *To Raise an Army: The Draft Comes to Modern America* (New York: The Free Press, 1987).
2. For the story of Mennonites in American society, see the three volumes of the Mennonite Experience in America Series, published by Herald Press, Scottdale, Pa.: Richard K. MacMaster, *Land, Piety, Peoplehood: The Establishment of Mennonite Communities in America 1683-1790* (1985); Theron F. Schlabach, *Peace, Faith, Nation: Mennonites and Amish in Nineteenth-Century America* (1988); and James C. Juhnke, *Vision, Doctrine, War: Mennonite Identity and Organization in America 1890-1930* (1989). A fourth volume by Paul Toews is forthcoming.

CHAPTER 1: The Mennonite Peace Witness Prior to 1917
1. The literature on early Anabaptism is rather extensive. Some good references are: C. Henry Smith, *Smith's Story of the Mennonites*, 5th ed., rev. and ed. by Cornelius Krahn (Newton, Kan., 1981), chap. 1; George H. Williams, *The Radical Reformation* (Philadelphia, Pa., 1962); Robert Friedmann, *The Theology of Anabaptism* (Scottdale, Pa., 1973); Franklin H. Littell, *The Anabaptist View of the Church* (Boston, 1958); Walter Klaassen, *Anabaptism: Neither Catholic nor Protestant* (Waterloo, Ont., 1973).
2. Smith, *Smith's Story of the Mennonites*, 283ff.
3. Ibid., passim.
4. U.S. Dept. of Commerce, Bureau of the Census, *Religious Bodies, 1916* (Washington, D.C., 1919), 178-79, 418.
5. On the General Conference Mennonites see Samuel Floyd Pannabecker, *Open Doors: The History of the General Conference Mennonite Church* (Newton, Kan., 1975).
6. On the Amish Mennonites see Paton Yoder, *Tradition and Transition: Amish Mennonites and Old Order Amish, 1800-1900* (Scottdale, Pa., 1991).
7. On the Mennonite Brethren Church see: John A. Toews, *A History of the Mennonite Brethren Church: Pilgrims and Pioneers* (Fresno, Calif., 1975); and A. H. Unruh, *Die Geschichte der Mennoniten-Brüdergemeinde, 1860-1954* (Hillsboro, Kan., 1954). On the Mennonite Brethren in Christ see: J. A. Huffman, *History of the Mennonite Brethren in Christ Church* (North Carlisle, Ohio, 1920), and *ME* III, 603.
8. On the Hutterites see A. J. F. Zieglschmid, *Das Klein-Geschichtsbuch der*

Hutterischen Brüder (Philadelphia, 1947). On the Brethren in Christ see Carlton O. Wittlinger, *Quest for Piety and Obedience: The Story of the Brethren in Christ* (Nappanee, Ind., 1978).

9. For more details on Mennonites and the outside world see: Theron F. Schlabach, *Peace, Faith, Nation: Mennonites and Amish in Nineteenth-Century America* (vol. II of the Mennonite Experience in America Series; Scottdale, Pa., 1988), passim; James C. Juhnke, *Vision, Doctrine, War: Mennonite Identity and Organization in America, 1890-1930* (vol. III of same series; Scottdale, Pa., 1989), passim; and James C. Juhnke, *A People of Mission: A History of General Conference Overseas Missions* (Newton, Kan., 1979). The literature on the Progressive movement is voluminous. For one good interpretative account, see Arthur S. Link and Richard L. McCormick, *Progressivism* (Arlington Heights, Ill., 1983).

10. Willard H. Smith, *Mennonites in Illinois* (Scottdale, Pa., 1983), 463; *Echoes: A Book Containing the Report of the Addresses Delivered at the First All-Mennonite Convention in America Assembled at Berne, Indiana, August, 19-20, 1913* (Hillsboro, Kan., n.d.).

11. Richard K. McMaster, *Land, Piety, Peoplehood: The Establishment of Mennonite Communities in America, 1683-1790* (vol. I of the Mennonite Experience in America Series; Scottdale, Pa., 1985), chap. 9; Richard K. McMaster, Samuel L. Horst, and Robert F. Ulle, *Conscience in Crisis: Mennonites and Other Peace Churches in America, 1739-1789. Interpretation and Documents* (Scottdale, Pa., 1979).

12. Schlabach, *Peace, Faith, Nation*, chap. 7; Samuel Horst, *Mennonites in the Confederacy: A Study in Civil War Pacifism* (Scottdale, Pa., 1967); Guy F. Hershberger, "Mennonites in the Civil War," *MQR* 38 (July 1944):131-144.

13. ([Ephrata, Pa.?], 1804).

14. (Winchester, Pa., 1837).

15. (Chicago, 1863).

16. (Chicago, 1863).

17. (Lancaster, Pa., 1864).

18. Ira S. Johns, J. S. Hartzler, and Amos O. Hostetler, comps., *Minutes of the Indiana-Michigan Conference, 1864-1929* (Scottdale, Pa., n.d.).

19. Among the Mennonite periodicals studied are *The Mennonite, Gospel Herald, The Christian Evangel, Herald of Truth, Messenger of Truth, Gospel Witness,* and *Gospel Banner.*

20. (Elkhart, Ind., 1898).

21. (Dayton, Ohio, 1894).

22. (Lancaster, Pa., 1886).

23. ([Lancaster, Pa.], 1888).

24. (Carthage, Mo., [1891]).

25. *TM,* June and July, 1895. In 1934 this essay was reprinted at Newton, Kan.

26. James C. Juhnke, "Kansas Mennonites During the Spanish-American War" *ML* 26 (Apr. 1971):70-71.

27. Schlabach, *Peace, Faith, Nation*, 317.

28. Juhnke, "Kansas Mennonites . . . Spanish-American War," 71. See also *TM*, Dec. 20, 1906.

29. *Echoes*, 15-16, 78-79.

30. On the diplomatic background see Thomas A. Bailey, *The Diplomatic History of the American People* (10th ed.; Englewood Cliffs, N.J., 1980), chaps. 38 and 39.

31. *GH,* Aug. 13, 1914. See also the issue of Sept. 14, 1916.

32. Ibid., May 20 and June 24, 1915.

33. *TM,* Aug. 6, 1914.

34. Ibid., May 13, 1915.

35. Ibid., Mar. 30, 1916.

36. Gregory J. Stuckey, "Fighting Against War: The Mennonite *Vorwaerts* from 1914 to 1919, *Kansas Historical Quarterly* 38 (Sum. 1972):169-86.

37. James C. Juhnke, *A People of Two Kingdoms: The Political Acculturation of the Kansas Mennonites* (Newton, Kan., 1975), 87-88.

38. See for instance *TM*, July 22, 1915, Sept. 14, 1916; *GH*, Sept. 9 and 16, 1915, Jan. 6, June 22, Aug. 17, and Nov. 23, 1916; *The Christian Evangel*, Jan. 1916.

39. Urbane Peachey, ed., *Mennonite Statements on Peace and Social Concerns, 1900-1978* (Akron, Pa., 1980), 166.

40. Ibid., 39-40.

41. *The Statutes at Large of the United States of America* (Washington, D.C., 1903), XXXII:775; *The Statutes at Large of the United States of America* (Washington, D.C., 1917), XXXIX:197.

42. U.S. Congress. House Committee on Military Affairs, *To Increase the Efficiency of the Military Establishment of the United States: Hearings Before the Committee on Military Affairs February 3, 9, 10, 11, 1916* (Washington, D.C., 1916), 14ff., 117, 147.

43. Peachey, *Mennonite Statements*, 39-40; Henry W. Lohrenz papers, CMBS.

44. Interview with Christian L. Graber, 28, SOHC.

45. Isaac M. Baer, "A CO in Camp Meade During World War I" (unpublished paper, 1981), 2-3, copy kindly provided by author, Mishakawa, Ind.

46. Mary S. Sprunger, ed., *Sourcebook: Oral History Interviews with World War One Conscientious Objectors* (Akron, Pa., 1985), 196.

47. Susan Krehbiel Ringleman to Henry Krehbiel, Sept. 2, 1918, Henry Krehbiel papers, microfilm, MLA.

48. *TM*, Dec. 6, 1917 and Apr. 18, 1918.

49. David C. Peterson, "Children of Freedom or Children of Menno? The Oregon Mennonite Church in Two World Wars" (M.A. thesis, University of Oregon, 1981), 18-19.

CHAPTER 2: The Initial Response to U.S. Involvement in the War, 1917

1. John W. Chambers, *To Raise an Army: The Draft Comes to Modern America* (New York, 1987), 105, 138; David M. Kennedy, *Over There: The First World War and American Society* (New York, 1980), 17-18.

2. Chambers, *To Raise an Army*, 131-135, 153-161.

3. U.S. Congress, House of Representatives, *Selective Service Act: Hearings Before the Committee on Military Affairs . . . April 7, 14, and 17, 1917* (Washington, D.C., 1918), 238ff.; U.S. Congress, Senate, Committee on Military Affairs, *Hearings Before the Committee on Military Affairs . . . on S 1871: A Bill to Authorize the President to Increase Temporarily the Military Establishment of the United States* (Washington, D.C., 1917), 20-24.

4. General Conference Mennonite Church, Western District Conference (hereafter GC Western Dist. Conf.), "Minutes, 1906-1917," MLA.

5. Jacob Klaassen, "Memories and Notations About My Life" (unpub. paper, n.d.), copy kindly provided by Mrs. Esther C. Bergen, Winnipeg, Man.

6. "Minutes of the Exemption Committee of the Western District General Conference Mennonite Church," MLA; on Peter Jansen see *ME* III:92; on Kratz see *ME* III:233.

7. Richert to Unruh, n.d. and to President Woodrow Wilson, Apr. 30, 1917, f. 89, box 16, H. P. Richert coll., MLA; records of Selective Service Committee, RG 163, NA, copies in MLA.

8. Ramseyer to Frank A. Nimrocks, Apr. 30, 1917, Ramseyer papers, University of Iowa Libraries, Iowa City. On Ramseyer, see U.S. Congress, Joint Committee on Printing, *Biographical Directory of the American Congress, 1774-1976* (Washington, D.C., 1971), 1583.

9. On Welty, see U.S. Congress, *Biographical Directory*, 1900.

10. Ibid., 1033-1034; see bishops of Lancaster Conference to Griest, Mar. 29, 1917, box 47, GHR.

11. Petition to Congress, Apr. 20, 1917, Lohrenz papers, CMBS—Fresno. For other Mennonite petitions, see House Military Affairs Committee records, RG 233, NA, copies in MLA; GC Western Dist. Conf., "Minutes, 1906-1917," MLA. President Kliewer was mistaken; Grant never made such a promise.

12. *Congressional Record* (Washington, D.C., 1917), LV:1502ff.

13. Ibid., 1610ff.

14. Ibid., 1474ff.

15. Ibid., 1476-77, 1610ff.

16. *The Statutes at Large of the United States* (Washington, D.C., 1919), XL:76-78, 955.

17. *Der Herold*, May 24, 1917, cited in James C. Juhnke, *A People of Two Kingdoms: The Political Acculturation of the Kansas Mennonites* (Newton, Kan., 1975), 97; Rose M. Klaassen "Mennonite Diary," *Liberty*, Sept.-Oct. 1985, 10. About one year later *TM* referred to the law as a "lemon," a "disappointment," and a "snare"; *TM*, Apr. 18, 1918.

18. Chambers, *To Raise an Army*, 211.

19. *The Berne Witness*, June 6, July 13, and Oct. 1, 1917.

20. "Minutes of the Exemption Committee of the Western District General Conference Mennonite Church," MLA. The German edition was written by William J. Ewert, D. E. Harder, and H. W. Lohrenz and entitled: *An die männlichen Glieder der Gemeinde, die in dem militärpflichtigen Alter sind* [To the male members of the congregation who are of draft age] ([Hillsboro, Kan., May 18, 1917]). H. P. Krehbiel wrote an English edition entitled: *Scriptural Foundation for the Doctrine of Non-Resistance* (Newton, Kan., 1917).

21. Lohrenz to draftees, May 5, 1917, Lohrenz papers, CMBS—Fresno.

22. On this see: Gerlof D. Homan, "World War I Registrants," *Mennonite Heritage* XV (1988):1ff.; Peter R. Krause to P. H. Richert, June 7, 1917, P. H. Richert papers, MLA.

23. Interview of Dan Lapp and I. B. Good, box 44 and 47, GHR; author's questionnaire received in 1988 from Mellinger Mennonite Church, Lancaster, Pa.

24. Michael Klaasen, "Autobiography" (unpub. paper, n.d.), 13, copy kindly provided by Mrs. Esther C. Bergen, Winnipeg, Man.

25. Board of Inquiry to Newton D. Baker, July 4, 1918, Selective Service System records, RG 163, NA, copy also in MLA; Chambers, *To Raise an Army*, 185.

26. For Wilson's view of conscientious objectors, see Arthur Link, ed., *The Papers of Woodrow Wilson* (Princeton, N.J., 1983-1985), XL:179; XLIV:293; XLIX:542.

27. Ibid., XLIV:74, 221; Walter G. Kellogg, *The Conscientious Objector* (New York, 1919; reprint ed., New York, 1970), xv; Frederick Palmer, *Newton D. Baker* (New York, 1931), I:341; Donald Johnson, *The Challenge to American Freedoms: World War I and the Rise of the American Civil Liberties Union* (Lexington, Ky., 1963), 26-27.

28. Western District Conference to Woodrow Wilson, June 12, 1917, Krehbiel papers, microfilm, MLA; GC Western Dist. Conf., "Minutes," Oct. 24-25, 1917, MLA.

29. Committee report, July 2, 1917, included in the "Minutes of the Exemption Committee of the Western District General Conference Mennonite Church," MLA.

30. "Minutes of the Middle District of the General Conference Mennonite Church, Yearbooks, 1888-1942," Aug. 19-22, 1918, BCHA.

31. *Verhandlungen und Berichte der 21 Allgemeine Konferenz der Mennoniten von Nord-Amerika: Beilage zum Christliche Bundesbote*, Nov. 22, 1917, 114-19.

32. Arlyn J. Parish, *Kansas Mennonites During World War I* (Hays, Kan., 1968), 27.

33. *GH*, Aug. 9, 1917; Ruth E. Stover, "The Franconia Conference and the Conscientious Objectors of World War I," *Mennonite Research Journal* 6 (Jan. 1965):7; John C. Wenger, *History of the Mennonites of the Franconia Conference* (Telford, Pa., 1937), 65-66.

34. Wenger, *History of Franconia Conference*, 65; "Lancaster Conference Minute Books," box 47, GHR.

35. *GH*, Sept. 6, 1917.

36. It is not clear if the committee was initially given an official designation. In the archival literature it is often referred to as the War Problems Committee but later it became also known as the Military Affairs Committee. After the war it was named the Peace Problems Committee. On Loucks see: *ME* III:400-401. On the War Problems Committee, see Guy F. Hershberger, "The Origin of the Peace Problems Committee," *The Youth's Christian Companion* 18 (Aug. 1, 1937):664.

37. Interview of D. D. Miller, box 44, GHR; Committee on Information, *Information to Mennonite Registrants Concerning Their Status under the Selective Draft Law* (n.p., 1918), 6.

38. Interview of D. D. Miller, box 44, GHR.

39. Klaassen, "Mennonite Diary," 10.

40. See Allan Teichroew, "Mennonites and the Conscription Trap," *ML* 30 (Sept. 1975):10-13.

41. *TM*, Feb. 8, 1917.

CHAPTER 3: Mennonites and Patriots

1. John Higham, *Strangers in the Land: Patterns of American Nativism, 1860-1925* (2nd ed.; New Brunswick, N.J., 1988), 195.

2. Ibid., 196-199, 204ff.; H. C. Peterson and Gilbert C. Fite, *Opponents of War, 1917-1918* (Madison, Wis., 1957), 18-19; Joan M. Jensen, *The Price of Vigilance* (Chicago, 1968), 96. On the clergy, see Ray H. Abrams, *Preachers Present Arms*, rev. ed. (Scottdale, Pa., 1969); an exception was Philip Mauro, a fundamentalist lawyer and writer who visited various military training camps where he urged young men to be conscientious objectors—see John Horsch, *The Mennonite Church and Modernism* (Scottdale, Pa., 1924), 67.

3. On mob violence see: Richard Hofstadter and Michael Wallace, eds., *American Violence: A Documentary History* (New York, 1970); Peterson and Fite, *Opponents of War*, 199ff.

4. Peterson and Fite, *Opponents of War*, 20.

5. Ibid., 17, 215

6. Higham, *Strangers in the Land*, 207, 216.

7. Frieda Pankratz Suderman, *You Just Can't Do That Anymore* ([Hillsboro, Kan.], 1977), 160.

8. *TM*, Apr. 5, 1917.

9. J. S. Hartzler to Jason O. Miller, Sept. 20, 1918, f. 2, box 2, PPC.

10. See for instance *GH*, Apr. 12; May 17, 24, 31; Oct. 11, 1917; and July 25, 1918; *TM*, May 3, Aug. 30, and Sept. 13, 1917; Feb. 14, Mar. 2, and Apr. 18, 1918; *The Weekly Budget*, Feb. 27, 1918; *Messenger of Truth*, Feb. 26, 1918.

11. *TM*, Sept. 26, 1918.

12. *The Berne Witness*, June 8, 1917; see also various 1918 issues of the same paper.

13. See *Der Herold*: Apr. 5, Oct. 11, 1917; Apr. 18, 1918.

14. Author's questionnaire received in 1988 from Germantown Mennonite Church, Philadelphia.

15. Edgar Schowalter to author, Aug. 22, 1987; Suderman, *You Just Can't Do That Anymore*, 160.

16. See various issues of *The Witmarsum*, especially Dec. 8, 1917.

17. On the "progressives" at Bethel College, see especially James C. Juhnke, "The Daniel Experience: Bethel's First Bible Crisis, *ML* 44 (Sept. 1989):20-25. On Burkhard's speech, see *Newton (Evening) Kansas Republican*, Sept. 20, 1918.

18. File 29159, reel 371, FBI records , RG 65, NA.

19. On these two churches, see *ME* III:168, and IV:900.

20. See various issues of the *The Pastor's Assistance*, especially Aug. 1917, and Apr., May, June, Aug., and Dec. 1918, copies kindly provided by the Wayland Mennonite Church; *Wayland News*, Nov. 14, 1918; John Neufeld to author, Sept. 1987. For more on the issue of Mennonite patriotism in World War I, see Susan Schultz Huxman, "In the World, But Not of It. Mennonite Rhetoric in World War I As an Enactment of a Paradox" (Ph.D. dissertation, University of Kansas, 1987), passim.

21. On anti-German sentiment, see Frederick C. Luebke, *Bonds of Loyalty: German-Americans and World War I* (De Kalb., Ill., 1974).

22. Author's questionnaire received in 1988 from First Mennonite Church of Christian, Moundridge, Kansas.

23. LaVernae Dick, "Early Mennonites in Oregon" (M.A. thesis, Oregon College of Education, 1972), 64.

24. Eldon B. Harder to author, Aug. 13, 1987.

25. *The Daily Pantagraph* [Bloomington, Ill.], July 17, 1918.

26. James A. Ray to John S. Foth, Apr. 1, 1918, copy kindly provided by Mrs. Velda Duerksen, Goessel, Kan.

27. Peter J. Wedel, *The Story of Bethel College,* ed. Edmund G. Kaufman (North Newton, Kan., 1954), 236-237; J. W. Kliewer, *Memoirs* (North Newton, Kan., 1943), 92-93; author's questionnaire received in 1988 from First Mennonite Church, Newton, Kan.

28. C. G. Wiens to Dept. of Justice, Sept. 14, 1917, Dept. of Justice records, RG 60, NA, copy also in MLA.

29. For complaints against the *Vorwärts,* see Gregory J. Stucky, "Fighting Against the War: The Mennonite *Vorwaerts* from 1914 to 1940" *Kansas Historical Quarterly* 38 (Sum. 1972):181-182; Solicitor W. H. Lamar to Hillsboro Postmaster, Dec. 6, 1917, Mar. 21, 1918, and other materials in U.S. Post Office Dept.'s Solicitor's Office records, RG 28, NA, copies in MLA.

30. Alan Teichroew has collected much material on Edward Krehbiel and has generously assisted the author in obtaining information on him. On Krehbiel's work with and dismissal from The Inquiry, see Lawrence E. Gelfand, *The Inquiry: American Preparations for Peace, 1917-1919* (New York, 1963), 53-57, 192, 306, 337.

31. LaVernae J. Dick, "A Noose for the Minister," *TM,* Apr. 21, 1964; Rufus M. Franz, "It Happened in Montana," *ML* 7 (Oct. 1952):181-184; Bethlehem Mennonite Church, Historical Committee, *75th Anniversary: Bethlehem Mennonite Church, 1910-1985* (n.p., [1985]), 4.

32. On anti-German sentiment in Oklahoma, see: Edeltraut L. Bilger, "The German-Americans in Oklahoma During World War I As Seen Through Three German-language Newspapers" (M.A. thesis, Oklahoma State University, 1976); Douglas Hale, *The Germans from Russia in Oklahoma* (Norman, Okla., 1980); and Wilma McKee, ed., *Growing Faith: General Conference Mennonites in Oklahoma* (Newton, Kan., 1988), 76-78, and 146ff. On the Mennonites in northeastern Oklahoma, see: Ruth Voth, "History of the Inola M. B. Church" (unpub. paper, 1986-1987), 1-2, copy kindly provided by Orlando Harms, Hillsboro, Kan.; John F. Harms, *Die Geschichte der Mennoniten Brüdergemeinde, 1860-1954* (Hillsboro, Kan., 1955), 183-184; *ME,* II:146. Information on the early beginning of the Amish settlement was kindly provided by letter by Bishop Levi M. Yoder, of Inola, Okla, Mar. 22, 1990.

33. *Mayes County Republican,* Sept. 20, 1917, Feb. 21, Mar. 7, and Apr. 25, 1918; *The Inola Register,* Apr. 4 and 11, 1918.

34. John J. Voth to author, Feb. 17, 1987 and Earl F. Cater to author, Feb. 4, 1987; *Zionsbote,* July 24, 1918.

35. Interview with Bender, and Bender, "War Experiences," box 44, GHR; Justus G. Holsinger, *Upon This Rock: Remembering Together the 75-Year Story of the Hesston Mennonite Church* (n.p., [1984]), 22.

36. Interview with Simon Gingerich, tape 28, SOHC; Stone to ?, n.d. and to ?, Mar. 28, 1918, file 10902, Military Intelligence Division of the War Dept., War Dept. General Staff records, RG 165, NA. Sanford Yoder to D. D. Miller, Mar. 18, 1918; Gingerich to L. O. King, Feb. 22, 1918; f. 7, box 13, Sanford Yoder papers, AMC. S. C. Yoder, "Reminiscences," box 44, GHR; *Burlington Hawkeye Gazette,* Feb. 19, 1918; *The Wayland News,* May 16, 1918.

37. Melvin Gingerich, "Incidents That Took Place in the Mennonite Community of Wayland, Iowa, During World War One as Experienced by Simon Gingerich Who Was the Bishop of Sugar Creek Mennonite Church at That Time," f. 25, box 15, S. C. Yoder papers, AMC.

38. Two letters to the author from local Mennonites who probably prefer to remain anonymous; Orlando Harms, Hillsboro, Kansas, Mar. 12, 1988; FBI report, 178293, rolls 573 and 577, FBI records, RG 65, NA; *Daily Oklahoman,* Apr. 20 and 22, 1918.

39. Ibid.

40. P. C. Hiebert "Memoirs," CMBS—Hillsboro, 41; Ernest G. Claassen to author Aug. 18, 1987; Margaret Entz, "War Bond Drives and the Kansas Mennonite Reponse," *ML* 30 (Sept. 1975):8.

41. Orlando Harms to author, June 6, 1988.

42. Lahla Seltzer to author, July 13, 1987; author's interview with D. Paul Miller, Normal, Illinois, July 1987; Marion Bontrager, "Sell 'em, Sell 'em," *GH*, Oct. 20, 1981.

43. *The Times Democrat*, June 19, 1918.

44. Author's questionnaire received in 1988 from Bethel College Mennonite Church, North Newton, Kansas; Henry A. Fast, "The Witness of Our Congregation. Over 75 Years" (unpub. paper, n.d.), 7, MLA.

45. Rachel Waltner Goossen, *Meetingplace: A History of the Mennonite Church of Normal* (Normal, Ill., 1987), 19; interview with John H. Miller, tape 119, SOHC.

46. *Urbana* [Ohio] *Citizen*, Mar. 19, 21, 27, 28, and 29, 1918.

47. Ibid., May 11, 18, 20, and 30, June 3 and 17, 1918.

48. Ibid., Mar. 27, 28, 1918.

49. Ibid., May 9, 1918. The Mennonite Children's Home in West Liberty canceled its agreement with the local schoolboard over the issue of flag saluting and decided to start its own school; L. L. Swartzendruber, *The Child: A History of the Mennonite Orphans' Home, West Liberty, Ohio* (Scottdale, Pa., 1931), 167-168.

50. File 14, Selective Service System records, RG 163, NA, copy also in MLA.

51. *The New York Times*, July 30, 1917.

52. See various draft board responses in file 14 (note 52).

53. Undated newspaper clipping from *The Sentinel*.

54. File 29159, roll 371, FBI records, RG 65, NA.

55. Correspondnce and reports in files 99-41 and 10902-94, Bureau of the Public Debt records, RG 53, NA; *The Daily Pantagraph*, July 12, 1918. On Christian Egle, see *ME* II:163.

56. Boxes 44 and 45, PPC; S. H. Miller to Loucks, Aug. 8, 1918, f. 11, box 1, PPC; File 29159, roll 371, RG 65, NA; *MHB* 33 (July 1972):7-8.

57. Wertz to Attorney General, Aug. 20, 1918, and other pertinent correspondence in file 194642, Dept. of Justice records, RG 60, NA, copies in MLA; Sanford C. Yoder to Loucks, Feb. 9, 1918, f. 10, box 13, S. C. Yoder papers, AMC.

58. *Urbana* (Ohio) *Citizen*, May 9, 13, 17, 22, and 28; Oct. 18, 1918; file OG 241390, FBI records, RG 65, NA; indictment, grand jury, Nov. 27, 1918, U.S. District Courts of the Southern District of Ohio records, RG 21, NA; file 193421-2, Dept. of Justice records, RG 60, NA.

59. Gerlof D. Homan, "The Burning of the Mennonite Church, Fairview, Michigan, in 1918," *MQR* 64 (Apr. 1990):104.

60. Ibid., 105.

61. Ibid., 105-107.

62. Ibid., 108-112.

63. Bontrager, "Sell'em, Sell'em," 778.

64. W. Churchill report, June 3, 1918, file 10902-18; and G. P. Perkins report, Aug. 12, 1918, file 10902-67, Bureau of the Public Debt records, RG 53, NA. See also Allan Teichroew, ed., "Military Surveillance of Mennonites in World War I," *MQR* 53 (Apr. 1979):100-101.

65. Memos by Captain T. A. Christen, Sept. 6 and 7, 1917, file 10902-18, War Dept. and Special Staffs records, RG 165, NA.

66. Krehbiel papers, microfilm, MLA.

67. Various isues of *TM*, esp. Apr. 18, Aug. 18, 1918.

68. *GH*, Apr. 11, 1918.

69. *Christian Evangel*, Jan. 1918.

70. [Hillsboro, Kan., 1917]. For a more detailed account of Mennonite efforts to defend themselves, see Susan Huxman Schultz, "In the World, But Not of It," chaps. 5-7.

71. File 49C36F, Minnesota Supreme Court, Minnesota Historical Society, St. Paul, Minn.

CHAPTER 4: Render unto Caesar the Things That Are Caesar's?
1. *Verhandlungen und Berichte der 21 Allgemeinen Konferenz der Mennoniten von Nord-Amerika: Beilage zum Christlicher Bundesbote,* November 22, 1917, 106; *TM*, Apr. 18, 1918.
2. *TM*, Apr. 18, 1918.
3. Susan Krehbiel Ringelman to Krehbiel, Sept. 20, 1918, Krehbiel papers, microfilm, MLA.
4. *GH*, Nov. 22, 1917.
5. D. U. Weld to Aaron Dick, May 20 and A. A. Penner to D. U. Weld, June 3, 1918, records Minnesota Public Safety Committee, Minnesota State Archives, St. Paul, Minnesota.
6. *Garden City Views*, May 23, 1918.
7. A. J. Hartzler to J. S. Hartzler, July 11, 1918; Sarah Hershberger to ?, Aug. 24, 1918; f. 3, box 2, PPC. Author's questionnaire received in 1988 from Sycamore Grove Mennonite Church, Garden City, Mo.; *Cass County Democrat*, June 6, 1918; Paul Erb, *South Central Frontiers: A History of the South Central Mennonite Conference* (Scottdale, Pa., 1974), 100. Most likely another local Mennonite bishop, John J. Hartzler, was also briefly imprisoned.
8. Samuel E. Allgyer, "War Experiences," and interview with Allgyer, boxes 44 and 47, GHR.
9. Gerlof D. Homan, "Niles M. Slabaugh's Ordeal in 1918," *MHB* 50 (Oct. 1989):4-5.
10. Ibid., 5.
11. Charles Gilbert, *American Financing of World War I* (Westport, Conn., 1970), 139; Nathaniel R. Whitney, *The Sale of War Bonds in Iowa* (Iowa City, 1923), 14ff., 29ff.
12. Whitney, *Sale of War Bonds*, 124ff.; Harvey County War Council to Krehbiel, Dec. 7, 1918. Krehbiel papers, microfilm, MLA.
13. Harvey County War Council to Krehbiel, Dec. 7, 1918, Krehbiel papers, microfilm, MLA; three vice-presidents of this War Council—Regier, Vogt, and Goerz—had "Mennonite" names.
14. *The Inola Register*, Apr. 4, 1918.
15. Margaret Entz, "Free to Buy: American World War I Financing and the Mennonite Response" (research paper, Bethel College, 1975; in MLA), 6-7.
16. Gilbert, *American Financing War*, 163-168.
17. See *ME* II:421.
18. N. van der Zijp, *Geschiedenis der Doopsgezinden in Nederland* (Enkhuizen, The Neth., 1952), 145-147. For the Mennonite experience in the Russian empire, see: Lawrence Klippenstein, "Mennonite Pacifism and State Service in Russia: A Case Study in Church-State Relations, 1789-1936" (Ph.D. dissertation, University of Minnesota, 1984), passim: and James Urry and Lawrence Klippenstein, "Mennonites and the Crimean War," *Journal of Mennonite Studies* 7 (1989):9-32.
19. Gilbert, *American Financing*, 75ff.
20. *TM*, Oct. 10, 1918.
21. On President Mosiman, see below p. 129. On the *Vorwärts*, see Gregory J. Stucky, "Fighting Against the War: The Mennonite *Vorwaerts* from 1914 to 1919," *Kansas Historical Quarterly* 38 (Sum. 1972):181-82.
22. J. E. Hartzler to R. Roth, Apr. 25, 1918, f. 10, box 3, J. E. Hartzler papers, AMC; J. S. Hartzler to D. W. Miller, Aug. 23, 1918, f. 3, box 2, PPC; S. C. Yoder to I. G. Shaver, June 11, 1917, f. 6, box 13, S. C. Yoder papers, AMC; *GH*, Aug. 29, 1918.
23. Aaron Loucks to Brethren, Apr. 4, 22, 1918, f. 7, box 13, S. C. Yoder papers, AMC.
24. LaVernae Dick, "Early Mennonites in Oregon" (M.A. thesis, Oregon College of Education, 1972), 61-62.

25. David W. Brubaker, "Suppression of the German Culture During World War One" (research paper, Bethel College, Apr. 1983; in MLA), 17.

26. J. Lamar and Lois Ann Mast, *As Long as Wood Grows and Water Flows: A History of the Conestoga Mennonite Church* (Pottstown, Pa., 1982), 132-133.

27. *Decatur Daily Democrat*, Apr. 11, 1918.

28. *Elkhart Truth*, June 27, 1918, copy in box 47, GHR.

29. Author's questionnaire received in 1988 from Fairview Mennonite Church, Milford, Nebraska.

30. Harold E. Huber, *With Eyes of Faith: A History of Greenwood Mennonite Church, Greenwood, Delaware, 1914-1974* (Greenwood, 1974), 70.

31. Interview with Charles Diener, 40, SOHC; Entz, "Free To Buy," 23-24; James J. Juhnke, "Mob Violence and Kansas Mennonites in 1918," *Kansas Historical Quarterly* 43 (Aug. 1977): 337-340; author's questionnaire received in 1988 from West Liberty Mennonite Church, Windom Kansas; Ida M. Kauffman to author, n.d. On other mob violence in Kansas, see Dale W. Fields, "My Father Was a Hero," *TM*, July 14, 1988.

32. Mary Sprunger, ed., *Sourcebook: Oral History Interviews with World War One Conscientious Objectors* (Akron, Pa., 1986), 205-208; Juhnke, "Mob Violence," 343-345; FBI report OG 334281, roll 757, FBI records, RG 65, NA; Peter J. P. Schrag to author, Sept. 2, 1987.

33. Information derived from questionnaires received in 1988 from various Mennonite congregations; *Goshen* Indiana *Democrat*, Sept. 3, 1918; Willard H. Smith, *Mennonites in Illinois* (Scottdale, Pa., 1983), 356.

34. James C. Juhnke, *A People of Two Kingdoms: The Political Acculturation of the Kansas Mennonites* (Newton, Kan., 1975), 106, 107; Edward Yoder, *Edward, Pilgrimage of a Mind: The Journal of Edward Yoder, 1931-1945*, ed. Ida Yoder (Wadsworth, Ohio, 1985), 22-23.

35. Luanne Habegger, "The Berne, Indiana, Mennonites During World War I" (unpublished research paper, 1976), 5-6, 10, copy kindly provided by Berne Mennonite Church, Berne, Ind.

36. *The Witmarsum*, Apr. 20, 1918.

37. Ibid., Apr. 27, 1918.

38. *Newton (Evening) Kansas Republican*, Apr. 2, Nov. 2, 1918; Peter J. Wedel, *The Story of Bethel College*, E. G. Kaufman, ed. (N. Newton, Kan., 1954), 240; *Bethel College Monthly*, June 15, 1918. Even at Goshen College students bought Thrift Stamps; see *Goshen News Times*, Aug. 24, 1918.

39. *The Pastor's Assistant*, Mar., Apr., Oct. 1918.

40. Entz, "Free To Buy," 20.

41. Gertrude Young, "The Mennonites in South Dakota," *South Dakota Historical Collection* 10 (1920):498; author's questionnaire received in 1988 from Salem Mennonite Church, Freeman, South Dakota.

42. David C. Peterson, "Children of Freedom or Children of Menno? The Oregon Mennonite Church in Two World Wars" (M.A. thesis, University of Oregon, 1981), 32.

43. Interview with Isaac B. Good, box 47, GHR.

44. Millard Osborne to author, Oct. 15, 1987.

45. Undated and unidentified newspaper clippings kindly sent to author by Paul F. Goossen.

46. "Agreement W. L. Crooks . . . and Representatives of the Mennonite Church" May 1918, f. 1, box 6, Elias Frey correspondence, PPC; Aaron Loucks? to S.C. Yoder, Oct. 8, 1918, f. 1, box 3, PPC; J. S. Hartzler to D. J. Johns, Aug. 31, 1918, f. 4, box 2, PPC; J. C. Frey to Loucks, June 27, 1918, f. 2, box 1, PPC; interview with Samuel E. Allgyer, box 47, GHR. Loucks to Crooks, June 7, 1918; W.L. Crooks report, June 10, 1918; Crooks to J. A. Huffman, Aug. 27, 1918; Edwin S. Wertz to Attorney General, Sept. 17, 1918; file 194642, Dept. of Justice records, RG 60, NA, copies in MLA. Lancaster Conference, "Minute Book," GHR; *GH*, June 27, 1918.

47. J. S. Hartzler to D. J. Johns, Aug. 31, 1918, f. 4, box 2, PPC.

48. Wertz to Attorney General, Sept. 17, 1918, and enclosures, file 194642, Dept. of Justice records, RG 60, NA, copies in MLA.

49. John C. Wenger, *History of the Mennonites of the Franconia Conference* (Telford, Pa., 1937), 75.

50. See: correspondence in f. 32, box 15, records Nebraska State Council of Defense records, RG 23, Nebraska State Historical Society, Lincoln, Nebraska; Robert N. Manley, "The Nebraska State Council of Defense . . . Loyalty Programs and Policies During World War I" (M.A. thesis, University of Nebraska, 1959), 89-93; "Nebraska Amish Mennonites and War Bonds in World War I, *MHB* 30 (Jan. 1969):4-5.

51. Smith, *Mennonites in Illinois*, 357.

52. Marion Bontrager "Sell 'em, Sell 'em," *GH*, Oct. 20, 1981; Lahla Seltzer to author, July 13, 1987.

53. See John D. Unruh, "The Hutterites During World War I," *ML*, 26 (July 1969):130-137.

54. Ibid.; Amos E. Ayres? to American Protection League, Aug. 24, 1918, file 99-23, War Dept. and Special Staffs records, RG 165, NA, copies in MLA; A. M. Allen to Henry C. Wallace, June 24, 1918, and copy of announcement of sale of Hutterite cattle, box 27, general correspondence, Dept. of the Treasury records, RG 56, NA, copies in MLA; Young, "Mennonites in South Dakota," 498; Donald W. Grebin, "The South Dakota Council of Defense, 1917-1919" (M.A. thesis, University of South Dakota, 1967), 51; Darrell Sawyer, "Anti-German Sentiment in South Dakota During World War I," *South Dakota Historical Collections* 38 (1976):468, 506; Allan Teichroew, ed., "Military Surveillance of Mennonites in World War I," *MQR* 53 (Apr. 1979):118-119; A. J. F. Zieglschmid, *Das Klein-Geschichtsbuch der Hutterischen Brüder* (Philadelphia, Pa., 1947), 486-487.

55. A. L. Wyman to Amos E. Ayres, Aug. 21, 1918, War Dept. and Special Staffs records, RG 165, NA; statement of sale of cattle, n.d., box 27, general correspondence, U.S. Treasury Dept. records, RG 53, NA, copies in MLA.

56. Unruh, "Hutterites," 136; Zieglschmidt, *Klein-Geschichtsbuch*, 486-487.

57. David Luthy, "The Arrest of an Amish Bishop in 1918," *Family Life* (Mar., 1972), 24-27; on *The Weekly Budget*, see *ME* I:462-463.

58. B. H. Miller to Loucks, June 27, Aug. 8, 1918; Hartzler to Miller June 25, 1918, folders 2 and 11, box 1, PPC; *The Weekly Budget*, Apr. 24, 1918; *Cleveland Plain Dealer*, Aug. 6, 1918.

59. Heatwole to Hartzler, June 27, f. 5, box 4, PPC; Heatwole to ?, Mar. 8, 1919; Benner statement, July 17, 1918, U.S. vs. Rev. L. J. Heatwole, Apr. 25, 1919, files 194896-5 and 194896-6, Dept. of Justice records, RG 60, NA, copies in MLA; LaVelle Wayne Smith, "Rockingham County Nonresistance and the First World War" (M.A. thesis, Madison College, 1967), 78-88; Harry A. Brunk, *History of the Mennonites in Virginia, 1900-1960* (Verona, Va., 1972), II:456-458.

60. *Christian Evangel*, Oct. 1918.

61. Mosiman to Wilbur K. Thomas, Sept. 26, 1918, Mosiman papers, BCHC.

CHAPTER 5: "Soldiers" of Uncle Sam

1. Edward J. B. Waltner, "A CO in the First World War" (unpublished paper, 1942), 3, MLA; Jacob Waldner, "An Account of Jacob Waldner: Diary of a Conscientious Objector in World War I," Theron Schlabach, ed.; Ilse Reist and Elizabeth Bender, trans.; *MQR* 48 (Jan. 1974):78; Isaac Baer, "A CO in Camp Meade," (unpublished paper, 1981), 5, copy kindly given to author, Mishawaka, Ind.; Michael Klaasen "Autobiography" (unpublished, n.d.), 14, copy kindly given to author by Mrs. Esther Bergen, Winnipeg, Man.; Lloy A. Kniss, *I Couldn't Fight. The Story of a CO in World War I* (Scottdale, Pa., 1971), 15; interview with E. L. Frey, box 47, GHR; author's questionnaire received in 1988 from Hoffnungsau Mennonite Church, Buhler, Kan.; Balko Mennonite Brethren Church, *Triumph: 75th Anniversary, Balko Mennonite Brethren Church, 1906-1981* (n.p., [1981]), 91. The Krimmer Mennonite Brethren passed a resolution advising men not to go to camp, but apparently all of them went. James C. Juhnke, *A People of Two Kingdoms: The Political Acculturation of the Kansas Mennonites* (Newton, Kan., 1975), 97.

2. Author's questionnaire received in 1988 from Mennonite Brethren Church, Corn, Okla.; Howard B. Seitz to Benjamin S. Ebersole, Sept. 21, 1917, Benjamin S. Ebersole collection, Lancaster Mennonite Historical Society, Lancaster, Pa.

3. Payson Miller to R. L. Hartzler, Mar. 31, 1918, BCHC; Waltner, "CO," 4.

4. Interview with Jacob N. Wiens, 263, SOHC, AMC.

5. *Decatur Daily Democrat*, Sept. 20, 21, 22, 26, 1917; *The Berne Witness*, Sept. 24, 1917. Aldie A. Gerber of Orrville, Ohio, failed to entrain in Aug. 1918. He was arrested and in Feb. 1919, fined $200, and sentenced to eight to twelve months incarceration in the House of Correction in Cleveland, Ohio; case 4193, District Courts of the United States, United States District Court for the Northern District of Ohio, Eastern Division records, RG 21, NA. In Apr. 1918, Ernest Gerber of Wooster, Ohio, was arrested for urging non-compliance with draft regulations; the outcome is not known. *Urbana* (Ohio) *Citizen*, Apr. 2, 1918.

6. On Jacob C. Meyer, see "Reflections of a Conscientious Objector in World War I," *MQR* 41 (Jan. 1967):79-96.

7. Harlan F. Stone, "The Conscientious Objector," *Columbia University Quarterly* 24 (Oct. 1919):260, 262.

8. *Walter G. Kellogg, The Conscientious Objector* (New York, 1919; reprint ed., New York, 1970), 42-43, 66-69.

9. Mark A. May, "The Psychological Examinations of Conscientious Objectors, *American Journal of Psychology* 31 (Apr. 1920):151, 153; Chief Psychological Examiner to Surgeon General, May 2, 1918, file 383.2; Captain Henry Vaughan to Commanding General, 83rd Div., May 2, 1918, file 382.2; Adjutant General's Office records, RG 94, copies in MLA. Military Intelligence report, Feb. 12, 1918, file 10902-18, Dept. of War and Special Staffs records, RG 165, NA, copy in MLA; Mary Sprunger, ed., *Sourcebook: Oral History Interviews with World War One Conscientious Objectors* (Akron, Pa., 1986), 217-218.

10. Leonard Wood, "Diary," 2; Wood to Adjutant General, Sept. 7, 1918; box 114, papers of General Wood, Library of Congress, Washington, D.C., copies in MLA.

11. *GH*, Oct. 11, 1917.

12. U.S. War Department, *Statement Concerning the Treatment of Conscientious Objectors in the Army*, prepared by J. S. Easby-Smith (Washington, D.C., 1919), 37.

13. Ibid.

14. Ibid., 16.

15. Baer, "CO," 11-15; John Hege, "Camp Meade Diary," (unpublished paper, n.d.), copy kindly given by William F. McLaughlin, Harpers Ferry, Va.; Benjamin S. Ebersole "Diary," Ebersole collection, AMC; *TM*, Oct. 18, 1917; *GH*, Oct. 4, 1917; Frederick Palmer, *Newton D. Baker* (New York, 1931), 1:342. For Camp Meade brutalities, see Maurice Hess papers, in possession of Fred Benedict, Union City, Ohio.

16. Much evidence can be cited, e.g.: interview with Albert Voth, 249, SOHC; Albert Voth to his father, Henry Voth, June 11, 1918; Gaeddert to Krehbiel, Oct. 8, 1917, Krehbiel papers, microfilm, MLA; Baer, "CO, "7-8; P. C. Hiebert, "Memoirs," CMBS—Hillsboro.

17. Ezra Deter to parents, July 4, 1918, private collection of Hazel Hassan, Goshen, Indiana.

18. Christophel to J. S. Hartzler, Feb. 8, 1919, f. 4, box 4, PPC.

19. Miller to J. S. Hartzler, June 2, 1918, BCHA.

20. *GH*, Oct. 4, 1917.

21. MRF project 24.

22. Meyer, "Reflections," 81.

23. Waltner, "CO," 20.

24. MRF project 24.

25. Waltner, "CO," 12.

26. Gaeddert to Krehbiel, Nov. 21, 1917, Krehbiel papers, microflim copy; Richert to J. U. Schmidt, Feb. 2, 1918, f. 87, Richert collection, MLA; interviews with Fred

Schroeder and Jacob N. Wiens, 10 and 24, SOHC; Leonard Wood to Adjutant General, Nov. 18, 1917, Adjutant General's Office records, RG 94, NA, microfilm in MLA.

27. Rose M. Klaassen, "Mennonite Diary," *Liberty* (Sept.-Oct. 1985), 10.

28. Court-Martial Record of Lee R. Swartzendruber, file 121498, Judge Advocate General records, RG 153, NA.

29. Nicholas Stoltzfus, ed., *Nonresistance Put to Test* (Aylmer, Ont., 1981), 15.

30. William Handrich, "Some of My Experiences at Camp" (unpublished paper, n.d.), copy kindly given to author by Ora Troyer, Fairview, Mich.

31. Cliff Landis, "A Soldier for Christ" (unpublished research paper, Goshen College, 1973; in AMC), 3.

32. Kellogg, *Conscientious Objector*, 133-138.

33. Many examples can be given. See: Stoltzfus, *Nonresistance*, 38; Lloy Kniss, *I Couldn't Fight: The Story of a CO in World War I* (Scottdale, Pa., 1971), 19; Ura H. Hostetler, "World War I Diary" (unpublished paper, n.d.), 1, copy kindly given to author by Mrs. Dewey Hostetler, Harper, Kan.; James Witmer, "John Witmer, A World War I Conscientious Objector," *MHB* 40 (Oct. 1963):3; author's interview with Howard Stutzman, Carlock, Ill., Feb. 1988.

34. Various examples could be given, e.g.: Stoltzfus, *Nonresistance*, 16-17; Unruh, "The Hutterites During World War I," 131-132; Edward R. Drange, *Peace Experiences of Conscientious Objectors at Camp Dodge, Iowa* (n.p., n.d.), 7.

35. Emanuel Swartzendruber, "Nonresistance Under Test" (unpublished paper, n.d.), box 47, GHR.

36. Letters by several draftees to Secretary of War, July 22, 1918, f. 8, box 13, S. C. Yoder papers, AMC; Major Percy Birdwell report, Aug. 13, 1918, file 383.2, Adjutant General's Office records, RG 94, NA, copy also in MLA.

37. Court-Martial Record of George B. Kennedy, file 121233, Judge Advocate General Records, RG 153, NA; interview with Elam R. Hernley by Rev. Robert N. Johnson, Scottdale, Pa., 1988-1989, copy kindly given to author.

38. George Miller, "Experiences in World War I COs in the Camp," in George S. Miller, *What Next?* (Kalona, Iowa, 1974), 27-28; S. C. Yoder to Hartzler, Aug. 30, 1918; Loucks to Commander of Camp Dodge, Aug. 26, 1918, folders 3, 4, box 3, PPC; interview with George S. Miller, Historical Committee Projects, World War I CO materials, f. 40, box 1, AMC.

39. J. G. Ewert to Keppel, Oct. 19, 1918, file 382.1, Adjutant's General's Office Records, RG 94, NA, copy also in MLA; Lohrenz papers, CMBS—Fresno.

40. MRF project 24.

41. Ray F. Yoder to Loucks, Aug. 24, 1918; Samuel Smeltzer to Loucks, Aug. 29, 1918; f. 3, box 2, PPC.

42. Joseph Kleinsasser to Keppel, Nov. 12, 1917, file 324.72, War Dept.'s U.S. Continental Commission, 1821-1920, Camp Funston, 1917-1920 records, RG 393, NA, copy also in MLA; Joseph Kleinsasser to Loucks, Dec. 6, 1918, f. 10, box 3, PPC; Waldner, "Diary," 77ff.; Noah Leatherman, *Diary Kept by Noah Leatherman While in Camp During World War I* (Salisbury, Pa., 1984), 7; Karl and Franziska Peter, eds. and trans., *Hutterite Conscientious Objectors and Their Treatment in the U.S. Army During World War I* (Cranford, Alta., 1982), 4ff.

43. Joseph Kleinsasser to Keppel, Mar. 28, Apr. 18, 1918, file 383.2, Adjutant General's Office records, RG 94, NA, copies in MLA.

44. Waldner, "Diary," 85-86; Leatherman, *Diary*, 21.

45. Fred Robertson, U.S. Attorney, District of Kansas to Attorney General, Feb. 27, 1918, file 186233-997; U.S. Attorney, District of Kansas to Attorney General, Feb. 5, 1920; and Attorney General to Robertson, Feb. 11, 1920, file #195216, Dept. of Justice records, RG 60, NA; U.S. vs. Hofer, Entz, and Wipf, Apr. 27, 1918, U.S. District Courts records, RG 21, Kansas City Record Branch, NA; *Kansas City Times*, Oct. 15, 1919, copies of some of these documents also in MLA.

46. Interview with George S. Miller, f. 40, box 1, Historical Committee projects,

World War I CO materials, AMC; Miller, "Experiences," 27-33; Adjutant General to Hartzler, Dec. 13, 1918, f. 11, box 3, PPC; Sprunger, *Sourcebook*, 164-165.

47. Eugene C. Brisbin report, Jan. 8, 1918, file 382.2, Adjutant General Records, RG 94, NA, copy also in MLA.

48. Kellogg, *Conscientious Objector*, 85.

49. Memo for Inspector General, Dec. 18, 1918, copy in f. 11, box 3, PPC.

50. Court-Martial Record of George B. Kennedy, file 121233, Judge Advocate General Records, RG 153, NA; interview with Hernley (note 37).

51. War Dept. to Adjutant General, Dec. 9, 1918; Jan. 3, 1919, file 383.2 and 383.4, Adjutant General's Office Records, RG 94, NA, copies in MLA.

52. Stoltzfus, *Nonresistance*, 33.

53. On Hough, see: Robert J. Hough to Inspector General, May 29, 1918, file 383.2, Adjutant General's Office Records, RG 94, NA, copy also in MLA; Stoltzfus, *Nonresistance*, 35. After the war Hough even attended CO reunions.

54. Interview with E. L. Frey, box 47, GHR. For a similar incident, see *GH*, Nov. 22, 1917, and Stoltzfus, *Nonresistance*, 68-69. See also Ernest H. Miller, "Experiences of a C.O. in World War I" (unpublished paper, n.d.), MSLA.

55. MRF project 24.

56. Interview with Jesse Hartzler, Historical Committee Projects, World War I CO materials, f. 40, box 1, AMC.

57. Interview with Elias Kleinsasser, 138, SOHC.

58. ? to Krehbiel, Nov. 3, 1917, Krehbiel papers, microfilm, MLA.

59. There is very little documentary material on the activities of this committee. It must not have met very often or have done very much. On it, see especially: Krehbiel papers, MLA; J. W. Kliewer, *Memoirs* (North Newton, Kan., 1943), 87-91.

60. On these various committees, see: Krehbiel papers, microfilm, passim and f. 16, box 3, John W. Kliewer papers, MLA; f. 7, box 13, Sanford Yoder papers, AMC; S. E. Allgyer, "War Experiences" and interview with Daniel Lapp, box 44, and interviews with S. E. Allgyer, Israel Good, and E. L. Frey, box 47, GHR.

61. See his papers at CMBS—Fresno.

62. *ME* II:275-276. The FBI spied on Ewert; see file 222182, FBI records, RG 65, NA. Especially interesting is a letter written by Dr. J. J. Entz of Hillsboro, Kan., to U.S. Representative Dudley Doolittle, June 4, 1918, in which Entz complained about Ewert's work with draftees. Entz urged that something be done to stop that propaganda, otherwise Ewert and others would be sowing the seeds of discontent. Most likely Entz was Mennonite or of Mennonite descent.

63. Krehbiel papers, microfilm, MLA; Kliewer, *Memoirs*, 87-91.

64. "Minute Book of the General Conference Mennonite Western District Executive Committee," MLA.

65. As previously indicated, its extensive records are in AMC.

66. Hartzler to J. C. Meyer, Oct. 30, 1918, f. 4, box 3, PPC; Hartzler to S. Honderich, Aug. 31, 1918, f. 4, box 2, AMC; Hartzler to L. J. Heatwole, Aug. 12, 1918, f. 1, box 2, PPC; interview with Loucks, box 44, GHR. On Loucks, see *ME* III:400-401.

67. Loucks to Krehbiel, Nov. 15, 1918, Krehbiel papers, microfilm, MLA.

68. Krehbiel to Gaeddert, Jan. 21, 1918, ibid.

69. "Minute Book Western District Exemption Committee," MLA.

70. Lohrenz papers, CMBS—Fresno; Krehbiel papers, microfilm, MLA; Committee on Information, *Information to Mennonite Registrants Concerning Their Status Under the Selective Draft Law* (n.p., Feb. 1918); *GH*, Jan. 31, 1918.

71. Yoder, "Reminiscences," and Gingerich to L. O. King, Feb. 22, 1917, box 44; Gingerich to Guy F. Hershberger, Sept. 20, 1962, box 47, GHR; Yoder to Loucks, Nov. 16, 1918 and to Major-General Plummer, Dec. 27, 1917, folders, 6, 7, 10, box 13, S. C. Yoder papers, AMC. Memo, Captain Brooks to P. Sparks, Dec. 6, 1917; Loucks to Baker, Jan. 24, 1918; Brigadier General Robert ? to Adjutant General, Feb. 1, 1918; file 383.2, Adjutant General's Office records, RG 94, NA, copies in MLA.

72. Unidentified newspaper clipping, Feb. 28, 1918; Perry Blosser to S. C. Yoder, Mar. 13, 1918, f. 13, box 3, S. C. Yoder papers, AMC. Military Intelligence Report; Stone to ? Feb. 2, 1918, and to Plummer, Mar. 4, 1918; file 10902-18, Adjutant General's Office records, RG 94, NA. Interview with Simon Gingerich, box 47, GHR; Roy Buchanan, "A Time To Say No," *Christian Living*, Sept. 1960, pp. 6-10.

73. Gingerich? to S. C. Yoder, Feb. 8, 1918; Perry Blosser to Yoder, Mar. 3, 1918; Harry Reschly to Yoder, Mar. 9, 1918; Yoder to Loucks, Mar. 15, 1918; Yoder to D. H. Bender, Mar. 18, 1918; Yoder to Perry Blosser, May 14, 1918; Yoder to S. G. Shetler, n.d.; folders 2, 3, 6, 7, box 13, AMC. S. C. Yoder, "Reminiscences," box 44, GHR; Buchanan, "Time To Say No," *Christian Living*, Sept. 1960, pp. 6-10. Various reports on Loucks's talk to the men can be found in file 10902-18, Adjutant General's Office Records, RG 94, NA, copies in MLA. Commanding General 68th Division to Adjutant General of the Army, Mar. 7, 1918, file 382.2, Adjutant General's Office records, RG 94, NA. After the war Stone left the community because he lost most of his Mennonite patients; interview with C. L. Graber, f. 5, box 73, Guy Hershberger collection, AMC.

74. Woodrow Wilson to H. C. Early, Jan. 1, 1918, reel 153, series 3, vol. 47, Wilson Papers, Manuscript Division, Library of Congress. Albert Keim of Eastern Mennonite College kindly called my attention to Early's correspondence with Wilson. Early represented the Church of the Brethren and in one of his letters referred to the president's reply. The published papers of Wilson do not refer to the letter of Jan. 1, but it was found among the unpublished materials. On Good, see interview with him, box 47, GHR.

75. *Congressional Record* (Washington, D.C., 1918), 56:passim.

76. It has been very difficult to find anything on this Committee of Nine; see Kratz to Mosiman, Apr. 5, 9, 29, Mosiman papers, BCHA.

77. Kellogg, *Conscientious Objector*, 18-21.

78. Adjutant General to all Commanding Generals, Apr. 18, 1918, file 382.3, Adjutant General's Office Records, RG 94, NA; Krehbiel papers, microfilm, MLA.

79. Keppel to Krehbiel, June 5, 1919, Krehbiel papers, microfilm, MLA. Keppel referred to the World War I hero Alvin York. York belonged to a small fundamentalist sect in eastern Tennessee. His pastor urged him to apply for conscientious objector status, but his draft board rejected him. In Camp Gordon, Georgia, a batallion commander persuaded York to become a regular soldier. In 1918 York became the greatest U.S. World War I hero. See David D. Lee, *Sergeant York: An American Hero* (Lexington, Ky., 1985).

80. Assistant U.S. Attorney General E. Moon to Attorney General, Mar. 21, 1918; U.S. Attorney General to Moon, May 2, 1918; file 191048, Dept. of Justice records, RG 60, NA, copies in MLA.

81. Henry County Council of Defense report, May 10, 1918, file 10902-18, War Dept. General and Specific Staffs records, RG 165, NA; Lafayette Young, Chairman Iowa Council of Defense to E. T. Meredith, Treasury Dept., June 5, 1918, and to M. Churchill, July 16, 1918, file 10902-18 just mentioned.

82. M. Churchill to Lafayette Young, July 10, 1918, file mentioned in n. 81; Military Intelligence report, July 3, 1918; M. Churchill to A. B. Bielaski, July 25, 1918; Keppel to Captain J. J. Kerrigan, Aug. 22, 1918; Military Intelligence report, Jan. 15, 1919, file mentioned n. 81. The report of Jan. 15, 1919, erred when it referred to the *Gospel Messenger*; it must have meant *Gospel Herald*. Keppel also wrote that the government had rejected Loucks's nomination for the "Advisory Commission of Mennonites." It is not clear what he meant by this commission unless Keppel was referring to the Mennonite membership on the advisory committee to assist the Secretary of Agriculture on farm furloughs.

83. Hartzler to Benjamin F. Hartzler, Sept. 24, 1918, f. 9, box 2, PPC.

84. See correspondence in folders 3, 7, 8, 9, box 2, and in f. 4, box 3, PPC.

85. *TM*, Apr. 18, 1918.

86. Unruh to Ben Sauer, Aug. 19, 1918, f. 2, box 1, P. H. Unruh papers, MLA.

87. *TM*, June 20, 1918.

88. *Trench Camp*, Sept. 23, 1918, copy in Krehbiel papers microfilm, MLA, and Mosiman papers, BCHA.

89. GC Western Dist. Conf. Exemption Committee to Brethren in Camp, Apr. 10, 1918, copy in f. 87, Richert papers, MLA. See also in the same folder Richert to D. D. Wipf, Apr. 24, 1918.

90. "Minute Book, Western District Exemption Committee," May 24, 1918, MLA.

91. Krehbiel to Otto Regier, Sept. 20, 1918, Krehbiel papers, microfilm, MLA.

92. Susan Krehbiel Ringelman to Krehbiel, Sept. 2, 1918; Krehbiel to Ringleman, Sept. 3, 1918; Krehbiel papers, microfilm, MLA.

93. "Minute Book Western District Conference," June 6, 1918, MLA.

94. Interview with Harry Graber, 96, SOHC.

95. "Minute Book Western District Exemption Committee," June 6, 1918, MLA.

96. Krehbiel and Richert papers, MLA.

CHAPTER 6: "Absolutists" and Soldiers

1. U.S. War Department, Statement Concerning the Treatment of *Conscientious Objectors in the Army* (Washington, D.C., 1919), 41-45. The idea of a three-man Board of Inquiry came from Felix Frankfurter, assistant to Secretary of War Baker and later chief justice of the U.S. Supreme Court; Frankfurter suggested this as early as Sept., 1917: container 132, reel 82, Frankfurter papers, Manuscript Div., Library of Congress. Allan Teichroew kindly called my attention to this Frankfurter connection.

2. Walter G. Kellogg, *The Conscientious Objector* (New York, 1919; reprint ed., 1970), 25, 111-112.

3. Ibid., v, 34, 38-41.

4. Deter to parents, Sept. 30, 1918, private collection of Hazel Hassan, Goshen, Ind. On Kellogg, see also: David Chris Peterson, "Children of Freedom or Children of Menno? The Oregon Mennonite Church in the Two World Wars" (M.A. thesis, University of Oregon, 1981), 40-41.

5. David M. Kennedy, *Over Here: The First World War and American Society* (New York, 1980), 164; Kellogg, *Conscientious Objector*, 27; Isaac M. Baer, "A CO in Camp Meade" (unpublished paper, 1981), 16-17, copy kindly given to author by Mr. Baer, Mishawaka, Ind.; John D. Roop, ed., *Christianity Versus War* (Ashland, Calif., 1949), 37-38; Peterson, "Children of Freedom," 44. Adam Mumaw, who was also interrogated by the Board of Inquiry, "marvelled" at the "fairness of their intelligence"; Mumaw, "Second Company Development Battalion" (unpublished paper, n.d.; in MSLA), 5.

6. Jonas S. Hartzler, *Mennonites in the World War: Or Nonresistance Under Test* (2nd ed.; Scottdale, Pa., 1922), 104-105; Kellogg, *Conscientious Objector*, 127; various so-called Summary Reports in file 383.2, Adjutant General's Office records, RG 94, NA, copies in MLA.

7. See: boxes 1 and 2, PPC; Kellogg, *Conscientious Objector*, 76-77.

8. Hartzler, *Mennonites*, 105-106.

9. Gerlof D. Homan, "Post-Armistice Courts-Martial of Conscientious Objectors in Camp Funston Kansas, 1918-1919," *ML*, 6 (Dec. 1989):6.

10. Interview with E. L. Frey, box 47, GHR. M. B. Brenneman to S. C. Yoder, Sept. 29, 1918; S. E. Allgyer to Yoder, Sept. 19, 1918; folders 3, 10, box 13, S. C. Yoder papers, AMC.

11. S. E. Allgyer, "War Experiences," box 44, GHR; interview with S. E. Allgyer, box 47, GHR; *West Liberty Banner*, Sept. 12, 1918; *Urbana Citizen*, Sept. 28, 1918.

12. S. C. Yoder to Loucks Sept. 4, 1918, and to Edward Z. Yoder, Oct. 12, 1918, f. 10, box 13, S. C. Yoder papers; ? to Loucks, Oct. 7, 1918, f. 1, box 3, PPC; S. C. Yoder "Reminiscences," box 44, GHR; interview with Jess Schwartzendruber, 212, SOHC. A military intelligence report of Feb. 19, 1919, charged that the episode near Kalona proved the "pigheaded, narrow, selfish, obstructive attitude of the Mennonites"; file 10902-18, Adjutant General's Office records, RG 94, NA, copy also in MLA.

13. Interview with Jess Schwartzendruber, 212, SOHC; Ezra Deter to parents, Nov. 16, 1918, private collection of Hazel Hassan, Goshen, Ind. Deter was well treated at the Adams ranch but did not like it there. On Dec. 16, 1918, he wrote, "I am still Adam's [*sic*] slave." But four days later he went home.

14. Gaedddert to Krehbiel, Aug. 31, 1918, Sept. 23, 1918, Krehbiel papers, microfilm, MLA; Simon Gingerich to Guy Hershberger, Sept. 20, 1962, f. 8, box 74, Guy F. Hershberger collection, AMC.

15. Hartzler to O. B. Gerig, Nov. 11, 1918; S. C. Yoder to Loucks, Oct. 5, 1918; Loucks to Moses Yoder, Oct. 28, 1918; folders 1, 4, box 3, PPC.

16. See above p. 53.

17. R. C. McCrea to Hartzler, Oct. 3, 1918; J. S. Hartzler to McCrea, Oct. 9, 1918; Hartzler to J. M. Kreider, Oct. 10, 1918; folders 1, 2, 3, 4, box 3, PPC. Some of this correspondence was published in *MHB* 33 (July 1972):10.

18. Commanding General of Camp Lee to Superintendent of State Central Hospital, Petersburg Va., Sept. 23, 1918, and other correspondence, file 382, Adjutant's General Office Records, RG 94, NA; Clarence S. Shank, *A Mennonite Boy's World War I Experience* (Marion, Pa., 1963), 25ff.

19. *TM*, May 9, 1918.

20. Allen B. Erb to Loucks, June 25, 1918, f. 2, box 1, PPC.

21. GC Western Dist. Conf. resolution, Aug. 9, 1918, f. 88, Richert papers, MLA; "Minute Book Western District General Conference Exemption Committee," MLA.

22. Krehbiel to Keppel, Oct. 12, 28; Nov. 12, 1918; McCrae to Krehbiel, Oct. 31, 1918; Krehbiel papers, microfilm, MLA.

23. O. B. Gerig to Hartzler, Oct. 9, 1918, f. 1, box 3, PPC.

24. Yoder to Loucks, Oct. 5, 1918, f. 10, box 13, S. C. Yoder papers, AMC.

25. War Dept. memos, Nov. 27, Dec. 2, 1918, file 383.2, Adjutant General's Office Records, RG 94, NA, copies in MLA; Krehbiel to Keppel, Jan. 1, 1919, Krehbiel papers, MLA.

26. *GH*, Nov. 22, 1917; Urbane Peachey, ed., *Mennonite Statements on Peace and Social Concerns* (Akron, Pa., 1980), 28.

27. There is much correspondence on the payroll issue in boxes, 1, 3, 4, PPC. See also: Noah Leatherman, *Diary Kept by Noah Leatherman While in Camp During World War I* (Linden, Alta.), 58-60; Loucks or Hartzler to editor of *Goshen* (Indiana) *Democrat*, Jan. 17, 1919, f. 1, box 4, PPC; *Topeka Capital*, Feb. 25, 1919, copy in Krehbiel papers, microfilm, MLA; Ruth E. Stover, "The Franconia Conference and the Conscientious Objectors of World War I," *Mennonite Research Journal* 6 (Jan. 1965):7.

28. MRF project 24.

29. Ibid. See also Mary Sprunger, ed., *Sourcebook: Oral History Interviews with World War One Conscientious Objectors* (Akron, Pa., 1986), 46.

30. Voth, "Experiences," 28-29.

31. MRF project 24.

32. This figure is based upon a great variety of sources in MLA and AMC.

33. On the courts-martial, see: Gerlof D. Homan, "Mennonites and Military Justice in World War I" *MQR*, 64 (July 1992):365-375; Post-Armistice Courts-Martial of Conscientious Objectors in Camp Funston, 1918-1919," *ML* 44 (Jan. 1989):4-9.

34. Homan, "Mennonites and Military Justice," 367-368.

35. Ibid.

36. Ibid, 369-370. Two other Mennonites, Peter Voth and Emil Becker who served as "regulars" in a military camp in Texas, also deserted. They were caught and tried; however, no court-martial or other records have been found on these two men. See interview with P. A. Voth, 251, SOHC.

37. Homan, Mennonites and Military Justice," 370-371. Because more court-martial records have been located in recent months, the court-martial figures in this chapter vary somewhat from those in my article "Mennonites and Military Justice." It is very difficult to determine the exact number of court-martialed Mennonites because by late 1918 not all of them were imprisoned in Fort Leavenworth. According to J. D. Mininger, in Dec. 1918 there were 135 Mennonites at that prison. Others were incarcerated in various camps or imprisoned in 1920. For four of the men listed by Mininger no records have been found. See J. D. Mininger, *Religious COs Imprisoned at the Disciplinary Barracks, Ft. Leavenworth, Kansas* (Kan., 1919).

38. Homan, "Mennonites and Military Justice," 372-373.

39. Court-martial record of Chris E. Miller, file 121854, Judge Advocate General Records, RG 153, NA.

40. Homan, "Mennonites and Military Justice," 372.

41. Ibid., 371; A. Voth to Captain P. G. Caldwell, Dec. 5, 1917, f. 1, Peter H. Unruh papers, MLA; Albert C. Voth, "Experiences of a War Objector in World War I (unpublished paper, n.d.; in MLA), 20-21; "Minutes Western District General Conference Exemption Committee"; Rose M. Klaassen, "Mennonite Diary," *Liberty* (Sept.-Oct., 1985, 10.

42. Homan, "Mennonites and Military Justice," 372; Homan, "Post-Armistice Courts-Martial," 4-9.

43. Homan, "Mennonites and Military Justice," 373-374.

44. Ibid., 374.

45. Court-martial record of Jacob E. Tschetter, file 116507, Judge Advocate General records, RG 153, NA. On the psychological testing, see above, chapter 4.

46. Court-martial record of Ray Metzler, file 118745, Judge Advocate General records, RG 153, NA.

47. On the Showalter trial, see Gerlof D. Homan, "A CO on Trial: The Court-Martial of Amos M. Showalter," *Mennonite Historian* 17 (Sept. 1991):5ff.; (Dec. 1991):2ff.

48. Ibid., (Dec. 1991):2ff.

49. Mininger, "Religious COs."

50. Jesse L. Brenneman, "Experiences and Trials in Military Service," (unpublished paper, n.d.), f. 7, box 4, PPC.

51. On prison conditions, see Allen B. Christophel to Hartzler, Feb. 2, 1919, f. 4, box 4, PPC; Edward J. B. Waltner, "A CO in the First World War I" (unpublished paper, 1942), 29-37, MLA; Jesse Brenneman's account is in f. 7, box 4, PPC; Voth, "Experiences of a War Objector," 24-25; Ernest H. Miller, "Experiences of a CO in World War I" (unpublished paper, n.d.; in MSLA), 14-20.

52. Krehbiel to P. H. Unruh, Oct. 3, 1918, Krehbiel papers, microfilm, MLA; "Minute Book Western District Exemption Committee," MLA.

53. Johannes Klaassen to parents, June 10, Aug. 27, 1918, Klaassen letters, Mennonite Heritage Centre Archives, Winnipeg, Man.

54. John Neufeld letters and diary, Illinois Mennonite Historical and Genealogical Library and Archives, Metamora, Ill.

55. Karl Peter and Franziska, trans. and eds., *Hutterite Conscientious Objectors and Their Treatment in the U.S. Army During World War I* (Crawford, Alta, 1982), 47-55.

56. Court-Martial record file 116306, Judge Advocate General Records, RG 153, NA.

57. Joseph Kleinsasser to Keppel, July 14, 1918, file 383.2, Adjutant General's Office Records, RG 94, copy also in MLA.

58. MRF project 24.

59. David Hofer and Andrew Wurz to Commanding Officer, Camp Lewis, Aug. 2, 1918, f. 10, box 1; and John J. Wipf to Loucks, Sept. 9, 1918, box 2, f. 9; PPC. F.H. Johnson, Secretary, Local board, County of Minnehaha, S.D., to Senator E. S. Johnson, Dec. 7, 1918, file 383.2, Adjutant General's Office Records, RG 94, NA, copy also in MLA; Leatherman, *Diary*, 41; Sprunger, *Sourcebook*, 194; Peter, *Hutterite Conscientious Objectors*, 29-36; A. J. F. Zieglschmid, *Das Klein-Geschichtsbuch der Hutterischen Brüder* (Philadelphia, Pa., 1947), 485-486.

60. Leatherman, *Diary*, 41; Peters, *Hutterite Conscientious Objectors*, 33.

61. John J. Wipf to Senator E. S. Johnson, Nov. 30, 1918, file 383.2, Adjutant General's Office records, RG 94, NA, copy also in MLA.

62. Jacob J. Wipf to his wife, Katharina, Dec. 8, 1918; f. 10, box 3, PPC. Adjutant General to Senator E. S. Johnson, Dec. 4, 9, 1918, Feb. 15, 1919, file 383.2; War Dept. memo Dec. 6, 1918, file 383.2; Adjutant General's Office Records, RG 94, NA, copies in MLA.

63. Report by Office of the Surgeon, U.S, Disciplinary Barracks, Fort Leavenworth, Kansas, Dec., 18, 1918; see also U.S. Disciplinary Barracks Report, Dec. 19, 1918; file 383.2, Adjutant General's Office records, RG 94, NA, copy in MLA.

64. Loucks or Hartzler to David Hofer, Oct. 17, 1918, f. 1, box, PPC.

65. Jakob Waldner, "An Account of Jakob Waldner: Diary of a Conscientious Objector in World War I," Theron Schlabach, ed.; Ilse Reist and Elizabeth Bender, trans., *MQR* (Jan. 1973):73-111.

66. J. G. Ewert, *The Martyrs of Alcatraz* (Hillsboro, Kan., n.d.), f. 9, box 22, Jacob D. Mininger papers, AMC.

67. Johannes Klaassen to parents, Sept. 14, 1918, Klaassen papers, Mennonite Heritage Centre, Winnipeg, Man.; Klaassen, "Diary," 10; Michael Klaassen, "Autobiography," (unpublished paper, n.d.), 13-17, copy kindly provided by Mrs Esther Bergen, Winnipeg, Man.; Sprunger, *Sourcebook*, 89, 98; *ME* III:189. Another Mennonite who died at Fort Leavenworth was Daniel S. Yoder; see box 6, Mininger papers, AMC.

68. Waltner, "CO," 31; Leatherman, *Diary*, 49; Jacob D. Mininger, *With God Behind Iron Bars* (Kansas City, Kan., 1919); interview with Mininger, box 44, GHR; *ME*, III:695.

69. *Kansas City Star*, Jan. 23, 1919.

70. Ibid., Jan. 27, 1919.

71. Neufeld, "Diary," Illinois Mennonite Historical and Genealogical Library and Archives, Metamora, Ill.

72. Voth, "Experiences," 28.

73. Ibid., "Addendum," 2; Christophel to Hartzler, Feb. 8, 1919, f. 4, box 4, PPC; David Johnson, *The Challenge to American Freedoms: World War I and the Rise of the American Civil Liberties Union* (Lexington, Ky., 1963), 50-51; Winthrop D. Lane, *The Strike at Fort Leavenworth* (New York, [1919]). Ora J. Hartzler, who was imprisoned in Fort Douglas, Utah, despaired of his release and wrote to his mother on Aug. 19 and Nov. 9, 1919, that he would not be released until 1943. Yet he was sure that he would be released some day even it if was "only a dead man's release"; box 22, Mininger papers, AMC.

74. Soldner to Mininger, Feb. 5, 1919, box 6, Mininger papers, AMC.

75. Miller, "Experiences," 33.

76. Allen Christophel to Hartzler, Feb. 2, 1918, f. 4, box 4, PPC.

77. Allan Teichroew, "World War I and the Mennonite Migration to Canada to Avoid the Draft," *MQR* 45 (July 1971):219-249; Sprunger, *Sourcebook*, 92-93, 95, 98-99; Jacob Klaassen, "Memories and Notations About My Life" (unpublished paper, n.d.), 30-31, copy kindly given to author by Mrs. Esther C. Bergen, Winnipeg, Man.; Klaasen, "Autobiography," 16-17. The Jacob Klaassen family's departure for Canada was hastened by a local gang's threat against them.

78. On Mennonite conscientious objectors in the Russian empire and the early Soviet Union, see: Lawrence Klippenstein, "Mennonite Pacificism and State Service in Russia: A Case Study in Church-State Relations, 1789-1936" (Ph.D dissertation, University of Minnesota, 1984), 42ff.; and John B. Toews, *Czars, Soviets, and Mennonites* (Newton, Kan., 1982), 63-68.

79. Warren Gish to Hartzler, June 29, 1918, and Eli Gish, father of Warren Gish, to Hartzler, July 5 and 10, 1918, folders 2, 4, and 5, box 1, PPC.

80. Gideon H. Amstutz, MRF project 24.

81. Waltner, "CO," 16.

82. A good example of strong Mennonite disapproval of noncombatant service is the attitude of Payson Miller; see especially his letters to R.L. Hartzler, May 12, 1918, July 7, 1918, BCHA.

83. Waltner, "CO, "16.

84. Loucks to Ernest Miller, Sept. 30, 1918, f. 9, box 2, PPC.

85. Hartzler to C. N. Amstutz, Sept. 23, 1918, f. 9, box 2, PPC.

86. Court-martial record of Rolla Wenger, file 122670, Judge Advocate General Records, RG 153, NA.

87. Gingerich to S. C. Yoder, Aug. 17, 1918, and undated, f. 3, box 13, S.C. Yoder papers, AMC; Gingerich to Loucks, Sept. 4, 1918, f. 6, box 2, PPC; copy of Gingerich's discharge, Federal Records Personnel Center, St. Louis, Missouri. There is further correspondence on the Gingerich case in file 382.2, Adjutant General's Office Records, RG 94, NA, copies in MLA.

88. Lester Detrow to parents, Aug. 16; Sept. 2, 8, 20; Oct. 13; Nov. 11, 1918, f. 6, box 1, Wilmer D. Swope papers, AMC.

89. David A. Janzen, "My Experiences as a Young Man in World War," rev. ed. (unpublished paper, n.d.), 1-9, 18-42, copy in MLA; interview with David Janzen, 129, SOHC.

90. Statement by Charles Kauffman, Apr. 20, 1950, copy kindly given by Ora Troyer, Fairview, Mich.; interview with Andrew C. Burky, 33, SOHC.

91. John Hege, "Camp Meade Diary," (unpublished, n.p.), copy kindly provided by William F. McLaughlin, Harpers Ferry, Va.; Roop, *Christianity Versus War*, 34.

92. E. E. Pierson and J. L. Hasbrouck, eds., *McLean County, Illinois in the World War, 1917-1918* (Bloomington, Ill., n.d.), 46, 94, 468; author's questionnaire received in 1988 from Hopedale Mennonite Church, Ill. A few years after the war some men—absolutists, noncombatants, or combatants—may have died because of the effects of maltreatment or other war-time experiences. Among them was Aldus Loganbill who may have been mistreated as a noncombatant at Camp Travis. He died in 1927 at age 32, allegedly because of maltreatment; David Habeggar to author, Aug. 28, 1992.

93. Lancaster Conference "Minute Book," box 47, GHR; Peachy, *Mennonite Statements*, 90; Wayne LaVelle Smith, "Rockingham County Nonresistance and the First World War" (M.A. thesis, Madison College, 1967), 73-74; information kindly furnished by Ora Troyer, Fairview, Mich.

94. Interviews with Abraham Eitzen, August Epp, and Frank Neufeld, 56, 64, 169, SOHC; William H. Regier papers, MLA; Sprunger, *Sourcebook*, 193.

95. Krehbiel to Susan Ringelman, Sept. 3, 1918, Krehbiel papers, microfilm, MLA.

96. See various issues of *The Pastor's Assistance*; Melvin Gingerich, *The Mennonites in Iowa* (Iowa City, 1939), 162-63.

97. Jake C. Regier to Emil Regier, Aug. 2, 1919, f. 4, box 4, Emil Regier papers, MLA.

98. Kurt M. Horst to author, Oct. 1, 1987.

99. Smith, "Rockingham County," 73.

100. *The Witmarsum*, Dec. 7, 1917; May 1, 1918.

101. James O. Lehman, *Salem's First Century: Worship and Witness* (Kidron, Ohio, 1986), 75, 80, 84-94.

102. *Decatur* [Indiana] *Daily Democrat*, May 15, 1918.

103. *MHB* 33 (July 1972):6; *Goshen* (Indiana) *Democrat*, Sept. 25, 1918; interview with D. D. Miller, box 44, GHR.

104. Information based a large number of sources most of which are in MLA and AMC.

105. Author's questionnaire received in 1988 from Holdeman Mennonite Church, Wakarusa, Ind.; unidentified newspaper clipping kindly furnished by Paul F. Goossen.

106. Lancaster Conference, "Minute Book," box 47, GHR; interview with John H. Miller, 163a, SOHC; John L. Ruth, *Maintaining the Right Fellowship* (Scottdale, Pa., 1984), 446. On Mennonite World War II combatants, see Keith L. Sprunger and John D. Thiesen, "Mennonite Military Service in World War II: An Oral History Approach," *MQR*, 66 (Oct. 1992), 481-91.

107. Ida M. Kauffman, Fairview, North Dakota, to author, n.d.

CHAPTER 7: The Aftermath
1. James C. Juhnke, *A People of Two Kingdoms: The Political Acculturation of the Kansas Mennonites* (Newton, Kan., 1975), 115.2. *ME* III:636-637; Guy F. Hershberger, "The Mennonite Church and Foreign Relief 189?: A Twentieth Century Expression of

the Anabaptist Theology of Discipleship" (unfinished book manuscript, n.d.; in AMC), chap. 4.

2. *ME*, III:636-637; Guy F. Hershberger, "The Mennonite Church and Foreign Relief 189?: A Twentieth Century Expression of the Anabaptist Theology of Discipleship" (unfinished book manuscript, n.d.; in AMC), ch 4.

3. James C. Juhnke, *Vision, Doctrine, War: Mennonite Identity and Organization in America, 1890-1930* (vol. III of The Mennonite Experience in America Series; Scottdale, Pa., 1989), 257; J. S. Hartzler, *Mennonites in the World War or Nonresistance Under Test* (2nd ed.; Scottdale, Pa., 1922), 184ff.; Vinora Weaver Salzman, *Day by Day, Year by Year* (n.p., 1982), 17ff.

4. Augsburger to Loucks, July 23, 1918, f. 7, box 43, PPC.

5. *The Goshen College Record*, Apr. 1918. Although Zook believed in nonresistance he wrote in February, 1918 that he could understand why so many young Frenchmen men in the Department of Haute Savoie, where he was staying for a brief period for reasons of health, enlisted in the army to fight for their beautiful country.

6. J. C. Meyer, "Preliminary Developments for the Young People's Conference in France in 1919," *MBH* 29 (Jan. 1968):1-4; Payson Miller's letter, BCHA; Elmer Jantz, "My Experiences as a Member of the Friends Reconstruction Unit in Europe (1919-1920)" (unpublished paper, n.d.), MLA; Roy Buchanan, "A Time to Say No," *Christian Living*, Jan. 1961, 24-35; *Goshen College Record*, Mar. 1919.

7. J. C. Meyer, "The Origins of the Young People's Conference Movement of 1918," *MHB* 29 (July 1969):4; *ME*, IV:262-263.

8. S. E. Allgyer, "War Experiences," box 44, GHR; Guy F. Hershberger, "Historical Background of the Formation of Mennonite Central Committee," *MQR* 44 (July 1970):233; Payson Miller to R. L. Hartzler, Oct. 18, 1919, Payson Miller letters, BCHA; *GH*, Jan. 23, 1919.

9. P. C. Hiebert and O.O. Miller, *Feeding the Hungry: Russia Famine, 1919, 1925. American Mennonite Relief Operations under the Auspices of Mennonite Central Committee* (Scottdale, Pa., 1929); *ME* III:605-609, V:562-564. On Kratz, see *ME* III:233. Hershberger concluded that MCC owed much of its origin and development to "the vision of the men in Clermont"; Hershberger, "Historical Background," 235.

10. Juhnke, *People of Two Kingdoms*, 114-115; Juhnke, *Vision*, 243ff.

11. Meyer, "Origins," 4-5; J. C. Meyer, "The Young People's Conference Held in Clermont, France, June 20-22, 1919," *MHB* 29 (July 1968): 5-7; *Report of General Conference of Mennonites in France in Reconstruction Work Held at Clermont-en-Argonne, Meuse, France, June 20-22, 1919* (n.p., n.d.); Walter Rutt to a friend, June 25, 1919, Walter Rutt collection, Mennonite Historical Society of Eastern Pennsylvania, Lansdale, Pa.

12. *Report of General Conference of Mennonites*, 14ff.; Rutt to a friend, June 25, 1919, Walter Rutt collection (note 11).

13. *Report of General Conference of Mennonites*, 8ff.

14. F. 27, box 1, J. C. Clemens collection, Mennonite Historical Society of Eastern Pennsylvania, Lansdale, Pa.; f. 2, box 4, J. C. Meyer collection, AMC; *ME* III:1009.

15. *The Daily* [Bloomington, Ill. *Pantagraph*, Feb. 17, 1919.

16. Statement by George W. Wright, chairman, Executive Committee of South Dakota Committee of National Defense, n.d., file 99-23, War Dept. General and Specific Staffs records, RG 165, NA; Paul K. Conkin, *Two Paths to Utopia: The Hutterites and the Llano Colony* (Lincoln, Neb., 1964), 62-64; Gertrude Young, "The Mennonites in South Dakota," *South Dakota Historical Collection* 10 (1920):500-502; Victor Peters, *All Things Common: The Hutterite Way of Life* (Minneapolis, 1965), 44-45; John D. Unruh, "The Hutterites During World War I," *ML* 26 (July 1969):136.

17. Unruh, "Hutterites," 136.

18. *Beilage zum Christliche Bundesbote*, Nov. 22, 1917; interview with S. G. Shetler, box 44, GHR; Juhnke, *Vision*, 272. See also: President Mosiman to Edmund Brunner, Apr. 9, 1918, Mosiman papers, BCHC.

19. On this division in the Mennonite Church, see especially Juhnke, *Vision*, 257ff.

20. On contacts with European Mennonites in the immediate postwar era, see Gerlof D. Homan, "Early Twentieth-Century Dutch-American Mennonite Contacts, *MHB* 53 (Apr. 1992):6-10.

21. Copy of this petition in AMC; Rodney J. Sawatsky, "The Influence of Fundamentalism on Mennonite Nonresistance, 1908-1944" (M.A. thesis, University of Minnesota, 1973), 133-134.

22. Paul Toews, "The Long Weekend or the Short Weekend: Mennonite Peace Theology," *MQR* 60 (Jan. 1986):44-55; Melvin Gingerich, *Service for Peace: A History of Mennonite Public Service* (Akron, Pa., 1949), 16ff.; Guy F. Hershberger, *The Mennonite Church in the Second World War* (Scottdale, Pa., 1951), 1-11; Juhnke, *People of Two Kingdoms*, 128-130, 146-148.

23. *ME* V:369.

24. *ME* IV:1006; Juhnke, *Vision*, 300-303; Edward Yoder, *Edward: Pilgrimage of a Mind. The Journal of Edward Yoder, 1931-1945*, Ida Yoder, ed. (Wadsworth, Ohio, 1985), passim.

25. Juhnke, *People of Two Kingdoms*, 130.

26. Sawatsky, "Influence of Fundamentalism," 138ff.

27. Scottdale, Pa., 1920. Another work by Horsch on nonresistance is *The Principle of Nonresistance as Held by the Mennonite Church: An Historical Survey* (Scottdale, Pa., 1927, 1939).

28. Juhnke, *People of Two Kingdoms*, 197.

APPENDIX: Some Statistics of Mennonite and Other Historic Peace Church Service in World War I

1. John W. Chambers, *To Raise an Army: The Draft Comes to Modern America* (New York, 1987), 216; Guy F. Hershberger, *War, Peace, and Nonresistance* (3rd ed.; Scottdale, Pa., 1953), 111.

2. Hershberger, *War, Peace and Nonresistance*, 111.

3. MRF project 24.

4. Arlyn Parish, *Kansas Mennonites During World War I* (Hays, Kan., 1968), 45.

5. John D. Unruh, "A Century of Mennonites in South Dakota," *South Dakota Historical Collections* 36 (1972):94.

6. *The Christian Evangel*, Oct. 1918.

7. Willard Hunsberger, *The Franconia Mennonites and War* (n.p., 1951), 12-13.

8. Cornelius C. Janzen, "A Social Study of the Mennonite Settlement in the Counties of Marion, McPherson, Harvey, Reno, and Butler, Kansas" (Ph.D. dissertation, University of Chicago, 1926), 66-67.

9. Willard H. Smith, *Mennonites in Illinois* (Scottdale, Pa., 1983), 357.

10. Author's questionnaire received in 1988 from Alexanderwohl Mennonite Church, Goessel, Kansas.

11. Naomi Lehman, *Pilgrimage of a Congregation: First Mennonite Church of Berne, Indiana* (Berne, Ind., 1982), 361.

12. Lohrenz papers, CMBS—Fresno.

13. Parish, *Kansas Mennonites*, 45; David V. Wiebe, *Scriptural Basis of the Principle of Nonresistance and Christian Love* (Inman, Kan., 1941), 76-77.

14. Parish, *Kansas Mennonites*, 45.

15. Guy F. Hershberger, "Mennonites and Conscription," box 44, GHR.

16. J. S. Hartzler, *Mennonites in the Great War: Or Nonresistance under Test* (2nd ed.; Scottdale, Pa., 1922), 93.

17. Elbert Russell, *The Story of Quakerism* (New York, 1942), 516.

18. Kenneth G. Long, "Attitudes of Brethren in Training Camps During the War," *Schwarzenau* 1 (July 1939):77.

19. Gilbert G. Buers to Loucks, Aug. 19, 1918, f. 2, box 2, PPC. On Brethren and World War I see Mininger to D. H. Bender, Oct. 16, 1918, box 5, Mininger papers, AMC; Lavelle Wayne Smith, *Rockingham County Nonresistance and the First World War* (M.A. thesis, Madison College, 1967), 114-115, 148-149.

Sources

Archival Holdings

The principal archival holdings on Mennonite experiences in World War I are in the Archives of the Mennonite Church (AMC) located at Goshen College, Goshen, Indiana, and in the Mennonite Library and Archives (MLA), at Bethel College, North Newton, Kansas. In the AMC, the papers of the Military or Peace Problems Committee are extensive and very valuable. Also important are various materials collected by Melvin Gingerich and Guy Hershberger. Among them is the collection "Mennonite Research Foundation Project 24," which consists of many questionnaires sent to and received from Mennonite conscientious objectors of World War I. All researchers owe these two Mennonite scholars more than words can express.

In the MLA, there are, most notably: the papers of Henry P. Krehbiel; the Minutes of the Western District Exemption Committee; microfilmed records of most court-martialed Mennonites; and materials from interviews with 270 Mennonite draftees, in the Schowalter Oral History Collection. In addition to those very important items, the MLA has copies of many valuable documents from the National Archives in Washington, D.C. Researchers are greatly indebted to many persons who have contributed to these and other MLA holdings, and to others who interviewed World War I draftees.

Much smaller but sometimes important archival holdings are in: the Center for Mennonite Brethren Studies in Fresno, California, and Hillsboro, Kansas; the Mennonite Historical Library at Bluffton College, Bluffton, Ohio; the Mennonite Library and Archives of Eastern Pennsylvania at Lansdale, Pennsylvania; the Menno Simons Historical Library and Archives at Eastern Mennonite College, Harrisonburg, Virginia; the Lancaster Mennonite Historical Society, Lancaster, Pennsylvania; and the Illinois Mennonite Historical and Genealogical Society at Metamora, Illinois.

I also found much material in the National Archives in Washington, D.C. Especially valuable there were various records of courts-martial and of the emerging Federal Bureau of Investigation. Finally, the author received documents from many private individuals and collected information from various Mennonite churches whose people filled out his questionnaire.

Selected Bibliography

Primary Works
Unpublished works without archival designation were donated by relatives or others.

Baer, Isaac. "A CO in Camp Meade During World War I." Unpublished, 1981.

Beiler, David. *Das wahre Christenthum: Eine Christliche Betrachtung nach dem Lehre der heiligen Schrift.* [Lancaster, Pa.], 1888.

Bender, Nevin and Emanuel Swartzendruber. *Nonresistance Under Test.* Irwin, Ohio, 1969.

Brenneman, Jesse L. "Experiences and Trials in Military Service." Unpublished, n.d., AMC.

Burkholder, Christian. *Nützliche und erbauliche Anrede an die Jugend der wahren Busse.* [Ephrata, Pa.?], 1804.

Burkholder, Peter. *Conference of Faith of the Christians Known by the Name of Mennonites.* Winchester, Pa., 1837.

Chambers, John W., ed. *Draftees or Volunteers: A Documentary History of the Debate over Military Conscription in the United States, 1787-1973.* New York, 1975.

Claassen, Menno. "Memoirs of a CO of World War I." Unpublished, n.d. MLA.

Committee of 100 Friends of Conscientious Objectors. *Who Are the Conscientious Objectors?* New York, 1919.

Committee on Information. *Information to Mennonite Registrants Concerning Their Status Under the Selective Draft Law.* N.p., 1918.

Dalke, Gerhard. *A Defense of the Mennonites Against Recent Attacks Made upon Them.* [Hillsboro, Kan., 1918].

Drange, Edward. R. *Peace Experiences of Conscientious Objectors at Camp Dodge, Iowa.* N.p., n.d.

Echoes: A Book Containing the Report of the Addresses Delivered at the

First All-Mennonite Convention in America. Assembled at Berne, Indiana, August, 19-20, 1913. Hillsboro, Kan. [n.d.].

Esch, Menno. *Autobiography of Menno Esch, 1879-1967.* N.p., n.d.

Ewert, William J., D. E. Harder, and H. W. Lohrenz. *An die männlichen Glieder der Gemeinde die in dem militärpflichtigen Alter sind.* [Hillsboro, Kan., 1917].

Funk, John F. *Warfare, Its Evils. Our Duty: Addressed to the Mennonite Churches of the United States and All Others Who Sincerly [sic] Seek and Love Truth.* Chicago, 1863.

Gaeddert, Gustave R. "Diary." Unpublished, n.d. Microfilm copy in MLA.

General Conference of Mennonites in France in Reconstruction. To Be Held at Clermont-en-Argonne, Meuse, June 20-22, 1919. Paris, [1919].

Handrich, William. "Some of My Experiences at Camp." Typewritten, n.d.

Haury, Samuel S. *Die Wehrlosigkeit in der Sontagschule.* Dayton, Ohio, 1894.

Hege, John. "Camp Meade Diary." Unpublished, n.d.

Hiebert, P. C. and Orie O. Miller. *Feeding the Hungry: Russia Famine, 1919-1925. American Mennonite Relief Operations under the Auspices of Mennonite Central Committee.* Scottdale, Pa., 1929.

Hofer, David. *Desecration of the Dead by American "Huns."* Chicago, Ill., [1919].

Holdeman, John. *A Treatise on Magistracy and War: Milennium, Holiness, and Manifestation of Spirits.* Jasper, Mo., 1891.

Hostetler, Ura H. "World War I Diary." Unpublished, n.d.

Jansen, Peter. *Memoirs: The Record of a Busy Life.* Beatrice, Neb., 1921.

Jantz, Elmer H. "My Experience as a Member of the Reconstruction Unit of the Friends in Europe (1919-1920)." Unpublished, n.d. Microfilm copy in MLA.

Janzen, David A. "My Experiences as a Young Man of Mennonite Faith in World War I, 1918-1919." Typewritten, n.d. MLA.

Johns, Ira S., J. Hartzler, and Amos O. Hostetler, eds. *Minutes of the Indiana-Michigan Conference, 1864-1929.* Scottdale, Pa., n.d.

Kauffman, Daniel. *Manual of Bible Doctrine: Setting Forth the General Principles of the Plan of Salvation.* Elkhart, Ind., 1898.

Klaassen, Jacob. "Memories and Notations of My Life." Unpublished, n.d.

Kliewer, John W. *Memoirs.* North Newton, Kan., 1943.

Kniss, Lloy A. *I Couldn't Fight: The Story of a CO in World War I*. Scottdale, Pa., 1971.

Krehbiel, Henry P. *Scriptural Foundation for the Doctrine of Nonresistance*. [Newton, Kan., 1917].

_____. *Status of Mennonites as to Military Service*. [Newton, Kan., 1918].

Landis, Cliff. "A Soldier for Christ." Unpublished, 1973. AMC.

Leatherman, Noah. *Diary Kept by Noah H. Leatherman While in Camp During World War I*. Linden, Alta., 1951; Salisbury, Pa., 1984.

Leisy, E. E. "The Martial Adventures of E. E. Leisy." Typewritten, n.d. MLA.

MacMaster, Richard, Samuel Horst, and Robert F. Ulle. *Conscience in Crisis: Mennonites and Other Peace Churches in America, 1739-1789. Interpretation and Documents*. Scottdale, Pa., 1979.

Miller, Chris E. "War Experiences." Unpublished, 1938. AMC.

Miller, Ernest H. "Experiences of a CO in World War I." Typewritten, n.d. MSLA.

Miller, George S. *What Next?* Kalona, Iowa, 1974.

Mininger, Jacob D. *Religious CO's Imprisoned at the U.S. Disciplinary Barracks, Ft. Leavenworth, Kansas*. Kansas City, Kan., 1919.

_____. *With God's People Behind Iron Bars*. Kansas City, Kan., 1919.

Moans from the Military Machine. N.p., 1918.

Mumaw, Adam H. "My Experiences as a Conscientious Objector in World War I." Unpublished, n.d. MSLA.

_____. "Second Company Development Battalion." Unpublished, n.d. MSLA.

Musser, Daniel. *Nonresistance Asserted or the Kingdom of Christ and the Kingdom of This World Separated*. Lancaster, Pa., 1864.

_____. *Nonresistance as Taught by Christ and His Apostles*. Lancaster, Pa., 1886.

Neufelt, John T. "Diary." Typewritten, n.d.

Peachey, Urbane, ed., *Mennonite Statements on Peace and Social Concerns, 1900-1978*. Akron, Pa., 1980.

Peter, Karl and Franziska, eds. and trans. *Hutterite Conscientious Objectors and Their Treatment in the U.S. Army During World War I*. Cranford, Alta., 1982.

Report of General Conference of Mennonites in France in Reconstruction Work Held in Clermont-en-Argonne, Meuse, France, June 20-22, 1919. N.p., 1919.

Salzman, Vinora Weaver. *Day by Day—Year by Year*. N.p., 1982.

Schlissel, Lillian, ed. *Conscience in America: A Documentary History of Conscientious Objectors in America, 1775-1967.* New York, 1968.

Shank, Clarence S. *A Mennonite Boy's World War I Experience.* Marion, Pa., 1963.

Shetler, Sanford G. "Memories of World War I." Unpublished, n.d.

_____. and A. J. Metzler, eds. *Resolutions: Mennonite Conference of the Southwestern Pennsylvania District, 1875-1933.* Scottdale, Pa., 1934.

Sprunger, Keith, James C. Juhnke, and John Waltner, eds. *Voices Against War: A Guide to the Schowalter Oral History Collection on World War I Conscientious Objection.* Rev. ed., North Newton, Kan., 1981.

Sprunger, Mary, ed. *Sourcebook: Oral History Interviews with World War One I Conscientious Objectors.* Akron, Pa., 1986.

Stoltzfus, Nicholas, comp. *Nonresistance Put to Test.* Aylmer, Ont., 1981.

Suderman Pankratz, Frieda. *You Just Can't Do That Anymore.* [Hillsboro, Kan.], 1977.

Swartzendruber, Emanuel. "Nonresistance Under Test." Unpublished, n.d. AMC.

U.S. House of Representatives. Committee on Military Affairs. *Hearings Before the Committee on Military Affairs . . . on the Bill Authorizing the President to Increase Temporarily the Military Establishment of the United States. April 7, 1917.* Washington, D.C., 1917.

_____. *Increase of Military Establishment. Hearings on the Bill Authorizing the President to Increase Temporarily the Military Establishment in the United States, April 7-17, 1917.* Washington, D.C., 1917.

_____. *Proposed War Measure Legislation. Hearings Before the Committee on Military Affairs on H.R. 9100 to Authorize the Secretary of War to Grant Furloughs Without Pay and Allowance to Enlisted Men of the Army of the United States and for Other Purposes.* Washington, D.C., 1918.

_____. *To Increase the Efficiency of the Military Establishment of the United States. Hearings Before the Committee on Military Affairs . . . February, 3, 9, 10, and 11, 1916.* Washington, D.C., 1916.

U.S. Provost Marshal-General. *Rules and Regulations Presented by the President for Local and District Boards.* Washington, D.C., 1917.

U.S. Secretary of War. *A Manual for Courts-Martial Court of Inquiry and of Other Precedures Under Military Law.* Washington, D.C., 1918.

U.S. Senate. Committee on Military Affairs. *Hearings Before the Committee on Military Affairs, United States Senate . . . on S 1871. A Bill to Authorize the President to Increase Temporarily the Military Establishment of the United States*. Washington, D.C., 1917.

U.S. War Department. *Statement Concerning the Treatment of Conscientious Objectors in the Army*. Prepared by James S. Easby Smith. Washington, D.C., 1919.

Verhandlungen der sechsten Peafic [sic] *Distrikt-Conferenz der Mennonitischen Brüdergemeinde von Nord Amerika. Reedley, 18-20 November, 1917*. N.p., n.d.

Verhandlungen und Berichte der 21 Allgemeinen Konferenz der Mennoniten von Nord Amerika. Beilage zum Christliche Bundesbote, November 22, 1917. N.p., n.d.

Voth, Albert C. "Experiences of a War Objector in World War I." Typewritten, n.d. MLA.

Waltner, Edward J. B. "A CO in the First World War." Typewritten, 1919. Rev. ed, 1942. MLA.

Western District Exemption Committee. *Information for Mennonite Men Drafted for Military Service under Act of May 18, 1917, But Who Wish to Be Exempt from Such Service*. [Newton, Kan., 1917].

Wilson, Woodrow. *The Papers of Woodrow Wilson*. Edited by Arthur Link. Vols. 42, 44, and 49. Princeton, N.J., 1983-1985.

Yoder, Sanford C. *The Days of My Years*. Scottdale, Pa., [1959].

——————. "Reminiscences of World War I." Unpublished, n.d. AMC.

Secondary Works

Abrams, Ray H. *Preachers Present Arms*. Rev. ed., Scottdale, Pa., 1969.

American Civil Liberties Bureau. *Political Prisoners in Federal Military Prisons*. New York, 1918.

Arn, John W. *The Herold Mennonite Church: 70th Anniversary (1899-1969)*. North Newton, Kan., 1969.

Bauman, Elizabeth Hershberger. *Coals of Fire*. Scottdale, Pa., 1964.

Beaver, Daniel R. *Newton D. Baker and the American War Effort, 1917-1919*. Lincoln, Neb., 1966.

Bethlehem Mennonite Church, Bloomfield, Montana, Historical Committee. *75th Anniversary: Bethlehem Mennonite Church, 1910-1985*. N.p., [1985].

Bilger, Edeltraut L. "The German-Americans in Oklahoma During World War I as Seen Through Three German-Language Newspapers." Master's thesis, Oklahoma State University, 1976.

Brunk, Harry A. *History of Mennonites in Virginia.* Vol. 2. Verona, Va., 1972.

Chambers, John W. *To Raise an Army: The Draft Comes to Modern America.* New York, 1987.

Crucifixions in the Twentieth Century: The Cases of Jacob Wipf and the Three Hofer Brothers, Religious Objectors to War. Chicago, n.d.

DeBenedetti, Charles. *The Peace Reform in American History.* Bloomington, Ind., 1980.

Dick, LaVernae. "Early Mennonites in Oregon." Master's thesis, Oregon College of Education, 1972.

Entz, Margaret. "Free to Buy: American World War I Financing and the Mennonite Response." Research paper, Bethel College, 1975. MLA.

Erb, Paul. *South Central Frontiers: A History of the South Central Mennonite Conference.* Scottdale, Pa., 1974.

Estes, Steven R. *A Goodly Heritage: A History of the North Danvers Mennonite Church.* Danvers, Ill., 1982.

_____. *Living Stones: A History of the Metamora Mennonite Church.* Metamora, Ill., 1974.

Falb, Timothy R. *Fruits of Diversity: Martins Mennonite Church and Pleasant View Mennonite Church, 1834-1984.* Orrville, Ohio, 1984.

Fast, Henry A. "The Witness of Our Congregation: Our 75 Years." Typewritten, n.d. MLA.

Federal Council of Churches of Christ in America. General War-Time Commission of the Churches. *Survey of the Moral and Religious Forces in the Military Camps and Naval Stations in the United States.* New York, 1918.

Finney, Torin R. *The Life and Witness of Ben Salmon: Unsung Hero of the Great War.* Mahwah, N.J., 1989.

Friedmann, Robert. *The Theology of Anabaptism.* Scottdale, Pa., 1973.

Gelfand, Lawrence E. *The Inquiry: American Preparations for Peace, 1917-1919.* New York, 1963.

Gilbert, Charles. *American Financing of World War I.* Westport, Conn., 1970.

Gingerich, Melvin. *The Mennonites in Iowa.* Iowa City, Iowa, 1939.

_____. *Service for Peace: A History of Mennonite Civilian Public Service.* Akron, Pa., 1949.

Goossen, Rachel Waltner. *Meetingplace: A History of the Mennonite Church of Normal, 1912-1987.* Normal, Ill., 1987.

Grebin, Donald W. "The South Dakota Council of Defense, 1917-1919." Master's thesis, Universty of South Dakota, 1967.

Habegger, Luannne. "The Berne, Indiana, Mennonite Church During World War I." Unpublished, 1976.

Hale, Douglas. *The Germans from Russia in Oklahoma*. Norman, Okla., 1980.

Harms, John F. *Geschichte der Mennoniten Brüdergemeinde*. Hillsboro, Kan., n.d.

Hartzler, J. S. *Mennonites in the World War: Or Nonresistance Under Test*. 2nd ed., Scottdale, Pa., 1922.

Haury, David A. *Prairie People: A History of the Western District Conference*. Newton, Kan., 1981.

Hershberger, Guy F. *The Mennonite Church in the Second World War*. Scottdale, Pa., 1951.

_____. "The Mennonite Church and Foreign Relief, A Twentieth-Century Expression of an Anabaptist Theology of Discipleship." Unfinished manuscript, n.d. MLA.

_____. "Mennonites and Conscription in the World War." Unpublished, 1940. MLA.

_____. *War, Peace, and Nonresistance*. 3d ed. Scottdale, Pa., 1969.

Hiebert, Clarence. *The Henderson Mennonite Brethren, 1878-1978*. Henderson, Neb., 1979.

Higham, John. *Strangers in the Land: Patterns of American Nativism, 1860-1925*. 2nd ed. New Brunswick, N.J., 1988.

Holsinger, Justus G. *Upon This Rock: Remembering Together the 75-Year Story of the Hesston Mennonite Church*. N.p., [1984].

Horsch, John. *Die biblische Lehre von der Wehrlosigkeit*. Scottdale, Pa., 1920.

_____. *The Failure of Modernism: A Reply to Harry Emerson Fosdick*. Chicago, 1925.

_____. *The Mennonite Church and Modernism*. Scottdale, Pa., 1924.

_____. *The Principle of Nonresistance as Held by the Mennonite Church*. Scottdale, Pa., 1939.

Horst, Samuel. *Mennonites in the Confederacy: A Study in Civil War Pacifism*. Scottdale, Pa., 1967.

Hostetler, John A. *Hutterite Society*. Baltimore, 1974.

Huber, Harold E. *With the Eyes of Faith: A History of Greenwood Mennonite Church, Greenwood, Delaware, 1914-1974*. Greenwood, Del., 1974.

Hunsberger, Willard. *The Franconia Mennonites and War*. N.p., 1951.

Huxman, Susan Schultz. "In the World, But Not of It: Mennonite Rhetoric in World War I as an Enactment of a Paradox." Ph.D. dissertation, University of Kansas, 1987.

Janzen, Cornelius C. "A Social Study of the Mennonite Settlement in the Counties of Marion, McPherson, Harvey, Reno, and Butler, Kansas." Ph.D. dissertation, University of Chicago, 1926.

Jensen, Joan M. *The Price of Vigilance*. Chicago, 1968.

Johnson, Donald. *The Challenge to American Freedoms: World War I and the Rise of the American Civil Liberties Union*. Lexington, Ky., 1963.

Juhnke, James C. *A People of Two Kingdoms: The Political Acculturation of the Kansas Mennonites*. Newton, Kan., 1975.

_____. *Vision, Doctrine, War: Mennonite Identity and Organization in America, 1890-1930* (Vol. III of The Mennonite Experience in America series). Scottdale, Pa., 1989.

Keim, Albert, and Grant M. Stoltzfus. *The Politics of Conscience*. Scottdale, Pa., 1988.

Kellogg, Walter G. *The Conscientious Objector*. New York, 1919; reprint, New York, 1970.

Kennedy, David M. *Over There: The First World War and American Society*. New York, 1980.

Klaassen, Walter. *Anabaptism: Neither Catholic Nor Protestant*. Waterloo, Ont., 1973.

Klippenstein, Lawrence. "Mennonite Pacifism and State Service: A Case Study in Church-State Relations, 1798-1936." Ph.D. dissertation, University of Minnesota, 1984.

Kohn, Stephen M. *Jailed for Peace: The History of American Draft Violators, 1658-1985*. Westport, Conn., 1986.

Kroeker, Marvin E. *The Mennonites of Oklahoma to 1907*. Norman, Okla., 1954.

Lane, Winthrop D. *The Strike at Fort Leavenworth*. New York, [1919].

Lehman, James O. *Creative Congregationalism: A History of Oak Grove Mennonite Church in Wayne County, Ohio*. Smithville, Ohio, 1978.

_____. *Salem's First Century Worship and Witness*. Kidron, Ohio, 1986.

_____. *Sonnenberg: A Haven and a Heritage*. Kidron, Ohio, 1969.

Lehman, Naomi. *Pilgrimage of a Congregation: First Mennonite Church Berne, Indiana*. Berne, Ind., 1982.

Lindley, John M. "A Soldier Is Also a Citizen: The Controversy over Military Justice in the U.S. Army, 1917-1920." Ph.D. dissertation, Duke University, 1974.

Littell, Franklin H. *The Anabaptist View of the Church.* Boston, Mass., 1958.

Lockmiller, David A. *Enoch H. Crowder.* Columbia, Mo. 1955.

Luebke, Frederick. *Bonds of Loyalty: German Americans and World War I.* DeKalb, Ill., 1974.

Manley, Robert N. "The Nebraska State Council of Defense. . . : Loyalty Programs and Policies During World War I." Master's thesis, University of Nebraska, 1959.

McKee, Wilma, ed. *Growing Faith: General Conference Mennonites in Oklahoma.* Newton, Kan., 1988.

McMaster, Richard K. *Land, Piety, and Peoplehood: The Establishment of Mennonite Communities in America, 1683-1790* (Vol. I of The Mennonite Experience in America series). Scottdale, Pa., 1985.

Palmer, Frederick. *Newton D. Baker.* 2 vols. New York, 1931.

Pankratz, Herbert L. "Loyalty-Disloyalty in Kansas During World War I." Master's thesis, University of Kansas, 1967.

Parish, Arlyn J. *Kansas Mennonites During World War I.* Hays, Kan., 1968.

Peters, Victor. *All Things Common: The Hutterite Way of Life.* Minneapolis, [1965].

Peterson, David C. "Children of Freedom or Children of Menno? The Oregon Mennonite Church in Two World Wars." M.A. thesis, University of Oregon, 1981.

Peterson, H. C., and Gilbert C. Fite. *Opponents of War, 1917-1918.* Madison, Wis., 1957.

Pierson, E. E., and J. L. Hasbrouck, eds. *McLean County, Illinois, in the World War, 1917-1918.* Bloomington, Ill., n.d.

Piper, John P. *The American Churches in World War I.* Athens, Ohio, 1985.

Rohrs, Richard C. *The Germans in Oklahoma.* Norman, Okla., 1980.

Roop, John D., ed. *Christianity Versus War.* Ashland, Ohio, 1949.

Russell, Elbert. *The History of Quakerism.* New York, 1942.

Ruth, John L. *Maintaining the Right Fellowship.* Scottdale, Pa., 1984.

Sawatsky, Rodney J. "The Influence of Fundamentalism on Mennonite Nonresistance, 1908-1944." Master's thesis, University of Minnesota, 1973.

Schellenberg, Tim. "Nonresistance Stand in the Krimmer Mennonite Brethren Church in World War I." Typewritten, 1981. CMBS-Fresno.

Schlabach, Theron F. *Peace, Faith, Nation* (Vol. II of The Mennonite Experience in America series). Scottdale, Pa., 1988.

Schmidt, Theodore. "The Mennonites of Nebraska." Master's thesis, University of Nebraska, 1933.

Seibert, R. H. "The Treatment of Conscientious Objectors in Wartime, 1775-1920." Ph.D. dissertation, Ohio State University, 1936.

Smith, Wayne L. "Rockingham County Nonresistance and the First World War." Master's thesis, Madison College, 1967.

Smith, Willard H. *Mennonites in Illinois.* Scottdale, Pa., 1983.

Stoltzfus, Grant. *Mennonites of the Ohio and Eastern Conference.* Scottdale, Pa., [1969].

Swartzentruber, L. L. *The Child: A History of the Mennonites Orphans' Home, West Liberty, Ohio.* Scottdale, Pa., 1931.

Thomas, Norman. *Is Conscience a Crime?* New York, 1972.

Toews, John B. *Czars, Soviets, and Mennonites.* Newton, Kan., 1982.

Troyer, Ora. *Fairview Mennonite Church: A Congregational History.* N.p., 1990

Ulmer, S. Sidney. *Military Justice and the Right to Counsel.* Lexington, Ky., 1970.

Unruh, A. H. *Die Geschichte der Mennoniten Brüdergemeinde, 1860-1954.* Hillsboro, Kan., 1955.

Warkentine, Kendal. "Military Justice in World War I: Court-Martial Troubles of Mennonite Conscientious Objectors." Typewritten, 1983. MLA.

Wedel, Peter J. *The Story of Bethel College.* E. G. Kaufman, ed. North Newton, Kan., 1954.

Wenger, John C. *History of the Mennonites of the Franconia Conference.* Telford, Pa., 1937.

_____. *The Mennonites of Indiana and Michigan.* Scottdale, Pa., 1961.

Whitney, Nathaniel R. *The Story of War Bonds in Iowa.* Iowa City, Iowa, 1923.

Zieglschmid, A. J. F. *Das Klein-Geschichtsbuch der Hutterischen Brüder.* Philadelphia, Pa., 1947.

Zijp, N. van der. *Geschiedenis der Doopsgezinden in Nederland.* Enkhuizen [The Netherlands], 1952.

Periodical Literature

Ansell, S. T. "Military Justice." *The Cornell Law Quarterly* 5 (Nov. 1919):1-17.

Berne Witness, The, 1917-1918

Bontrager, Marion. "Sell 'em, Sell 'em." *GH,* Oct. 20, 1981.

Buchanan, Roy. "A Time to Say No." *Christian Living,* Sept. 1960, pp. 6-

35; Oct. 1960, pp.12-35; Nov. 1960, pp. 14-34; Dec. 1960, pp. 22-33; Jan. 1961, pp. 24-35; Feb. 1961, pp. 25-35.

Christian Evangel, 1917-1919.

Christian Exponent, The.

"Court-Martial 1918, Pvt. Ura V. Aschliman (420382)." *ML* 31 (Sept. 1976):18-21.

Dick, LaVernae J. "A Noose for the Minister." *TM,* Apr. 21, 1964.

Entz, Margaret. "War Bond Drives and the Kansas Mennonite Response." *ML* 30 (Sept. 1975):4-9.

Fields, Dale W. "My Father Was a Hero." *TM,* July 14, 1988.

"The First World War and Mennonite Nonresistance." *MHB* 3 (July 1972):4-10.

Franz, Rufus M. "It Happened in Montana." *ML* 7 (Oct. 1952):181-184.

"From the Boys at Camp Meade." *Newsletter: Mennonites of Eastern Pennsylvania* 17 (Mar. 1990):no pagination.

Gospel Banner, 1900-1918.

Gospel Herald, 1917-1919.

Gospel Witness, 1905-1908.

Hartman, Oscar E. "An Original Draft Resister." *Sword and Trumpet,* June 1974, pp. 24-26.

Hernley, Elam R. "My Experiences During the World War," *Christian Monitor,* Nov. 1939-May 1940, no pagination.

Herald of Truth, 1900-1908.

Herold, Der 1917-1918.

Hershberger, Guy F. "Historical Background of the Formation of the Mennonite Central Committee." *MQR* 44 (July 1970):213-244.

—————————. "The Origins of the Peace Problems Committee." *The Youth's Christian Companion* 18, Aug. 1, 1937.

—————————. "Mennonites in the Civil War." *MQR* 18 (July 1944):131-144.

—————————. "To Keep Alive Our Scriptural Peace Testimony. The Origins of the Peace Problems Committee." *The Youth's Christian Companion,* Nov. 5, 1939, p.776.

Homan, Gerlof D. "Americanism, Pro-Germanism, and Conscientious Objection During World War I." *MHB* 55 (Jan. 1994):1-4.

—————————. "The Burning of the Mennonite Church Fairview, Michigan, in 1918." *MQR* 64 (Apr. 1990):99-112.

—————————. "The Court-Martial of Amos M. Showalter." *Mennonite Historian* 17 (Sept. 1991):5+; (Dec. 1991):2ff.

—————————. "Early Twentieth-Century Dutch-American Mennonite Contacts." *MHB* 53 (Apr. 1992):6-10.

_____. "Mennonites and Military Justice in World War I." *MQR* 65 (July 1992):365-375.

_____. "Post-Armistice Courts-Martial of Conscientious Objectors in Camp Funston, Kansas, 1918-1919." *ML* 44 (Dec. 1989):4-9.

_____. "World War I Draft Registrants." *Mennonite Heritage* 15 (June 1988):1ff.

Horsch, John. "The Principle of Nonresistance Compared with Popular Pacificism." *GH*, Sept. 1, 1938.

Joseph, Ted. "The United States vs. Miller: The Strange Case of a Mennonite Editor Convicted of Violating the 1917 Espionage Act." *ML* 30 (Sept. 1975):14-18.

Juhnke, James C. "The Agony of Civic Isolation: Mennonites in World War I." *ML* 25 (Jan. 1970):27-33.

_____. "The Daniel Explosion: Bethel's First Bible Crisis." *ML* 44 (Sept. 1989):20-25.

_____. "John Schrag Espionage Case." *ML* 22 (July 1967):121-122.

_____. "Kansas Mennonites During the Spanish-American War." *ML* 26 (Apr. 1971):70-72.

_____. "Mob Violence and Kansas Mennonites." *Kansas Historical Quarterly* 43 (Aug. 1977):334-350.

_____. "The Wilhelm Galle Family and Camp Funston: The 'Lost Battalion.' " *ML* 44 (Dec. 1989):10-15.

Kauffman, J. Howard. "The Mennonite Community of Fairview, Michigan." *MQR* 21 (Oct. 1947):252-274.

Klaassen, Rose M. "Mennonite Diary." *Liberty*. Sept.-Oct. 1985, pp. 9-10.

Krehbiel, Henry P. "War Inconsistent with the Teaching and Spirit of Christ and Hence Unwise and Unnecessary." *TM*, June and July 1895. The article was reprinted at Newton, Kansas, in 1934.

Long, Kenneth G. "Attitudes of Brethren in Training Camps During the War." *Schwarzenau* 1 (July 1939):57-77.

May, Mark A. "The Psychological Examinations of Conscientious Objectors." *American Journal of Psychology* 31 (Apr. 1920):152-165.

Mennonite, The, 1917-1919.

Messenger of Truth, 1917-1918.

Meyer, Jacob C. "The Origin of the Young People's Conference Movement of 1918." *MHB* 28 (Apr. 1967):4-5.

_____. "Preliminary Developments for the Young People's Conference in France in 1919." *MHB* 29 (Jan. 1968):1-4; (Apr. 1968):3-4.

_____. "Reflections of a Conscientious Objector in World War I." *MQR* 41 (Jan. 1967):79-96.

_____. "The Young People's Conference Held in Clermont, France, June 20-22, 1919." *MHB* 29 (Jan. 1968):5-7.

Miller, Ernest H. "I Tried to Be Reasonable." *GH*, Jan. 22, 1974.

Miller, Payson. "A Nonresistant Soldier." *The Christian Exponent*. May 9, 1924.

"Nebraska Amish Mennonites and War Bonds in World War I." *MHB* 30 (Jan. 1969):4-5.

Pankratz, Herbert. "The Suppression of Alleged Disloyalty in Kansas During World War I." *Kansas Historical Quarterly* 42 (Fall 1976):277-307.

Pastor's Assistant, The, 1917-1919.

Sawyer, Darrell. "Anti-German Sentiment in South Dakota During World War I." *South Dakota Historical Collection* 38 (1976):439-512.

Shields, Sarah D. "The Treatment of Conscientious Objectors During World War I." *Kansas Historical Quarterly* 4 (Win. 1981):255-269.

Slagel, Arthur. "From the Diary of a Relief Worker." *The Christian Exponent*, Jan. 4-May 23, 1924.

Smith, C. Henry. "Keeping the Faith. The Story of the Mennonites During the War." *The Christian Exponent*, June 5-July 31, 1928.

Stone, Harlan F. "The Conscientious Objector." *The Columbia University Quarterly* 21 (Oct. 1919):253-272.

Stover, Ruth E. "The Franconia Conference and the Conscientious Objectors of World War I." *Mennonite Research Journal* 6 (Jan. 1965):1ff.

Stucky, Gregory J. "Fighting Against the Mennonite *Vorwaerts* from 1914 to 1919." *Kansas Historical Quarterly* 38 (Sum. 1972):169-186.

Teichroew, Allan. "Mennonites and the Conscription Trap." *ML* 30 (Sept. 1975):10-13.

_____. "Military Surveillance of Mennonites During World War." *MQR* 53 (Apr. 1979):95-127.

_____. "World War I and the Mennonite Migration to Canada to Avoid the Draft." *MQR* 45 (July 1971):219-249.

Toews, Paul. "The Long Weekend and the Short Week: Mennonite Peace Theology." *MQR* 60 (Jan. 1986):38-57.

Unruh, John D. "A Century of Mennonites in South Dakota." *South Dakota Historical Collections* 36 (1972):1-142.

_____. "The Hutterites During World War I." *ML* 26 (July 1969):130-137.

Urry, James, and Lawrence Klippenstein. "Mennonites in the Crimean War, 1854-1856." *Journal of Mennonite Studies* 7 (1989):9-32.

Waldner, Jacob. "An Account by Jacob Waldner: Diary of a Conscientious Objector in World War I." Ed. by Theron F. Schlabach; trans. by Ilse Reist and Elizabeth Bender. *MQR* 48 (Jan. 1974):73-111.

Weekly Budget, The, 1917-1918.

Witmer, James. "John Witmer: A World War I Conscientious Objector." *MHB* 24 (Oct. 1963):3-4.

Young, Gertrude. "The Mennonites in South Dakota." *South Dakota Historical Collection* 10 (1920):470-506.

Index

The Author

Gerlof D. Homan was born in 1929 in the Netherlands. After arriving in United States in 1952, he attended Bethel College (Kan.) and the University of Kansas, where he received his Ph.D. He has taught history at Central State University (Okla.), the University of Oklahoma, and Kansas State University at Pittsburg. During most of his academic career, Homan studied and taught European history.

He is currently teaching peace history (a course he introduced), contemporary world history, and graduate seminars at Illinois State University and is active in peace and conflict resolution studies. *American Mennonites and the Great War, 1914-1918* is the result of his research in various Mennonite and other archives and libraries, interviews, and extensive correspondence. He considers the U.S. Mennonite World War I experience a twentieth-century faith story.

Homan's spouse, Roelie (Noord), is a church secretary. Both are members of the Normal (Ill.) Mennonite Church. They have three children—Paul (manager of public affairs, State Farm Insurance Office, Birmingham, Ala.), Robert (evaluator, General Accounting Office, Washington, D.C.), and Chris, third grade teacher (International Embassy School, Banjul, The Gambia, West Africa).